Assessment, Risk & Decision Making in Social Work

Sara Miller McCune founded Sage Publishing in 1965 to support the dissemination of usable knowledge and educate a global community. Sage publishes more than 1000 journals and over 800 new books each year, spanning a wide range of subject areas. Our growing selection of library products includes archives, data, case studies and video. Sage remains majority owned by our founder and after her lifetime will become owned by a charitable trust that secures the company's continued independence.

Los Angeles | London | New Delhi | Singapore | Washington DC | Melbourne

2nd Edition

Assessment, Risk & Decision Making in Social Work

An Introduction

Campbell Killick & Brian J. Taylor

Learning Matters
A Sage Publishing Company
1 Oliver's Yard
55 City Road
London EC1Y 1SP

Sage Publications Inc.
2455 Teller Road
Thousand Oaks, California 91320

Sage Publications India Pvt Ltd
B 1/I 1 Mohan Cooperative Industrial Area
Mathura Road
New Delhi 110 044

Sage Publications Asia-Pacific Pte Ltd
3 Church Street
#10-04 Samsung Hub
Singapore 049483

Editor: Kate Keers
Senior project editor: Chris Marke
Project management: Westchester Publishing Services UK
Marketing manager: Camille Richmond
Cover design: Sheila Tong
Typeset by: C&M Digitals (P) Ltd, Chennai, India

Library of Congress Control Number: 9781529621358

British Library Cataloguing in Publication Data

A catalogue record for this book is available from the British Library

ISBN 978-1-5296-2136-5
ISBN 978-1-5296-2135-8 (pbk)

Contents

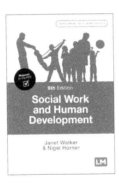
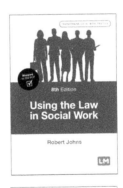
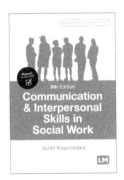
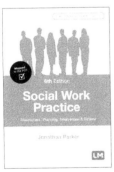
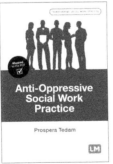
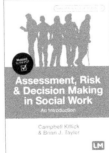
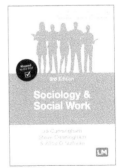

About the authors

Campbell Killick is Lecturer in Social Work at the University of Ulster. He teaches on undergraduate (qualifying) and post-graduate (post-qualifying) courses, including being Course Director for the postgraduate Research Methods Programme and the MSc in Development and Co-Production of Social Care Research designed for people who use services and carers. Prior to joining the University, Campbell held the role of Research Officer: Social Work at one of the Health and Social Care Trusts in Northern Ireland. His social work experience includes work with people who have disabilities and mental health problems, as well as older people. Campbell's PhD was on professional decision making in relation to the abuse of older people, and his research focuses particularly on adult safeguarding. He is an author on *Understanding and Using Research in Social Work* and *Working with Aggression and Risk in Social Work*, and an editor of *Handbook of Decision Making, Assessment and Risk in Social Work*, all published by Sage.

Brian J. Taylor is Professor of Social Work at Ulster University, Northern Ireland where he leads the research cluster on Decision, Assessment, Risk and Evidence Studies in Social Work and contributes to qualifying and post-qualifying social work education. He spent 12 years as a practitioner and manager in social work, residential childcare, primary school teaching and youth work, and 15 years in social work training and organisation development in health and social care. This included three years as project manager implementing new children's legislation. His doctorate was on risk and decision making in community care, and he had a lead role in developing the Northern Ireland Single Assessment Tool for the health and social care of older people. He is an author on *Understanding and Using Research in Social Work* and editor of *Handbook of Decision Making, Assessment and Risk in Social Work* and *Working with Aggression and Risk in Social Work*, all published by Sage.

Acknowledgements

We are grateful to people we have worked with, colleagues and students for all that we have learnt from them. In particular we would like to acknowledge the students on the Assessment and Risk Assessment in Practice Settings (undergraduate, qualifying) module, and the candidates on the Professional Decision Making in Social Work (post-graduate, post-qualifying) module for newly qualified social workers. We would like to acknowledge the advice of Dr Roger Manktelow and Robyn Lennox with case study material. Thanks to Josie Lister for artistic support. We are grateful to the staff at Sage for their encouragement and helpful advice. Last but not least, thanks to our families for their forbearance with this writing adventure.

Series editor's preface

This updated edition of Campbell Killick and Brian J. Taylor's significant text provides a refreshed and enhanced introduction to key concepts in practice, providing a deeper focus on the analysis of assessment and risk assessment in an uncertain world. During recent teaching sessions for student social workers, I have been struck keenly by the changes permeating our contemporary world. This book acknowledges the ambiguities and uncertainties in practice and makes for the inculcation of measured decision making. Values and ethics lie at the heart of social work and social work education, and we address these throughout all the books in the series. The positions that we take in the world are to an extent determined by context, time and experience, and these are expressed in different ways by students coming into social work education today and, of course, by the different routes students take through their educational experience. This book will help you develop practice that is driven by values, helping you to reflect on core issues, risks and the need for safeguarding that centres around the people with whom you will be working.

Since the turn of this century we have witnessed shifts and challenges as the marketised neoliberal landscape of politics, economy and social life may attract little comment or contest from some and even the acceptance of populist Right Wing positions. We have also observed the political machinery directing much of statutory social work towards a focus on individuals apart from their environment. However, on a more positive note, we have also seen a new turn to the social in the #MeToo campaign, where unquestioned entitlement to women's bodies and psychology is exposed and resisted. We have seen defiance of those perpetuating social injustices that see long-term migrants alongside today's migrants abused and shunned by society and institutions, as well as individuals.

It is likely that, as a student of social work, you will lay bare and face many previously unquestioned assumptions, which can be very perplexing, and uncover needs for learning, support and understanding. This series of books acts as an aid as you make these steps. Each book stands in a long and international tradition of social work that promotes social justice and human rights, introducing you to the importance of sometimes new and difficult concepts, and inculcating the importance of close questioning of yourself as you make your journey towards becoming part of that tradition.

There are numerous contemporary challenges for the wider world, and for all four countries of the UK. These include political shifts to the 'popular' Right, a growing antipathy to care and support, and dealing with lies and 'alternative truths' in our daily lives. Alongside this is the need to address the impact of an increasingly ageing population with its attendant social care needs and working with the financial implications that such a changing demography brings. At the other end of the lifespan, the need for high quality childcare, welfare and safeguarding services has been highlighted as society develops and responds to the changing complexion. All these areas demand complex decision making, understanding of risk and clear assessment skills. This book will help focus your attention in these matters.

As a social worker you will work with a diverse range of people throughout your career, many of whom have experienced significant, even traumatic, events that require a professional and caring response. As well as working with individuals, however, you may be required to respond to the needs of a particular community disadvantaged by local, national or world events or groups excluded within their local communities because of assumptions made about them.

The importance of high-quality social work education remains if we are to adequately address the complexities of modern life. We should continually strive for excellence in education as this allows us to focus clearly on what knowledge it is useful to engage with when learning to be a social worker. Questioning everything, especially from a position of knowledge, is central to being a social worker.

The books in this series respond to the agendas driven by changes brought about by professional bodies, governments and disciplinary reviews. They aim to build on and offer introductory texts based on up-to-date knowledge and to help communicate this in an accessible way, so preparing the ground for future study and for encouraging good practice as you develop your social work career. Each book is written by people passionate about social work and social services and aims to instil that passion in others. The current text introduces you to the central processes involved in social work practice, namely assessment, risk assessment and decision making. The book is introductory and, therefore, sets the scene for exploring more specialised areas of practice and providing you with a grounding from which to enhance your learning. In our current era of 'post-truth' statements and claims, it is fundamental that we have this book to begin to guide you to a questioning and reflective approach that cuts through unhelpful relativities while retaining a necessary uncertainty.

Professor Jonathan Parker
November 2023

Introduction

The place of assessment in social work

All social work is about **assessment** and all assessment is about relationship. A recurring theme in this book is that social work, and particularly assessment, is about human connection. Irrespective of the setting, social work involves trying to understand the reality of people's lives and experiences. The primary source of such understanding comes from engagement with the people themselves. Case notes and professional reports may help, but they cannot replace face-to-face engagement and honest interaction. Everything that a social worker does is some form of assessment: every conversation, every home visit and every telephone call. Although social workers may participate in specific assessment processes, the quest for understanding is ongoing. Each piece of new information adds to our comprehension of the dynamic reality of the individual and those around them. This brings us to one of the central dilemmas that face social workers. Social work inhabits a world of uncertainty. We are not able to gather all the necessary information and we cannot be sure that the information we have is accurate. Social work assessment is about achieving the best understanding when faced with these limitations. We are gathering jigsaw pieces of information to produce a picture that describes a person's reality, but some pieces are missing and others don't fit together.

This does not mean that our task is hopeless. We wrote this book because we believe that practitioners can use knowledge, skills and values to achieve clarity and consensus around the issues that they face. This includes being honest about what we don't know or where we don't agree. Chapter 1 explores some of these issues in more depth. It describes the stages of the assessment process. Social work assessments cannot be formulaic, but they should be methodical, and participants should understand what is happening at each stage.

Assessing what?

When teaching assessment to undergraduate social work students, I often start with the case study below. Like many case studies there is limited information, but I ask the group to try to identify the key issue or area of concern.

Case Study   What's the Problem?

Alice has been reported to social services by neighbours who say that she and her partner, Daniel, are often drunk. Their three young children are unfed and unkempt. They are
living in emergency accommodation that is dirty and unsafe. On occasions the family
have been without heat or electricity. Daniel is described as a violent man who is known
to police because of petty crime and anti-social behaviour. Alice has recently discovered
that she is pregnant.

What would you say is the key problem in the above case study? Students considering
this case study come up with a range of issues.

- It seems that the needs of the three children are not being met
- There are a number of housing issues
- There is a danger to Alice and the children from Daniel's violence
- Another child may put further pressure on a struggling family.

All of these are genuine concerns, but it is possible that they are actually symptoms of
something bigger. It is possible that there are larger structural issues at play such as poverty, trauma or discrimination. Much of today's social work practice relies on individual
methods and interventions but it is important that we recognise the societal context of
issues like disability and distress (Frazer-Carroll 2003). The chapters of this book will
sometimes focus on the concerning symptoms, but these are best understood in the
context of the broader issues. Chapter 2 argues that assessments are most effective when
conducted in collaboration with the individuals and families at the centre of the process.

Uncertainty and emotion

Social work assessment is both a science and an art. It employs objective processes to
weigh up evidence while also acknowledging subjective aspects of human life such as
emotion and creativity. In this book we will suggest that intuitive practice wisdom can
be supported by a structured approach to obtaining the most reliable information about
the problem, strengths and situation of the individual (and where appropriate, family).
This may include the use of the best evidence of the effectiveness of possible interventions and a sound understanding of knowledge, legislation and policy. We propose a
rational approach to assessment and **decision making** but we do recognise that emotion
plays a significant role in social work and we need to be in tune to feelings as well as facts
(Ingram 2013). This is because many aspects of human existence cannot be described by
facts. Social work assessment and decision making must take account of subjectivity and
uncertainty. There always remains the unknown and unknowable about the individual
and family dynamics. As a practitioner you will need to draw upon knowledge, skills and
values when undertaking complex and sensitive judgements and decisions in uncertain
('risky') situations where harm may ensue.

The value (and danger) of a risk perspective

The social work role has always included elements of care and elements of control. At the heart of our profession is a duality that obliges us to empower but also to protect. It is possible to map out a spectrum of social work practice from inclusive, empowering approaches like coproduction and community development through supportive interventions to the most controlling aspects of our work (see Figure 0.1). Sometimes it is not possible to achieve our goals through collaboration and the wellbeing of vulnerable individuals requires the use of more coercive approaches.

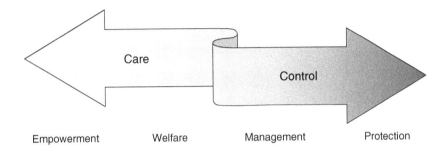

Figure 0.1 Care and control

To protect children and adults from harm, social workers should use the most empowering interventions possible, but this often necessitates some form of social control. Connolly (2017 pxii) describes how an over-emphasis on harm can undermine our ability to collaborate with families.

Tensions exist between society's need to assess, understand, and effectively mitigate risk, and the need to engage children, young people and families within processes that address their concerns and uphold their rights as citizens.

(Marie Connolly 2017, pxii)

A number of commentators have described a drift from social work traditional principles of empowerment to the more controlling aspects of practice.

An emphasis on risk pushes social work away from inclusive, emancipatory approaches towards exclusionary, controlling practices which do not necessarily cohere with traditional values. Social work has been transformed from a profession with a commitment to enhancing individual well-being to one concerned to prevent harm, either to service users themselves, or to other members of the community.

(Hardy 2017, p395)

This book argues that the principles of protection and social justice are not mutually exclusive. The challenge for today's practitioners is to be risk aware without being risk averse, to work with individuals and families to promote both well-being and safety.

A clear understanding of potential dangers is an important aspect of a holistic assessment, but that is only one aspect and it should not be allowed to dominate the decision-making process. Hopefully, in this book we have articulated the importance of a balanced approach that incorporates strengths as well as deficits and benefits as well as harms.

The need for professional decision making

The primary reason for assessing need and risk is to help guide good **decision making**. Our understanding of the situation enables us to agree the best course of action to address the identified issues. Like assessment, decision making is a complex and challenging task with legal, ethical and cultural implications. Decision making in social work frequently involves your professional supervisor and other professionals, but you will have an important role weighing the available information and supporting the decision-making process. In the current climate with limited resources and services, it is often necessary to decide if there is sufficient risk or need to justify an intervention (Crossland 2019). Similarly, we may need to decide if an individual or family meets the eligibility criteria or which service best meets a person's needs. Practitioners can experience tensions between their responsibility to people who use services and their employing agency. Symonds et al (2018) describe how professionals can find themselves at an interface between the needs of their client and a bureaucratic system of resource allocation.

Research suggests that one of the most challenging aspects of assessment is the interpretation or analysis of the gathered information. This book provides practical guidance to help practitioners synthesise their findings into clear and well-evidenced conclusions. We also describe how collaborative discussions of risk and need can help to manage conflict and achieve consensus on the best course of action.

Structure of this book

This book is in two parts. Part One comprises the first five chapters, which provide an overview of the assessment and decision-making processes. Chapter 1 introduces the theme of assessment and defines key terms. It goes on to outline a six-stage process and considers good practice in relation to each stage. In Chapter 2 we outline the need to include individuals and their families in assessment of needs, strengths and risks. In Chapter 3 we discuss how assessment frameworks provide prompts and help us to structure information when used, employing professional assessment skills and social work values. Good assessments draw on the expertise of others and in Chapter 4 we look at ways in which other professionals and other agencies can contribute to a multidisciplinary process. Research suggests that social workers are good at gathering information from a range of sources but sometimes struggle to pull this together in a way that highlights the key messages. Chapter 5 suggests ways to use criticality and analysis throughout the assessment and decision-making process.

Part Two of the book considers more specialist aspects of the assessment and decision-making process that are important for social workers in a range of practice settings. This uses the decision ecology of Baumann et al (2014) as a general framework. Statutory social work is conducted within a legal framework and Chapter 6 considers legal aspects of assessment including duties and standards of care. In all areas of practice, social workers are required to engage in reasoned, reasonable risk taking. They have a duty of care and a duty to communicate about the risks. Legislation upholds the equality (Equality Act 2010) and rights (Human Rights Act 1998) of every person subject to social work assessments and decisions. Practice is subject to scrutiny and challenges such as inquiries and judicial reviews, but we argue that it is possible to be a competent, confident, caring professional through a fuller appreciation of how the law supports reasonable, reasoned decision making.

There is ongoing debate as to what constitutes sound evidence and how this can inform assessments and decisions. Chapter 7 takes a closer look at the role of professional judgement and the use of available information and knowledge. We highlight the importance of having a clear, conceptual understanding to underpin any assessment. Issues of objectivity, subjectivity and bias are considered in more depth than in Part One. **Assessment tools** are discussed as a key mechanism to bring knowledge into practice.

Chapter 8 focuses on 'threshold' decisions such as in safeguarding adults and children from abuse, and making decisions about eligibility for services. The potential and pitfalls of statistical models for predicting a harmful outcome are outlined, including reference to static, dynamic and mitigating (strength) factors. Reference will be made to statistical models, professional consensus tools and eligibility criteria such as in *Fair Access to Care*.

Robust assessments should be used as the basis for positive risk management as opposed to risk avoidance. Chapter 9 focuses on decisions that choose between options, such as in care planning. Reasonable and reasoned positive 'risk taking' (including supporting clients to take reasonable, reasoned risks) in situations where no option is risk-free are emphasised. The idea of 'balancing risk and harms' is introduced and the need for professional values in such decision making is emphasised.

The final chapter focuses on the process of developing skills related to assessment, working with risk, making professional judgements and engaging in effective decision processes. The effective use of professional supervision is highlighted as a key mechanism for learning as well as avoiding bias in judgements and making reasoned, reasonable decisions in contexts of risk. Developing knowledge and skills within a multi-professional team or working environment is discussed in the context of ensuring that your role as a social work professional is respected just as you must respect other professions.

Learning outcomes

To aid you in your learning process, each chapter of this book has been mapped against the Social Work Subject Benchmark Statement produced by the Quality Assurance Agency for Higher Education (2016). This is designed to ensure consistency of standards across qualifying social work courses in the UK. In addition, each chapter of this book has been mapped against the Professional Capabilities Framework for England (British Association of Social Workers 2018). This is designed to aid the continuing development of knowledge and skills at various career stages. A diagrammatic representation of this is provided in Appendix 1. These learning outcomes are listed at the start of each chapter, and we hope that you will find them helpful.

Theoretical underpinnings

Each chapter in this new edition concludes with links identifying some broad theoretical material which is relevant to the chapter themes. There is not always a single theory that informs the material, but we hope that the pointers are useful in helping you to understand the broader context.

What this book isn't

As the title suggests, this book is an introduction to the concepts of assessment, risk and decision making. It is primarily aimed at students and practitioners at the start of their careers. Brian Taylor's *Decision Making, Assessment and Risk in Social Work*, also by Sage, is aimed at more experienced practitioners. This book is an attempt to provide a framework to help social workers understand their role in assessment and decision making. It highlights some of the challenges and complexities inherent in this role and encourages practitioners to apply the principles of person-centred relational practice. As we introduce our core themes it is worth clarifying what this book will not provide.

1. This book is not a manual for practice. Social work is diverse and complex and it is not possible or helpful to produce a formulaic approach to practice. Any assessment or decision needs to take into account the legal, policy and organisational context. While some frameworks are referenced as illustrations, we do not provide or recommend specific models. Simply reading this book is only a start in creating competent practice; developing knowledge, skills and values to assess and support individuals and families takes time and practice.
2. This book is not specific to any group or programme of care. Rather it is an effort to identify themes, principles and concepts that relate to all social work decision-making settings. Practitioners need to think through the application to their own areas of work.
3. This book is not 'the silver bullet'; a magical solution to the challenges of uncertainty and risk is attractive, but mythical. We argue that the most effective response to social issues is compassionate engagement, competent assessment and robust and fair decision processes. Reasoned and reasonable decisions cannot be guaranteed to achieve predicable outcomes, but they are the best response to the situations in which we find ourselves.

Terminology

Key terms are discussed in the text at appropriate places and a Glossary is provided. Some social workers in the UK prefer the term *service user* to *client*, although the best evidence suggests that this is not a preference of people who come to social workers (Lloyd et al 2001; Keaney et al 2004; Covell et al 2007; Taylor and McKeown 2013). As there is no consensus on this issue, when possible we endeavour to use general terms like people, individuals or families.

New material in the second edition

We are grateful for feedback received on the first edition. This second edition has retained the same basic structure, but it has been updated and developed in the following ways.

- Chapter 5 has been expanded to include more practical guidance on analysis within assessment.
- We have endeavoured to make more explicit reference to recognition of spirituality and cultural competence within assessment and decision making.
- We have extended our discussion of the potential for bias within assessment and professional judgement.
- We have tried to ensure that the book has equal relevance to all aspects of social work including adult social care, families and children, and justice.
- Where possible we have supplemented the statutory services focus with material relating to the voluntary sector
- Legal and policy aspects of UK services have been updated.
- Feedback indicates that readers value the visual representations used in the first edition. Where possible we have included additional illustrations.

Concluding comments

This brief book attempts to provide social workers with an overview of the exciting topics of assessment and risk. References have been limited to readily available books, documents and articles that are likely to be of most interest. For further study you may wish to consider how the following relate to your own area of work:

- inter-professional working;
- evidence-based practice;
- legislation and statutory duties;
- professional standards;
- decision-making processes; and
- decision aids including assessment tools and computerised systems.

Hopefully, this book will prompt you to think about your role as a professional in the critical task of making judgements and being involved in decisions for the benefit of clients, families and society.

Part One

Introducing key concepts

1

A framework for assessment, risk and decisions

Achieving a Social Work Degree

This chapter will help you develop the following capabilities from the Professional Capabilities Framework (2018):

2. Values and ethics
5. Knowledge
6. Critical reflection and analysis
7. Skills and interventions
8. Contexts and organisations

See Appendix 1 for the Professional Capabilities Framework Fan and a description of the 9 domains.

(Continued)

(Continued)

It will also introduce you to the following standards as set out in the Social Work Subject Benchmark Statement (2019):

5.2 Knowledge of social work theory
5. 3 Values and ethics

See Appendix 2 for a detailed description of these standards.

Introduction

This first chapter will define the concept of **assessment** as it applies to social work practice. It will argue that assessment is central to the social work process but it is a challenging task given the complexity of the world we live in. Assessments help us make decisions about supporting people and keeping them safe so we will think about the context of **risk**, decision making and the broader care planning cycle. Assessment does not always happen in a linear way, but six foundational elements of assessment and decision making will be explored using case studies to illustrate their practical application. Assessment will be shown to be both an art (involving skills in working with people) and a science (involving understanding and using a relevant knowledge base). Hopefully by the end of the chapter you will be aware of the ways in which a collaborative assessment will provide a better understanding of people and the situations that they live in.

Activity 1.1   Being Assessed

Think of a time when you have been the subject of an assessment. This may be medical, educational or in relation to your employment.

- Did you find the process to be helpful?
- Do you think that the outcome was accurate?
- How involved did you feel in the process?

Comment

You may have had a positive experience where you were part of a process that accurately described your situation. It is also possible that you were dissatisfied by a process where you felt that it failed to accurately reflect your situation. Feedback from people who use our services suggests that the assessment process can have a powerful impact promoting hope or causing distress and that the attitude of the worker is a key factor.

The importance of assessment in social work

Social work is about working with people, empowering them and promoting change. The assessment phase of any intervention is crucial as it sets the scene for any further work. It is an opportunity to clearly articulate *why* social services are involved. Unfortunately, this is not always explained to the people who use our service and it is difficult to achieve a good outcome if people do not know why we are there. The initial stage of intervention is also the time to agree *what* information is required. The social worker needs to combine their knowledge of the issues (theoretical knowledge) with information about the specific situation (case information). Case information is gathered at the start of a helping process and then throughout the period of engagement, providing an understanding of the dynamic situation. It is central to the social work process as it forms the basis of decisions made about the case. Often these decisions will have a major impact on the lives of people who use our services, so the assessment process needs to be as accurate as possible. Whether it is a two-minute phone call or a 25-page court report, we need to make sure that we are gathering and presenting information in an accurate manner.

Defining assessment

Within social work, the term 'assessment' generally relates to a process that helps professionals make a decision. The following definition may be helpful in breaking down the core components of an assessment.

> Assessment is a purposeful, systematic, collaborative process of information gathering which supports analysis, recommendations and shared decision making.

An assessment needs to be based on knowledge. Before we begin the process, we need to have a clear understanding of the issues being investigated. This will help us know what questions to ask and how to ask them and there may be specific **assessment tools** that can be used. It will help if we can explain our rationale to the people who might be providing answers. This is why the assessment needs to be purposeful. The assessor should know what information is required and the decisions that will eventually be made. They will use a systematic approach to engage all key stakeholders based on the knowledge and experience that they bring. Information gathering should be collaborative, ideally based on a relationship of trust between the assessor and the people who provide information. Social work assessment is not just about information gathering. Pertinent information needs to be synthesised and analysed to produce conclusions and recommendations that a decision-making forum, like a case conference or a care review meeting, can use as the basis for its deliberations.

Figure 1.1 shows how assessment fits within the broader social work process. A good assessment will describe the current situation and help us to plan the best way to intervene. Interventions may be provided by a range of professionals and agencies and it is good practice to regularly review (reassess) the progress that has been made. It is possible that the process will terminate after initial intervention but for many cases this cycle will repeat multiple times.

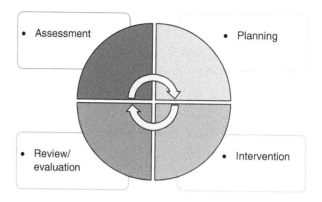

Figure 1.1 The social work process

Defining needs, risks and capacity

Most social work assessments and interventions focus on promoting the well-being of an individual, family or group. In most situations this involves the three overlapping areas illustrated in Figure 1.2. In reality, these three concepts are closely related. A lack of capacity impacts on a parent's ability to meet the needs of a child, which could result in the risk of harm. Similarly, in adult services, a brain injury or dementia may impact on a person's ability to recognise dangers, resulting in potential harm.

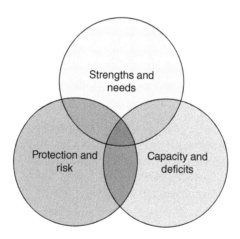

Figure 1.2 Needs, Risks and Capacity

The term 'needs' describes those things that are required to promote safety, well-being and fulfilment. Assessments focusing primarily on needs might ask:

- if the current accommodation is appropriate;
- if a child's health and developmental needs are being met;
- if appropriate services are being provided.

Risk relates to the potential for something going wrong. A situation where harm *might* occur. The word *might* suggests uncertainty because it is not possible to be sure if harm will occur. A **risk assessment** tries to understand how likely the harm is and how severe the outcome might be. Risk is a normal part of human existence (Ponton 1997) but social workers need to differentiate between positive risk taking that achieves benefits with minimal harm, and negative risk taking that results in harm but achieves minimal benefits.

Assessments focusing primarily on risk might ask:

- Is there a danger that an older person might fall?
- What is the likelihood of reoffending?
- Is there a danger of exploitation?

It is important to recognise that any planned interventions may themselves have inherent **risks** as consequences (Carson and Bain 2008). Our understanding of 'risk' will be developed further in later chapters.

Capacity describes the ability of an individual or family to meet needs and protect from harm. This might relate to themselves or someone in their care. When change is required, a good assessment will describe how willing or able key individuals are to achieve this change. Assessments focusing primarily on capacity might ask:

- if parents understand and can meet the needs of a child;
- if a person has sufficient understanding to make an informed decision;
- if a person understands the implications of a service or intervention.

Key Definitions

Needs

Human needs are the aspects of life which an individual requires to be healthy and happy. Maslow's hierarchy (1954) categorised these as basic needs, psychological needs and self-fulfilment. While agencies may recognise the importance of all needs, they are often required to make a pragmatic decision as to which they are able to support. Such prioritisation can result in unmet needs. Some needs are deemed to be the moral entitlement of every person and these rights are protected in law.

Risk

Risk is a situation where undesirable as well as desirable outcomes are possible and the outcome is not known. Risk management involves the balancing of benefits and harms.

Capacity

Capacity is the ability of a person to understand their needs or the needs of another person and weigh up the benefits and risks of any course of action.

Knowledge as a basis for assessment

The practitioner undertaking an assessment is equipped with:

- knowledge that helps them conceptualise the issue at hand;
- skills to engage people, gather information and analyse the findings;
- values that uphold the worth and dignity of the people involved.

Pawson et al. (2003) categorised five types of knowledge that underpin social work.

- Organisational: Knowledge gained from organising social care.
- Practitioner: Knowledge gained from doing social care.
- Policy: Knowledge gained from wider policy context.
- Research: Knowledge gathered systematically with a planned design.
- People who use our services and carers: Knowledge gained from experience of and reflection on service use.

These combined forms of knowledge form the bedrock of an assessment, which helps us to:

- define the key concepts (what is happening?);
- understand possible causes (why is it happening?);
- identify the impact (what is the harm or benefit?);
- inform professional judgement (how do I understand it and how does this frame the decision?); and
- consider necessary change (what would help?).

As our understanding of social issues is constantly changing, it is important that practitioners keep themselves informed. Professional development opportunities should enable participants to engage with up-to-date information relating to their specific area of practice. The use of knowledge to inform assessment and analysis will be further developed in Chapter 5.

Assessing complex situations

For some professional groups, assessing conditions and recommending responses is a reasonably simple process. However, the world inhabited by social workers is notoriously complex. For example, social workers sometimes help older people and their families to decide if it is better to remain at home or move to a supported care setting, but:

- it is difficult to predict the outcome of each option;
- such decisions raise powerful emotions;
- stakeholders may have very different opinions on the potential benefits and harms; and
- social workers may need to coordinate the assessment roles of other professions in order to create a holistic assessment and to provide coordinated care.

As a result, the task of assessment is difficult, requiring a high level of skill (Horwarth 2018). The information available may be based on concrete facts, but equally it could be based on subjective opinion or gut feelings. The Brunswik Lens Model (Brunswik 1956; Figure 1.3) provides a graphic illustration of the dilemma inherent in the social work assessment process. The assessor must choose which information (cues) are important, how to weigh them and what to do if there is disagreement. A different approach to choosing, weighing and interpreting cues will result in a different conclusion.

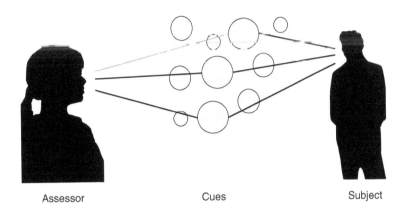

Assessor   Cues   Subject

Figure 1.3   Brunswik lens model (adapted from Brunswik 1956)

A range of factors affect the quality of information available to us, as below.

- Complexity – the difficulties faced by families and individuals can be multifaceted and interconnected.
- Context – we need to interpret information in the light of the wider situation.
- Uncertainty – we cannot be 100 per cent sure that information is correct as sources and measures can be fallible.
- Incompleteness – often there are gaps in the available information.
- Contested information – the key players in a situation do not always agree on the information or its importance.

One of the challenges of the social work profession is the requirement to make important decisions that affect people's lives using complex and/or incomplete information. It is the social worker's job to predict the unpredictable. When there is a negative outcome and somebody gets hurt it is not the quality of the information that is criticised. Most often **hindsight** (see Glossary) is used to criticise the decision process or the decision makers. The 'damned if you do, damned if you don't' dilemma can be profoundly uncomfortable for practitioners and there is a danger that we can unconsciously allow our fear for ourselves to influence how we support other people. This 'defensive practice' can distort how we engage with individuals and families and how we perceive the risks that they are experiencing (Whittaker and Havard 2015). The potential for defensive practice was highlighted by Munro in her review of child protection processes.

Child protection work involves working with uncertainty: we cannot know for sure what is going on in families; we cannot be sure that improvements in family circumstances will last.

Many of the problems in current practice seem to arise from the defensive ways in which professionals are expected to manage that uncertainty. For some, following rules and being compliant can appear less risky than carrying the personal responsibility for exercising judgment.

(Munro 2011, p6)

Practitioners need to recognise the potential for defensive practice and the way that this could distort their assessments and decision making.

Theory and methods that inform assessment

There is no single social work theory that explains how and why assessments should be completed. Knowledge does, however, help us understand social issues and therefore the role of assessment as part of the wider helping process. Some examples of how theories and methods can influence assessments are provided below and in Table 1.1.

Table 1.1   Examples of theories and methods

Theory	Method	Application
Systems theory	Systems models	The individual in context
Problem-solving theory	Task-centred casework	The social work process
Change theory	Motivational interviewing	Recognising ambivalence
Psychoanalytical theory	Relationship-based practice	Relationship as the basis of assessment

Social work relates to human behaviour and any assessment process needs to be based on an understanding of emotional and interpersonal factors. Relationships may not always be free from conflict, but the skilled social worker will seek to understand the situation from the client perspective, and try to view conflict from the client or family perspective. For more detailed attention to working in situations of ambivalence and conflict, see Taylor 2011 in the Further Reading section.

Social work intervention relates to a person or family who exists within a wider social system. Houston (2015b) suggests that the individual person needs to be understood within the context of relationships, culture, organisations and politics. The individual and the system factors are so intertwined that it is not possible to explain any part in isolation. Any assessment that seeks to understand a person's experience, motivation and behaviour must be able to appreciate the world that they inhabit.

Social work practice is strongly influenced by task-oriented casework approaches based on **problem solving** theory. They tend to focus on the practitioner as an expert helper who endeavours to assess and then resolve problems by agreeing a methodical, staged approach. The inconvenient reality is that people often don't want to be fixed. They do not always agree that a problem exists and they can be ambivalent or resistant to social work involvement. Change theory and motivational interviewing recognise the possibility of such ambivalence and incorporate this into the approach to intervention.

Art or science?

There is an ongoing debate as to whether or not social work can be a purely rational, logical, linear process. Social work assessments involve subjective information and subjective information needs to be interpreted. A skilled assessor is able to explain why they chose information, how they interpreted it and what it means for future decisions. They will be able to justify why some sources of information were given priority over others and how contested issues were addressed. Unfortunately, there have been a number of very public failings where the assessment process did not keep children or vulnerable adults safe. In cases like Steven Hoskin (Flynn 2007) or Child C (Fife Child Protection Committee 2017), deaths have been linked to inadequacies in information gathering, communication and risk recognition. With each inquiry, recommendations are made and procedures are reviewed.

Professionals and agencies are often criticised in the media for not identifying problems that, with the benefit of hindsight, seem all too obvious. Public anger is understandable, but it is often based on a flawed understanding of risk assessment that presumes a capable practitioner using appropriate procedures will effectively identify and eliminate risk (Fengler and Taylor 2019). This oversimplification supposes a linear relationship between social work skills and outcomes for families. It presumes the task is similar to a car production line where every stage can be assessed and quality assured to provide uniform and predictable results. This technical/scientific perspective overlooks the influence of multiple factors outside the practitioner's control.

We know that working with subjectivity and complexity is not an exact science, but this does not mean we should abandon efforts to measure impact and effectiveness. As a profession, we agree that people on our caseloads deserve to receive support that is based on the current best evidence. Some might argue that the selection and application of evidence is more of an art than a science. In reality, social work is a combination of both. Connolly et al. (2009) argue that social work must incorporate methodically developed theory with skills and creativity to meet the needs of families and individuals. The importance of using evidence to form a clear conceptual understanding as the basis of a skilled assessment will be discussed in Chapter 7.

Research Summary   A Good Quality Assessment

In a review of research relating to assessment in child protection, Turney et al. (2011 p13) identified five elements of a good quality assessment:

1. Ensure that the child remains central
2. Contain full, concise, relevant and accurate information
3. Include a chronology and/or family and social history
4. Make good use of information from a range of sources
5. Include analysis that makes clear links between the recorded information and plans for intervention (or decisions not to take any further action).

The assessment and decision-making process

We have discussed above the importance of assessments being purposeful and systematic if they are going to be effective. Assessments are not always a single linear process but it is possible to identify specific stages of the task. Figure 1.4 divides the assessment into stages so that we can explore them in more depth.

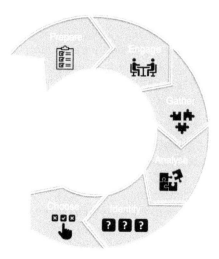

Figure 1.4 The assessment and decision-making process

1. Prepare – Who will be involved and what do we need to know?
2. Engage – Make contact with the key individual/s to agree the process
3. Gather – Use a range of techniques to collect necessary information
4. Analyse – Combine, order and make sense of the collected information
5. Identify – Make recommendations of the possible options
6. Choose – Work with others to select the most favourable option.

You will see in the diagram that the six dimensions of assessment progress from planning to decision making. It is possible that some elements will be replicated during the overall assessment. Similarly, the cycle may reoccur a number of times during our work. Let's look at each of the six stages in more detail.

Stage 1: Prepare

It is important to know why we are undertaking an assessment and what information we need, but how we undertake that task is an equally significant factor in achieving success. The complexity of social issues means that no two assessments will be identical and a formulaic approach will fail to meet the needs of families or professionals. Taylor and Devine (1993) describe a process of 'tuning-in' similar to getting the best reception on a radio. They suggest that in planning an intervention, the practitioner should take time to formally consider:

- the client group – knowledge of the issues;
- the individual – understanding of their culture, beliefs and perceptions;
- the phase of work – fitting this visit into the wider involvement; and
- their own feelings.

These aspects can be used to develop specific questions that might assist a formal preparation process. The theme of the person uses theory and existing knowledge to consider how the person may be feeling. The theme of work considers how this interaction will fit within the wider involvement of our agencies and others identifying specific objectives for this element of the work. The theme of self analyses the practitioner's own thoughts and feelings and identifies ways that they might contribute to a positive outcome. Taylor and Devine's approach to tuning-in can be developed to produce a range of planning questions relating to the subject of the assessment, the potential work and the practitioner (Table 1.2).

Table 1.2   Tuning in to the work (based on Taylor and Devine (1993))

The Context	What is the local setting of my team?
	What are the issues for people who use this service?
	What is the policy and legal context?
The Person	What knowledge (theory) will help me understand the situation?
	What information has already been gathered?
	What hopes and fears might the person have?
The Work	How does this specific interaction fit within the broader work?
	What would a good outcome look like?
	What are my key objectives for this interaction?
My self	What presumptions do I bring?
	What anxieties do I have/what might go wrong?
	What skills will I use to achieve my objectives?

Case Study   Preparing for an Initial Meeting

The duty social worker has received a telephone call from Dr Baxter about a young mother called Alison Morrison (age 21 years old). Alison has a 2-year-old son called Zac, and they recently moved to your area from the town where her parents live.

Alison's doctor suggests she has little support and needs reassurance and advice about her care of Zac. There are concerns that Zac may have some form of developmental delay. He is very active and Alison is struggling to manage in her small, city centre flat.

Clearly the doctor feels there is a need for intervention, but the referral is vague.

- What aspects of the referral stand out for you?
- How would you prepare for an initial meeting?

On receipt of the referral, it is useful to give some thought to the task ahead. The available information is limited, which complicates the task. The planning stage allows the social worker to prepare for initial contact: how they will engage, who they will engage with and what will be the focus of the assessment. This planning requires some basic information and, in this case, it may be necessary to go back to the GP to clarify some details.

There is a range of information that might be gathered during any social work assessment. It is never possible to find out and record everything, so the early stages will involve ascertaining the primary issue of concern. In the above case study, the focus might be about:

- support for a parent who is struggling (strengths and needs);
- Alison's ability to care for Zac (capacity and deficits); and
- potential harm to Alison or Zac (protection and risk).

When identifying the focus of the assessment, it is also important to recognise the context within which the individual lives. This may include immediate family members, extended family, social networks and communities. Careful preparation will allow you to structure your first contact with the family. It will also allow you to clearly explain to participants what you hope to achieve. This may come as second nature to experienced practitioners who are able to prepare the assessment as they drive to the house. Less experienced social workers and students may benefit from undertaking a formal tuning-in which will consider the possible issues, the expectations of the people they will be meeting, and the skills that they will need to use. Being clear on the focus of your assessment does not mean you are blind to other possibilities. Social workers should always be alert to underlying factors or related issues that need attention. Often during interviews, we receive information seemingly at a tangent to the primary focus, and this may require further consideration. Any indication of risk to people in or outside the family group will need to be followed up (see Chapter 6 on legal and ethical aspects for further discussion on this topic).

Stage 2: Engage

The engagement stage is an opportunity for the social worker to introduce themselves and explain the reason for their involvement. The family at the centre of the assessment has the right to know why we are there, how we plan to proceed and how the information will be used. During this early stage we initiate human connection, listen to the individual and endeavour to empathise with their situation. The experience of being listened to and being understood can, in itself, be powerfully therapeutic. Unfortunately, this is not always how people feel when receiving our services.

Research Summary   Empathy in Assessment

When organising a student event at a day centre for people who have mental health difficulties, we asked the members what characteristics made a good social worker. It didn't take them long to come up with a unanimous response:

That's easy. They treat you like a human being.

When we asked how we might teach this vital skill they said:

You can't teach it. They either have it or they don't.

Assessment is a collaborative process and often it is an opportunity to build a relationship that will be the basis for future involvement. If the key stakeholders feel that their input is valued, they are more likely to engage in the process and in any following intervention. Whenever possible we strive to do assessments *with* people rather than doing assessments *of* people. It is not always possible to engage individuals in the assessment process but, in most cases, it is possible to identify areas of agreement on which to base a working relationship. The initial meeting is an opportunity to seek permission to contact other professionals who may have information to contribute. Chapter 2 of this book focuses on the importance of engaging with clients and families in the processes of assessment and decision making.

Case Study   Beginnings of Meetings

At an initial home visit, you meet Alison and Zac. Alison apologises for the sparsely furnished flat, but it seems clean and comfortable with a range of toys and books on the floor. As you talk, Zac runs about the room climbing on furniture and trying to turn on the TV. Alison seems to be very anxious about your presence and Zac's behaviour. She says she is glad you have visited as she is not sure she can cope.

- How might you put Alison at ease?
- What might be the focus of your assessment?

Stage 3: Gathering information

Once we have got to know more about Alison and Zac, we are able to agree how the assessment will be completed, what information will be gathered and how this will be achieved. The primary sources of information may be:

- speaking to the child or adult who is the subject of the assessment;
- speaking to carers and family members;
- observing the home environment;
- observing the interaction of the key individuals;
- speaking to other professionals;
- reading existing case records;
- contacting any other people who could contribute to the process.

As the assessment progresses, the practitioner will decide where to go for information and what aspects are important. This selectivity introduces potential dangers that could influence the outcome of the assessment. Firstly, because we are concerned about harm, there is a danger that social work assessments will focus on the negative aspects of an individual or family's life, taking the positive aspects for granted. This presents a skewed picture that could result in poor decisions and demoralised participants. Equally, there is a danger that the practitioner unconsciously prioritises data that supports their existing beliefs (Spratt 2023) or that describes what they would like to see rather than what they actually see (Kettle 2023). These and other forms of bias are discussed further in Chapter 7. To reduce the impact of bias, the gathering of evidence needs to be thorough and balanced. The assessment should consider strengths as well as needs, and **protective factors** as well as risks. It should also assess the capacity for individuals to respond and the **likelihood** of change. The potential to engage family members using person-centred or solution-focused techniques will be further discussed in Chapter 2.

A range of assessment tools has been devised to assist in the gathering of information and the understanding of specific issues that families might face. These cannot replace assessment skills but they can support the practitioner to gather and order the necessary information in a methodical way. Chapter 3 of this book discusses some of the available tools and how they can best be used within an assessment.

Other professionals and family members can be a key asset in providing information, bringing their specific knowledge or experience to the assessment. Chapter 4 considers the importance of collaborating, communicating and managing conflict in assessment and decision making.

Stage 4: Analyse

A good assessment is much more than collecting information from a range of sources. The social worker needs to draw the material together and use it to tell the story of the people at the centre of the process. Describing the 'big picture' helps decision makers understand what the primary issues are and why they might be occurring. Munro (1996) likens this task to completing a jigsaw puzzle when some of the pieces are missing and we do not know what the final picture will look like. To develop this metaphor further, the pieces that we are able to gather do not always fit easily together and they do not always provide an accurate image. A key social work skill is the ability to evaluate each source of evidence to establish its credibility. This professional curiosity or 'respectful uncertainty' (Taylor and White 2006) should be applied to all information rather than taking it at face value. Chapter 5 will discuss how professional judgements can be used as a basis for analysis and conclusions.

Case Study   Reconciling Conflicting Information

Your subsequent case work produces differing accounts of the family situation.

Alison tells you that her critical and unsupportive parents told her she was no longer welcome in the family home. She moved to her current flat as it was the first available option and she wants a fresh start. Alison feels that she is able to care for Zac despite her lack of support.

A health visitor from Alison's hometown reports that Alison's parents seemed to be supportive, caring for both Alison and Zac. Their efforts to provide support and direction resulted in an argument and Alison walked out. The health visitor feels that Alison is immature and struggling with the demands of parenthood. She provides examples of Alison's inability or unwillingness to provide boundaries for Zac.

- How might you make sense of these two different accounts?

Stage 5: Identify

Once the relevant information has been gathered and analysed, it is possible to consider the options that might help to achieve change. At this stage it is possible to recognise differing opinions and articulate the potential value of each course of action. Before formal decisions are made it can help to consider all available options and often this process can be undertaken in partnership with the people being assessed.

Use of Terms 'Judgements' and 'Decisions'

It is important to distinguish between two aspects of assessment that are often used interchangeably. In this book the term judgement relates to a mental process where an individual assesses or weighs up information. The term decision making relates to an individual or group choosing between alternatives, often to inform future action.

For example, in a mental health assessment, a professional makes judgements about information relating to circumstances and behaviour that will ultimately allow a decision if the subject should be detained in hospital.

A social worker will judge how well a child is progressing in foster care and write a report helping a multidisciplinary group to make a decision about the future.

Stage 6: Choose

The final stage of assessment is to indicate the preferred course of action, justifying why it has been selected. Macdonald (2001) argues that quality of any assessment depends on its prescriptive value: 'The value of assessment lies in its ability to direct future action – soundly' (p236). Practitioners can sometimes be reluctant to use and express their professional opinion, but without this it is impossible for decision makers to develop an effective **care plan**. Too often professionals hedge their bets by suggesting a broad range of actions that are too general to address the issue and too extensive for families to be able to achieve.

Theoretical underpinnings

In this chapter we discuss how social work practice theories can be linked to the assessment process, in particular:

- Systems theory which helps us understand the individual within the context of family and society.
- Problem-solving theories, including Task-Centred Practice, which focus on specific aspects of the situation that need to be addressed and the actions that might enable progress.

Knowledge and skills summary

This first chapter has introduced the assessment process and suggested that it is central to the social work role. Assessment needs to be based on a framework of knowledge that helps us understand the issues and the potential impact that they may have. It is a skilled task as the information is often complex, context bound, incomplete and contested. An assessment may incorporate information from one or more of the overlapping domains of needs, risk and capacity. In **assessing risk**, it is important to include the potential benefits as well as potential harms. Key assessment skills are:

- People skills, which include the ability to build a rapport and explain the purpose of the assessment
- Communication skills, which include asking questions, listening, probing and recognising non-verbal communication
- Information-gathering skills, which include the ability to identify sources of information and draw out the pertinent data using questioning and observation
- Analytical skills, which involve synthesising the gathered data to present the 'big picture' of the child or adult's life.

Further Reading

Martin, R. (2010). *Social work assessment*. Exeter: Learning Matters.

This book defines social work assessment and discusses the knowledge, skills and values that underpin it. Specific chapters are included considering the application of assessment in children's services, adult services and mental health settings.

Parker, J. (2020). *Social work practice: assessment, planning, intervention and review* (Sixth Edition). London: Learning Matters.

The sixth edition of Jonathan Parker's popular book outlines the key social work roles of assessment, planning, intervention and review.

Taylor, B.J. (Ed.) (2011). *Working with aggression and resistance in social work*. London: Sage (Learning Matters Transforming Social Work Series).

This book focuses on the challenges of working in situations of aggressiveness and resistance to social work involvement. Three general chapters on topics such as understanding and defusing aggression are followed by chapters relating to specific client groups.

2

Involving individuals and families in assessment and decisions

(Continued)

It will also introduce you to the following standards as set out in the Social Work Subject Benchmark Statement (2019):

5.4   Service users and carers
5.16 Skills in working with others

See Appendix 2 for a detailed description of these standards.

Introduction

Social work is about relationships. The best social work involves human connection, honesty and respect and ideally this is a two-way process. Assessments build on relationships to develop an understanding of the complex lives and experiences of individuals and families. It is this understanding that will help us make reasonable and reasoned decisions about needs, risks and capacity. The people we are working with should be active participants in the assessment process and their well-being should be central to assessments and decisions.

This chapter will consider the benefits of cooperation in assessment. People will not always be willing or able to be fully involved, but it is the role of the social worker to maximise their contribution. Occasionally, because of the risk of harm and limited time constraints we will have no choice but to require unwilling individuals to engage. This chapter explores the way our attitudes can affect how people experience our services, and provides a brief introduction to some strengths-based approaches. We will consider the crucial social work skill of working with resistance and we will draw from motivational interviewing to understand the relevance of ambivalence to the change process.

Who is the assessment for?

Before we commence an assessment, we need to ask who will be using the material that we gather. Who will be involved in making decisions based on your findings? Hopefully, the families and individuals at the centre of the process will have access to the central reports. If that is the case, this documentation needs to be written in a way that people can understand. We need to be careful about jargon, acronyms or terminology that can cause confusion. People who receive social work support say that the language that we use can be alienating and stigmatising (Goddard 2021). The language used can also build relationships or undermine collaboration. In a 'Ways of Writing' initiative, Wiltshire Council encourages staff to write in a way that a child would understand and find helpful (Hayward 2023). A clear and sensitive description of the situation allows all stakeholders to participate on an equal footing and helps families and practitioners to work together in identifying the best way forward.

The importance of cooperation

Activity 2.1   The Importance of Cooperation

Think of a professional in your life who influenced your development and growth. This might be a teacher, a youth worker, a religious leader, a counsellor or a manager.

- What was it about them that helped you?
- Can you think of practical examples of this helping?
- Have you experiences of people whose efforts to assist you were unhelpful?

Comment

Your thoughts may have related to the person's attitude and the way they made you feel about yourself. In my own case, one particular mentor seemed to understand me and believe in me. His belief was infectious and it encouraged me to believe in myself. Positive attitudes can be seen in practical examples. My mentor was always quick to identify and celebrate success. Similarly, he was understanding and supportive when things went wrong.

The assessment process, like other aspects of social work, is based on the interaction between two or more people. Research suggests that the quality of the relationship will affect the quality of the work. There are ethical and practical reasons to promote a relational approach to assessment in children's (McLeod 2010, Rice et al. 2002) and adult services (Duffy et al. 2016, Dix et al. 2019).

Chapter 1 discussed how each individual's experience is subjective and empathy is required to gain an understanding of the world from their perspective. The more involved the individual is in the assessment process, the more likely it is that an accurate assessment and a positive outcome will be achieved. What's more, people who have participated in the early stages of the work are more likely to remain engaged in the subsequent intervention. Partnership working is central to the provision of care and protection to children or adults and the principle is often central to policy documents and practice guidance.

Cooperation may be the ideal form of engagement, but it is not always possible. Individuals and families can resist social work involvement and occasionally undermine the assessment process. As Figure 2.1 shows, the risk of harm can force the practitioner

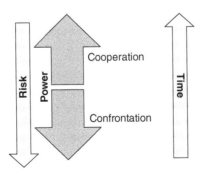

Figure 2.1   Cooperation and Confrontation

to take a more directive approach, as can limitations to the available time. The reality of much social work is that full cooperation is not achieved, but the good practitioner will seek opportunities to maximise the engagement of individuals and families in the process.

In undertaking an assessment, the social worker uses a range of skills to engage with the key stakeholders, explaining the process and encouraging their participation. The potential experience of the worker and the recipient have been added in Figure 2.2 to show that this way of working benefits all parties. The opposite is also true; coercive approaches can be disempowering for the recipient and demoralising for the practitioner. People who receive our service may not always be able to engage, but it is the role of practitioners in all areas of social work to be ready and willing to cooperate while also being prepared to work with resistance.

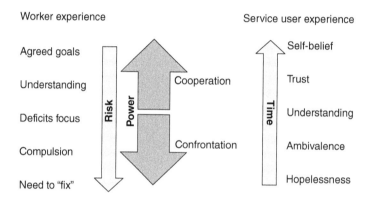

Figure 2.2   Worker and recipient experience

What families want

Butler and Williamson (1994) gathered the views of children on social work support. Since then, there has been a growing body of research that helps us to understand how families experience social work support and how they wish to be treated (McLeod 2010; Ghaffar et al. 2011; Chambers et al. 2014). Similar themes are identified across all programmes of care, and they may echo your thoughts from Activity 2.1 above.

People want social workers to be:

- **Able to listen**. Perhaps the most commonly identified characteristic is the ability to take the time to listen. Active listening helps people to feel understood and has a powerful impact. Equally a frequent criticism is that workers don't take the time to listen.
- **Accessible**. Responding promptly by telephone or in person is seen as essential, and it can be frustrating to hear that your social worker is 'on a course' or 'busy in the office'.
- **Dependable**. Similarly, families expect us to do what we say we will do. When you are anxious or distressed it is unhelpful for the social worker to delay or cancel your visit.
- **Honest**. Children and adults who use our services frequently comment on the practitioner's willingness to share information and 'tell the truth'. It is upsetting if you feel a professional has exaggerated or told lies about you.

- **Compassionate**. It is important that practitioners recognise the pain, shame or distress that individuals might be feeling. In all situations social workers should be able to recognise strengths and encourage hope.
- **A good communicator**. Individuals and families value clear and understandable communication, particularly where there are language or communication difficulties. This includes providing information in an understandable format and in sufficient time for the person to read it.

It is not always easy to predict how individuals and families will experience our involvement, but it is important that we reflect on the type of feedback gathered above. Complaints received are an equally useful insight into the way that we make people feel. Reviewing complaints to the Northern Ireland Social Care Council, Hayes (2018) found that the majority related to attitudes rather than outcomes. Hayes used the acronym HURT to summarise issues relating to Honesty, Unequal practice, lack of Respect or lack of Technical competence.

Research Summary   The World's Worst Professional (Turner 2003)

In research conducted for the Welsh Assembly Government, Claire Turner spoke to 105 disabled children and young people who were between the ages of 5–25 years old. They provided their opinions on the best and worst aspects of a range of professionals including social workers. In their view, the world's worst professional had attributes including:

- someone who doesn't listen
- someone who decides what is best for you instead of asking you
- someone who talks to your parents instead of you
- someone who doesn't explain what they are doing to you
- someone who doesn't give you the right information
- someone who doesn't have enough time and is always too busy
- someone who isn't interested in you
- someone who isn't dedicated to their job
- someone who talks to you but you can't understand them
- someone who is boring.

Clearly these perceptions do not always reflect the workers' motivation or ability, but they provide a sobering reminder that people's perceptions of our attitudes have a significant impact.

Relationship-based practice

The concept of relationship-based social work has recently received renewed attention, partly as a reaction to the perceived proceduralisation of the role. A relationship-based approach recognises that every family is unique, and the relationship between worker and recipient is not just a means-to-an-end but rather a core element of the intervention (Ruch 2005). As Figure 2.3 shows, any worker/subject relationship is in the broader context of the agency setting, which will influence the priorities of the worker and the nature of the engagement. The legal basis and purpose of the employing organisation shapes the role of the social worker in this particular job, and therefore frames the discussion with clients about the helping process. High caseloads, tight time frames and frequent staff turnover make it difficult to build meaningful working relationships with children (Winter 2009) or adults (McLaughlin 2016), but there is a growing recognition that social work may need to rediscover the value of human connection between the practitioner and the recipient. Relationship-based approaches have been applied to settings including adult mental health, residential child-care, care of older people and children's services (McColgan and McMullin 2017).

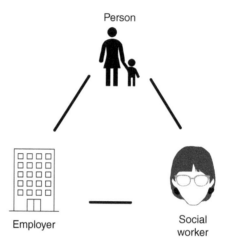

Figure 2.3   Influence of agency setting

There is a tendency to think of relationship-based work as applying only to adults, but this approach is equally important when working with young children. Working together to safeguard children (Government 2018) stresses the importance of engaging with children whatever their age. This should not simply be interpreted as seeing the children but also involves observing them, engaging with them, talking to them and participating in activities that will help to build trust.

Case Study   Planning a Home Visit

Today you will be visiting a Romanian family consisting of Ana-Maria and her three children. Ana-Maria works in a local factory. She is trying to learn English but she often asks her children to interpret. Marius (14) has mild autism but is doing well at school, where he excels in maths and IT. Cristina (9) loves sports and has won awards for running. Daniela (4) is very quiet and reluctant to leave her mother's side. She likes animals.

- How will you plan your home visit so that you have the opportunity to build your understanding of each of the four family members?

Strengths-based approaches

A key step in building effective working relationships is the ability to recognise the strengths and assets that individuals have in addition to any needs and deficits. Social workers tend to be attuned to the potential for harm and areas for improvement and it is possible that they pay less attention to the aspects of family life that are working well. Strengths-based practice celebrates the positive aspects of a person's life and in so doing encourages optimism. The Department of Health (2017) lists the benefits of strengths-based practice, including that it:

- *acknowledges that people are more than their care needs*
- *acknowledges that notions of community are subjective*
- *reframes the narrative and tells the 'good' stories*
- *draws upon a person's resources, skills and networks*
- *uses explicit methods to identify strengths and assets*
- *is goal orientated and outcomes focused*
- *is collaborative and based on reflective conversation*
- *is respectful – not making assumptions, non-judgemental*
- *is hope-inducing!*

(Department of Health 2017, p12)

It is important that strengths-based approaches do not ignore areas of difficulty or risks as an aspect of the helping process. Moore (2022) provides a valuable model that uses a relational and reciprocal approach to identify strengths, needs and those things that the individual can contribute.

One strengths-based approach is Solution Focused Brief Therapy, which encourages individuals to reflect on the positive aspects of their situation (De Jong and Miller 1995; Finlay 2011). The approach to questioning is of particular value for the assessment process as it encourages the individual to identify their strengths and assets. Social work practitioners may not be providing all aspects of Solution Focused Therapy in a particular case, but the following questions can usually be incorporated into the assessment and adapted to suit the specific situation. It is often helpful to start an assessment with some form of miracle question. What outcome would you like us to achieve?

- **Coping questions** – What has helped you to keep going?
- **Exception questions** –When were things better?
- **What's better questions** – What progress have you seen?
- **Scaling questions** – What number is a goal right now?
- **The miracle question** – In an ideal world what would things be like?

Research Summary   Empathy (Forrester et al. 2008)

Forrester and colleagues analysed taped interviews between qualified social workers and actors who simulated parents in child protection cases. They found that the social workers were good at identifying concerns but less able to identify positives. The research showed that social workers rarely used empathy but when they did it reduced resistance and improved information sharing.

Signs of Safety approach

Turnell and Edwards (1997) applied the above strengths-based and brief therapy concepts to child protection. Their Signs of Safety approach was designed to assess both strengths and limitations in a cooperative and transparent manner. The Signs of Safety assessment and planning framework is based on three broad questions:

1. What are we worried about?
2. What is working well?
3. What needs to happen?

All parties are encouraged to use their answers to provide a numerical rating between 0 (Emergency – child cannot remain at home) and 10 (Things could not be better). By placing a conversation about risk at the heart of a strengths-based approach, Signs of Safety claims to achieve better outcomes for families and a better working experience for staff. Internal evaluations in a range of legislatures have reported fewer re-referrals, registrations and admissions to care. Proponents of the approach also suggest that it does result in greater safety for children, but results from the few independent evaluations that have been completed (e.g. Baginsky et al. 2019 and Baginsky et al. 2020) have been mixed. Sustained improvements require resources and commitment, and some authors have argued that the short-term enthusiasm may not result in long-term benefits for families or organisations (Spratt et al. 2019).

Person-centred planning

While Signs of Safety was developing in Australia, a new understanding of adult services was gathering momentum in America. There was a growing recognition that adults with disabilities were being segregated into services that, while designed to support them, were inadvertently limiting their hopes and dreams. As the name suggests, Person-centred planning (Sanderson 2000) or personalisation (Lewis and Sanderson 2011) puts the person at the centre of the assessment and planning process. It seeks to understand their dreams and aspirations and to gather a community of supporters that can help to achieve these (Burke 2006).

Activity 2.2   Living the dream!

Take some time to think about your personal dreams and aspirations. What aspects of your life would you like to be different in five years' time?

1. Try to describe these in one sentence.
2. What positive and possible steps could you take to move towards your goal?
3. Who might be able to help you?

Comment

You may have found this activity challenging. We are rarely asked about our dreams and we automatically think about the barriers. You can see how this approach turns the assessment process on its head and the different process could result in a different understanding of the way forward. Previously we were asking 'which of our services is best for you?' Now we are asking 'what needs to happen to achieve your goals?'

Person-centred planning is more than an assessment; it provides an ethos that can be used with individuals in any setting. It also uses a range of creative approaches to gathering information. A MAP is a facilitated group process that produces a visual representation of the person and their wishes. A facilitator encourages participants to work with the individual in eight steps, each of which is illustrated on a giant sheet of paper.

Step 1 – Introduce the MAP process

Step 2 – Discuss the person's story to date

Step 3 – Identify their dreams

Step 4 – Identify their nightmares

Step 5 – Find out who the person is

Step 6 – What are their gifts, strengths and talents?

Step 7 – What do they need to achieve the dream?

Step 8 – Action Plan

A path is a similar process that focuses on the action plan and identifies ways to overcome the complex and difficult aspects of everyday reality. When faced with disagreements, challenges or limitations, the path allows key stakeholders to work together to imagine a way forward.

Step 1 – Remember the dream

Step 2 – Agree the goal

Step 3 – Where are we now?

Step 4 – Who might help?

Step 5 – How are we going to build strength?

Step 6 – Three/six-month goals

Case Study   Eva's Path

Eva wasn't happy at the day centre, which was large and noisy. She particularly disliked the bus journey, which took 45 minutes each way. She did, however, enjoy socialising and she had friends at the centre whom she wanted to keep in contact with. Her path meeting was the first time that her sister had met her key worker from the centre. Eva also invited her social worker and some of her friends. At the meeting everybody got to contribute. By the end people agreed that things needed to change. The group agreed that Eva would reduce her attendance at the centre to Thursdays and Fridays (her favourite days). On one of the other days she would attend the church social group. Two aspects of the plan were longer term objectives. The group agreed to explore whether someone could accompany Eva to do her own shopping. Staff at the centre would also investigate if Eva could use a taxi to get to the day centre. Until these were achieved, Eva's sister agreed to provide the necessary support.

- In what ways is this different to traditional planning meetings?
- Could this approach be used for different client groups?

The above case study illustrates how it is possible to build services around an individual's wishes rather than squeezing them into our available services. Person-centred planning, also known as Essential Lifestyle planning, has had a significant influence in many countries and has been incorporated into government policies such as 'Valuing People' (Department of Health 2001) and 'Caring for our future' (Department of Health 2012). The ethos has also been used in other programmes of care including older people, mental health, criminal justice and children's services. Advocates have developed specific models and tools to incorporate person-centred principles into various aspects of assessment and planning. One good example is a person-centred approach to risk (Kinsella 2000; Neill et al. 2009). This promotes a realistic analysis of the positive and negative consequences of any action. It moves beyond risk aversion to support the informed management of risk. Kinsella (2000) has produced a graphical framework that considers the potential for happiness as well as safety (Figure 2.4). This is helpful as it allows the identification of safe

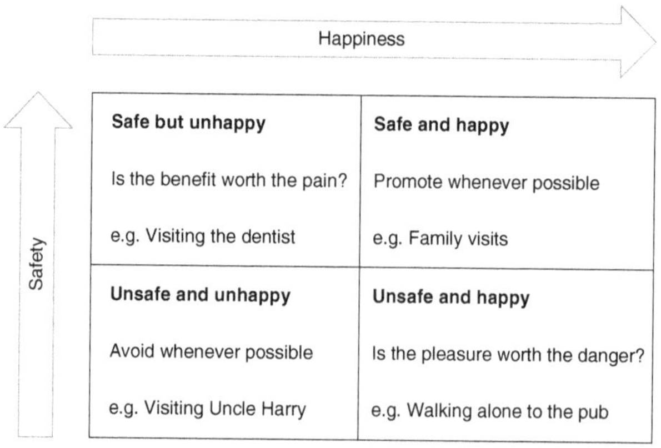

	Happiness →	
↑	**Safe but unhappy** Is the benefit worth the pain? e.g. Visiting the dentist	**Safe and happy** Promote whenever possible e.g. Family visits
Safety	**Unsafe and unhappy** Avoid whenever possible e.g. Visiting Uncle Harry	**Unsafe and happy** Is the pleasure worth the danger? e.g. Walking alone to the pub

Figure 2.4   Person-centred risk assessment (Adapted from Kinsella 2000)

activities that promote happiness and should be encouraged, harmful activities that reduce happiness and should be avoided, and other combinations where careful management is required.

The recovery model

Strengths-based and person-centred approaches have also developed in the area of adult mental health. As a reaction to the 'medical approach' to the assessment and treatment of mental illness based on binary notions of 'health' and 'illness', the recovery model emphasises the personal journey of individuals towards goals that they have identified (Slade et al. 2017). Taking control of their own recovery provides the individual with a sense of purpose and greater self-belief. The approach emphasises the importance of social connection in promoting well-being. It recognises the challenges of choice and risk taking and encourages collaborative approaches where professionals support positive action. Proponents of the recovery approach see it as improving engagement and therefore supporting a more honest approach to risk assessment and management. It has also been suggested that the approach could be used when parental mental health interfaces with child protection concerns (Duffy et al. 2016).

Working with resistance

So far in this chapter we have highlighted the importance of cooperation in the assessment process. Empowering individuals or families results in better outcomes and greater satisfaction for the assessor and the person being assessed. But it is naïve to presume that people will always want to work with us, be assessed or engage in a process of change. Social workers need to recognise this resistance and have the knowledge and skills to work with involuntary families.

Case Study   A Resistant Client

Despite your best efforts you have not been able to make contact with Ana-Maria. You have sent letters and made phone calls but to no avail. Today you called at the house. There were clearly people at home but nobody answered the door.

- Why might the family be reluctant to meet with social workers?
- What more could be done to engage?

Comment

Let's presume that Ana-Maria knows that we are from social services. There are many reasons why she might be avoiding contact:

(Continued)

(Continued)

1. Shame – Few people want to have a social worker if they can avoid it. Our presence is a reminder to the family and those around them that they are not managing. Social work carries stigma.
2. Fear – Families often fear that social workers come to judge, punish or, worst-case scenario – remove a child.
3. Secrecy – There may be things that a family wants to hide. Child abuse, neglect or domestic violence may be factors, but equally debt, criminal behaviour, drugs or immigration status may make families wary of officials.
4. Previous experience – If Ana-Maria has had a negative previous experience of social workers, she might have learnt to stay out of their way.

In the case above, resistance resulted in an unwillingness to engage with social services. Even when contact has been made, children, families and adults can openly or subtly resist or disrupt the social work process. Often this is a struggle for power. People rarely want to be 'fixed' unless it is on their terms when they are in control. Working with resistance is challenging and can result in practitioners being as reluctant as the families to engage in the work (Rooney and Mirick 2018). Involuntary practitioners working with involuntary clients are unlikely to achieve positive outcomes.

Motivational interviewing

Forrester et al. (2012) suggest that motivational interviewing recognises the reality of ambivalence and can therefore be useful for social workers working with resistant individuals or families. Motivational interviewing, based on theories of change (Prochaska and DiClemente 1986), identifies specific forms of intervention depending on the individual's readiness to move forward. Understanding a person's motivation is a key component of any assessment and is helpful in planning any further intervention. There is little value in referring someone for drug treatment if they don't accept that they have an addiction. Motivational interviewing is a skilled role that requires specific training and this chapter can only provide an indication of the way in which it can support a social work assessment. For a fuller understanding the reader is directed to Miller and Rollnick (2012).

Figure 2.5 provides descriptions for possible attitudes to change. People may not be willing to consider that a problem exists; they may recognise the need for change but feel powerless to move forward; or they may be taking the first steps into the unknown. For each person the journey and the timescale will be different. Unfortunately, as social workers we often want to see significant change accomplished within a very short time due to multiple demands on our time.

Table 2.1 provides some examples of forms of help that relate to the stages of change. In the initial stages we need to resist the desire to demand action. The person at the pre-contemplative and contemplative stages may respond better to empathy and open

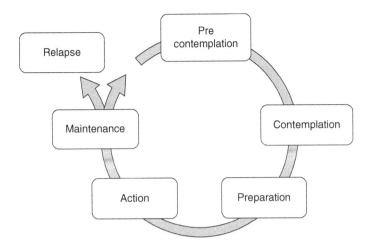

Figure 2.5   Cycle of change

Adapted from Prochaska, J.O. and DiClemente C.C., *Toward a comprehensive model of change*, In Miller, W.R. & Heather, N. (Eds.) Treating Addictive Behaviors: Processes of Change © (1986) Reprinted by permission from Springer Nature: Springer, Boston, MA.

questions that will encourage them to reflect on their situation. The person preparing to take action or taking action may require information, while at the maintenance stage they may need encouragement to keep going, or during relapse the person may require encouragement to identify progress and overcome obstacles.

Table 2.1   Helping the change cycle

Phase	Pre-Contemplation	Contemplation	Preparation	Action	Relapse	Maintenance
Attitude	Nothing is Wrong	Maybe you're right	What do I need to do?	I'm doing it	It has all gone wrong	One day at a time
Assistance	Empathy and questioning		Information and options		Encouragement	

Some change models have been critiqued as taking a simplistic view of very complex and interconnected difficulties (Ward et al. 2014; Platt and Riches 2016). Social workers need to understand how environmental factors can undermine an individual's ability to make significant changes in their life.

Case Study   Pace of Change

Because you are a persistent social worker you finally make contact with Ana-Maria and her children. She did not answer the telephone because she is very anxious, and she was

(Continued)

(Continued)

unable to read the letters that you had sent her. The children seem to be well looked after, although Ana-Maria admits she struggles to provide consistency around their use of TV and bedtimes.

- At a subsequent case discussion, it was agreed that Ana-Maria be referred to a literacy class, an assertiveness group, and a parenting course, and the case was subsequently closed.
- How likely is Ana-Maria to benefit from the three referrals?
- What more could we do to assist this family?

Comment

It is a big ask to expect Ana-Maria to make these major changes in a short period of time. We are not sure how she feels about the situation and how motivated she is to engage. We know she is anxious and if she is not committed it may be easier not to attend. It is likely that we will see this non-attendance as a failing on her part and not ours.

If someone took the time and energy to get to know and understand Ana-Maria they might be more able to offer the appropriate service at an appropriate time. If she was helped to imagine a better life for her children and herself, she could then discuss the initial steps to achieve this.

Compassion and 'good authority'

This chapter has highlighted the importance of recognising strengths when building cooperation with individuals and families. Perhaps our focus has been too much on what is wrong rather than what is strong. There is a growing recognition that social workers need to be able to assess and address the positive and negative aspects of families and individuals. Forrester et al. (2019) found that compassion influenced the satisfaction of

Figure 2.6 Good authority

families but outcomes were more related to the use of 'good authority'. Good authority is the ability to be clear about the needs of the child and the changes that are required.

Figure 2.6 illustrates the different ways in which social workers might respond when families or individuals do not agree with their intervention. Some practitioners assert their power in a harsh and controlling manner which can ostracise the people we work with. Equally dangerous is the tendency to concede control, which limits our ability to influence progress. The middle position of good authority combines sensitive compassion with a recognition of the potential risks.

Ferguson (2011) has described eight elements of good authority.

1. Recognise and be prepared to work with resistance
2. Encourage people to express their emotions
3. Explore the reasons for resistance
4. Keep the focus on the needs of the child
5. Be clear on what has to change
6. Be open to discuss the negotiable aspects of the work
7. Provide a very clear plan
8. Be able to describe what progress would look like.

Research Summary   Harsh but Fair

Munford and Sanders (2017) interviewed young people about their resistance towards social work and other services. They found that young people used avoidant or hostile behaviours to protect themselves from interfering professionals.

'... don't like them knowing ... had people nosing around my whole life'

However, they found that skilled workers were often able to harness young people's resistance, encouraging their participation. The young people valued staff who could enforce boundaries in a compassionate and understanding manner. This echoed Forrester's concept of good authority.

'... he was harsh but fair ... he didn't beat around the bush, he listened to what I said ...'

Skills and values for relationship

This chapter on relationship is all about skills and values. Engaging people in assessment and decision making is an advanced skill that requires the practitioner to use themselves to develop human connection (Hennessey 2011). We have discussed above a range of person-centred approaches and strengths questions that can be used in assessment processes. Some of these require specialist training but many can be generalised within a relationship-based approach to assessment.

Good authority is a combination of skill and values, and it may take time and support to learn. Students tend to be comfortable exhibiting compassion or authority, and Forrester et al.'s work (2008) suggests that it is not always easy to combine the two.

Reflective listening is a powerful skill based on attending and responding that helps the speaker to feel heard and the listener to check their understanding of the issues (Fuller et al. 2019).

Warmth, empathy and non-judgemental attitudes are the basis of relationship-based assessments. While these values are recognised as central there is some evidence that they are not always evident in social work practice (Lynch et al. 2019). It is easier to empathise with people who are like us and sometimes we struggle to understand or engage with people who are different (Beckett et al. 2017). Each of us needs to constantly monitor our own feelings and attitudes to ensure that they do not hamper our ability to engage in cooperative relationship-based assessments (Tedam 2020).

Theoretical underpinnings

In this chapter we discuss how practitioners can collaborate with individuals and families in the assessment and decision-making process. Theoretical perspectives that support this include:

- Strengths-based and solution-focused approaches that identify future possibilities and build upon the positive aspects of the case to reach these.
- Theories of change help us understand the process of transformation, the reasons why this might be difficult and the way that we might help.

Knowledge and skills summary

- Assessment and decision making work best in cooperation with the people that they are about.
- When working with people who are reluctant or resistant, we should try to maximise cooperation.
- Relationship-based practice is an empowering approach that can benefit all participants.
- Strengths-based approaches have been developed in most areas of social work.
- Good practice recognises both strengths and concerns.
- Motivational interviewing provides a helpful framework for assessing and supporting the potential for change.
- Some individuals and families exhibit resistance or even hostility.
- The use of 'good authority' combines compassion with a clear focus on the needs of the child.

Further Reading

Hennessey, R. (2011). *Relationship skills in social work*. London: Sage Publications.

Roger Hennessey's book describes how the practitioner can use self-knowledge and an understanding of the situation to promote positive and effective interaction.

McColgan, M. and McMullin, C. (2017). *Doing relationship based social work: a practical guide to building relationships and enabling change*. London: Jessica Kingsley.

Each of the chapters in this edited book considers how relationship-based practice can apply to a specific group or setting.

Miller, W.R. and Rollnick, S. (2012). *Motivational interviewing: helping people change*. New York: Guilford Press.

Seen by many as the bible for motivational interviewing, this comprehensive book provides a guide to the method and the necessary skills.

3

Assessing risk, needs and strengths: tools and processes

Achieving a Social Work Degree

This chapter will help you develop the following capabilities from the Professional Capabilities Framework (2018):

2.   Values and ethics
5.   Knowledge
6.   Critical reflection and analysis
7.   Skills and interventions

See Appendix 1 for the Professional Capabilities Framework Fan and a description of the 9 domains.

(Continued)

(Continued)

It will also introduce you to the following standards as set out in the Social Work Subject Benchmark Statement (2019):

5.2   Knowledge of social work theory
5.10 Problem-solving skills

See Appendix 2 for a detailed description of these standards.

Introduction

Chapter 3 describes the value of frameworks and tools to support the assessment process. Various types of assessment tools are described relating to the range of social work activity. The Triangle Diagram from Working together to safeguard children (HM Government 2018) is used as an exemplar of assessment domains in child welfare, and the Single Assessment Process in Adult Social Care as an exemplar of coordinating multi-professional assessment. It is not possible to provide an exhaustive list of assessment tools, but the reader is signposted to other potential resources.

Case Study   Assessment Tools in Everyday Life

John and Andrew share the hobby of photography. They have exactly the same camera but Andrew consistently produces better photographs than John. John bought an extra lens in the hope that it would help, but it didn't. In frustration John bought a much more expensive camera with a range of different lenses, but he still could not take photographs as good as Andrew's.

Comment

Any assessment tool is only an instrument that assists the assessment process. There is a danger that practitioners and managers can be beguiled by attractive frameworks and layouts, but the quality of the assessment will always depend on the skills of the social worker.

In social work, clear assessment and effective decisions are critical to good practice. In general, social workers are good at gathering and synthesising information to support decisions, but there are times when we get it wrong. It is tempting to think that a better framework or tool will produce a better result, particularly when it comes to safeguarding children and adults. In recent years we have seen the development of frameworks with accompanying tools that seek to standardise the assessment process, synthesise the most important information and enable effective decision making, but there is a danger that standardising assessment could erode professional discretion (Munro 2011) and constrain social work practice (White, Hall and Peckover 2009). At the outset of a chapter on assessment tools it is important to dispel some common myths.

- Assessment is a process, not a piece of paper.
- No assessment framework is perfect.
- 'Good' assessments are the result of knowledge, skills and values.
- 'Good' decisions do not always produce positive outcomes.

Assessment frameworks and tools are not guaranteed to produce a good outcome, but there are a number of ways in which they can be used to support the process. Figure 3.1 illustrates how knowledge, skills and values inform an assessment framework and enable the relationships that in turn support a strong assessment. If the practitioner has limited understanding of the situation, if they do not have the necessary skills or values, the use of the framework and the professional relationship will be impeded, as will the resulting assessment and decision making.

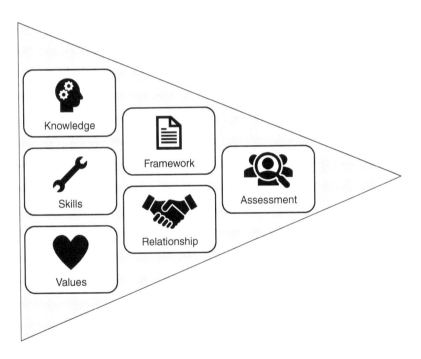

Figure 3.1 The role of the assessment framework

Assessment tools as decision support systems

Assessment frameworks and the related tools help us to understand what information is important and they often support the organising and analysis of our findings. As discussed in the chapter on legal issues (Chapter 6), it is the role of the assessor to produce reasoned, reasonable judgements. A good assessment framework will support the skilled practitioner as they seek to present a logical rationale for their conclusions and recommendations. Below are five ways in which a framework can support assessment and decision making:

1. Incorporating current best evidence
2. Structuring the available information
3. Encouraging a holistic and balanced overview
4. Facilitating communication and engagement in the process
5. Promoting clarity and understanding for decision making.

Evidence-informed assessment tools

Assessment tools are a key mechanism to bring wider knowledge to bear in the assessment process. Hopefully the architects of the framework will have incorporated the current knowledge base that describes the key issues and their potential impact. Obviously, the rigour with which assessment tools are created will affect their value as a tool for bringing knowledge into practice. There are also examples of assessment tools that have incorporated the perspectives of people who use our services and carers in their design (Taylor 2012a).

Assessment Framework   The Graded Care Profile (Srivastava et al. 2015)

This assessment framework is based on a detailed understanding of the needs of children and the behaviours that support child development. Now in its second version, the framework is accompanied by assessment tools that prompt the practitioner to observe practical indicators as to whether key needs are being met. The four main areas of need are identified as

1. Esteem
2. Love
3. Safety
4. Physical care

These are subdivided into more specific aspects of need which are graded from 1 (needs always met) to 5 (needs never met). As one example, the assessment of nutrition includes a history of meals provided, an evaluation of the carer's knowledge about nutrition, and potentially an observation of mealtimes. Johnson et al. (2015) evaluated the tool and found that it provided consistent results (reliability) and was effective in measuring neglect (validity).

Structuring information

A good assessment tool helps the practitioner to structure the process and the information gathered in a coherent manner. Many frameworks identify broad areas or *domains* that are subdivided into specific elements. Figure 3.2 illustrates the assessment framework from Working together to safeguard children (HM Government 2018). The three areas of needs, capacity and environment subdivided into specific areas are similar to other child safeguarding frameworks in Scotland (Scottish Government 2008) and Northern Ireland (DHSSPS 2008).

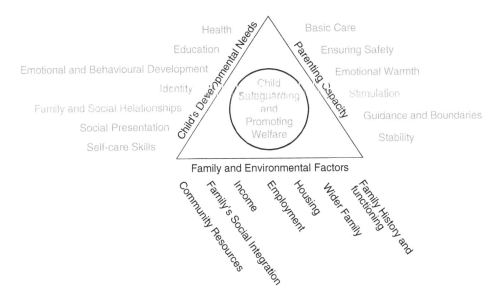

Figure 3.2 Assessment Framework from Working together to safeguard children (HM Government 2018 p30).

Using this type of framework, the social worker can methodically gather information relating to each domain. Training in the framework will explain the importance of each domain and encourage the practitioner to identify strengths as well as weaknesses. The provided domains cannot cover all aspects of family life and it is the role of the trained worker to explore potential areas for inclusion. You will notice that the DoH framework diagram does not specifically mention domestic violence or parental substance abuse, but these might be areas that the worker asks about when addressing family functioning. It is possible that the worker may use an additional specific assessment tool to gather detailed information about one or more domains.

Assessment frameworks for child and adult safeguarding have been criticised for failing to recognise the importance of risks outside the family. Carlene Firmin (2020) argues that dangers like exploitation, radicalisation and criminality are not adequately addressed in existing processes. She argues for 'contextual safeguarding' that recognises the influence of peer groups, neighbourhoods and institutional settings such as schools.

Holistic understanding

Assessment tools should assist the professional to gather all the relevant information about the client and family. The absence of important information can cause bias in decision making or overlook the wishes of a key stakeholder. During the assessment the practitioner must constantly ask themselves if any important information may be missing, including contextual material that may help explain the individual's motivation or behaviours. A holistic understanding might involve a person's health, thinking, relationships, culture and beliefs. This biopsychosocial-spiritual (BPSS) approach (Gale 2022) recognises the importance of all aspects of a person's lived experience. When assessing families, our focus is often drawn to the most obvious and immediate factors that are facing us and there is a danger that we oversimplify complex situations, identifying symptoms like a lack of food, but not the overarching problems such as poverty (Johnson et al. 2015). There is growing evidence that social services are more likely to initiate child protection and child removal with poorer families (Webb et al. 2020; Goldacre and Hood 2022).

A holistic assessment that explicitly recognises socioeconomic factors could help decision makers to differentiate poor parenting from parents experiencing poverty.

Case Study   Travel Assessment

Victor is 23 years old and he has a learning difficulty. He would like to travel to the day centre independently, using the public bus. Staff recognise there are benefits to this and have agreed to assess the potential risks. Initially we might focus on the specific task. Can Victor get to the bus stop, does he know when the bus arrives and can he get off at the right stop? A more holistic assessment will require some understanding of broader issues that may impact on the situation.

- Is it relevant that Victor is black and from a working-class family?
- Should the concerns of his parents be incorporated into an assessment?

Assessment frameworks are always open to critique and revision. The lack of structural domains, such as poverty, in assessments has been highlighted, as has the need to recognise specific factors such as identity (Thomas and Holland 2009) and community (Jack and Gill 2003).

Communication and engagement

In Chapter 2 we discussed the importance of relationship in the assessment process. Ideally information gathering is a collaboration between the people who receive services and the professionals. Any assessment will involve the professional interpreting or translating the information that they have gathered.

This involves setting the scene for dialogue, understanding and interpretation, as opposed to a 'fact finding' or data collection interview. If we assume that what we are doing is collaboratively constructing a story of a problem situation which will allow service users to gain assistance then this potentially transforms the way we relate to each other.

(Fook 2016, p154)

An assessment tool can support this process of dialogue and understanding if it is constructed to encourage collaboration. Mooney and Bunting (2019) developed a Family Life Story Workbook that uses visual, understandable techniques to help social workers and parents to work collaboratively as they consider how adverse childhood experiences (ACEs) might impact on parenting.

Often social work assessments require participants to share complex ideas and meanings that they may not fully understand themselves. A questioning approach can be dull and tedious for all concerned and so it may not be an effective way to gain full participation. Thankfully there is an increasing range of creative techniques that can be used to promote thought, discussion and engagement. Tools like genograms and ecomaps (Parker 2020) allow practitioners and family members to work together to produce a visual representation of family groups and wider social systems. Often this helps participants to consolidate and articulate their own perception of the situation. Creative approaches can move the process from a questioning model to an exchange model (Smale et al. 2000), shifting the balance of control and expertise. Most importantly, creative approaches can be fun and participants who are enjoying the process will be less defensive and more forthcoming. Creative approaches may be particularly important when working with children who struggle to articulate their experience within traditional processes and time frames. Katie Wrench (2018) argues that spoken dialogue is an adult-centred form of communication and practitioners need to develop more relational and creative approaches if they wish to understand children's thoughts, feelings and experiences. Similarly, Pipi (2016) suggests that creative arts allow the collaborative development of understanding.

Activity 3.1   Drawing and Thinking

'Drawing is a thinking tool and a medium for making meaning'

(Pipi 2016, p47)

Figure 3.3   The Blob Tree

© Pip Wilson and Ian Long 2005
Available from www.blobtree.com

Have a look at the blob tree in Figure 3.3.

Which of the blob people illustrates how you are feeling right now?

If none are appropriate you could draw an extra one.

Think about why you made this choice.

This creative and playful approach is a great way to begin an assessment with many of the people who use our services. For some reason the exercise is less threatening than direct questioning and questions can be developed to prompt reflection in specific areas, e.g.

- Which blob might your child pick?
- Which blob is like you when you are at school?
- Which blob would you like to be?

Clarity and understanding

The ultimate aim for any assessment is to synthesise information in a way that allows informed decisions to be made. Key stakeholders should understand the rationale for the assessment, the process that was used and the reasons why specific recommendations were made. A key challenge is presenting complex information in a way that the subjects can comprehend. The contents of an assessment tool should make sense to the people at the centre of the process, be they children, parents, older people or people who have disabilities or mental health problems.

Research Summary   Use of Assessment Tools (Brown et al. 2017)

Brown et al. gathered data from professionals working in a range of agencies in relation to child sexual exploitation. Most participants found assessment tools and checklists to be helpful in their role. They suggested that the tools:

- help staff to focus on the area of concern
- provide a structure for interviews
- show children and families that the issue is being taken seriously
- guide decision making
- provide information to support ongoing protection
- provide clarity.

Types of assessment tools

To continue with the camera analogy from the start of this chapter, some assessment tools take a macro approach gathering a wide range of information, while others zoom in to provide micro detail on a very specific area. With each assessment we need to decide on the required scope. Contextual information without sufficient detail prevents effective decision making. Potentially worse is a detailed assessment that lacks sufficient context to make sense of the information.

Assessment, like research, can be quantitative (concerned with measurement), qualitative (concerned with meaning) or a combination of both. Both approaches are necessary and both have particular value. Quantitative approaches attempt to claim objectivity while qualitative approaches embrace the subjectivity of the situation. The quantitative aspects of an assessment will ask when, how often and how many, while qualitative aspects ask what happened or what does this mean? Increasingly quantitative tools are being developed to explore (e.g. the impact of specific factors), compare (e.g. is this a greater risk than that?) or predict (e.g. how likely is this to happen again?).

Predictive tools

Most assessment tools help social workers to gather and structure information, but there are some that aim to assist the practitioner in the analysis of their findings and prompt the subsequent decision making. Decision processes are becoming increasingly complex and open to challenge and increasingly sophisticated assessment tools are required to support professional judgements.

Some assessment frameworks will use the information to indicate the level of risk (low, medium or high) or use a formula to provide a numeric measurement. There is ongoing debate as to whether actuarial (i.e. statistical) approaches are better than clinical (i.e. individual or 'intuitive') approaches which are not based on numerical calculation of risk factors. The use of these approaches in risk assessment will be discussed further in Chapter 8. Research shows that in some situations statistical approaches are better at prediction than human beings, but they are often more effective to guide decisions than to predict outcomes (Saunders et al. 2014). Empirical evidence relating to the effectiveness of specific tools is limited (McNellan et al. 2022). Prediction of harm is only one dimension of professional judgement. The 'art' of social work in terms of engaging with clients, families and other professionals will still be required to complement the 'science' of social work knowledge. Increasingly practitioners need to develop the skill to use statistical information (understanding its potential and also its limitations) to inform professional judgement (Søbjerg et al. 2020; Taylor 2017a; Taylor 2020).

Specialist assessment tools

Often social work assessments gather information from a range of different sources including other professionals, but they might also undertake specialist assessments relating to a specific aspect of the case. This is an aspect of social work that is generally under-developed at present. Social workers should be able to undertake basic assessments that relate to substance misuse or violence. Similarly, they should be able to assess challenging issues facing a client or family such as carer support, anxiety, depression or stress. More specialist areas like trauma, attachment or parental capacity may require training on the knowledge base and the use of a particular tool. Adding additional items to the assessment toolkit should be seen as standard practice in social work, as in other professions. Discuss your ideas for developing your assessment practice with your professional supervisor or line manager.

Safeguarding assessments and thresholds

Frameworks for safeguarding children or adults often include guidelines for the categorisation of levels of need or risk. Each category of need will have related interventions to address the issues. Most child safeguarding frameworks incorporate a thresholds of needs model based on the work of Hardiker et al. (1991). This identifies four categories of need with indicators that assist the practitioner to choose the most appropriate category. Many of the thresholding models have mapped service provision to the levels of need as in Table 3.1.

Table 3.1 Levels of Need – Children (adapted from Hardiker et al. 1991).

Level of need	Response
Level One: Base Population	Universal Services
Level Two: Additional Needs	Enhanced Universal Services
Level Three: Complex Needs	Tailored Support
Level Four: Potential harm	Child Protection

A similar approach has been taken in some areas of adult safeguarding as in Table 3.2.

Table 3.2 Levels of Need – Adults

Level of need	Response
All Adults	Prevention
Adults at risk of harm	Safeguarding
Adults in need of protection	Protection

These conceptual frameworks are used in decision-making forums and can be incorporated into the assessment process. They have the potential to recognise strengths as well as deficits in each domain of a person's life and clearly identify areas where change is needed.

Multi-professional assessments

Social workers may be required to coordinate or contribute to an assessment that involves a range of other professionals or agencies. The Northern Ireland Single Assessment Tool (NISAT) is an example of an integrated assessment tool (see Glossary: **Integrated Assessment System**) that incorporates the views of older people, their carers and key social and health care staff. Taylor (2012a) stresses the need to incorporate the various perspectives rather than simply assembling them in one place. The tool has three components for: Screening, Core and Complex assessments. As Figure 3.4 shows, the Core Assessment has three domains regarded as central to every assessment. There are seven other domains in the Core Assessment, designed to be included whenever deemed to be relevant to the assessment based on the presenting information.

Narrative approaches

Perhaps the most qualitative approach to assessment is the free narrative where participants are encouraged to tell their story without any imposed structure or prompts. It is used where depth of meaning, or experience, is more important than the order in which it is provided.

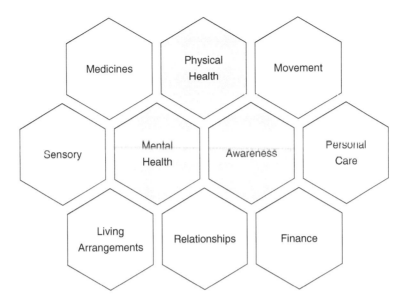

Figure 3.4   Northern Ireland Single Assessment Tool

Research Summary   Your Friend TED (Brandon, Wells and Seale 2018)

Police forces have developed the science of 'cognitive interviewing' based on the work of Fisher and Gieselman (1992) to maximise the quantity and quality of information provided by witnesses without contamination by leading questions.

First, the witness is encouraged to provide their own account of the event, for example:

Tell me in as much detail as you can everything that happened after you left the house on Thursday.

When this account is exhausted, open questions can be used to explore specific aspects. Effective questions often start with the words tell, explain or describe (TED):

Tell me more about the driver of the car.

Ideally these techniques obtain all the necessary information. However, in some circumstances it might be necessary to ask a closed question:

How long did that take?

Or request specific confirmation:

Was he alone?

There may be times in a social work assessment where a free narrative account is the most suitable approach, particularly where the practitioner does not want to influence the information that is being provided.

Cook and Miller (2012) have developed the Talking Points: Personal Outcomes Approach, which uses storytelling or conversations to discover what is important to individuals and their carers. As with other person-centred approaches, these agreed outcomes become the focus of intervention and support. Cook and Miller found that participants valued this alternative above a 'tick box' service-driven approach. Staff also found it liberating, although some found it difficult to 'unlearn' traditional habits.

Assessment skills

So far we have described the benefits of assessment frameworks and outlined the types of tools that can support social work practice. We have argued that a good tool in the hands of a skilled worker can support reasoned and reasonable decision making, but an assessment tool can never make up for a deficit of knowledge skills or values. Below we outline some specific skills that practitioners should have.

Relational skills – It is the role of the practitioner to engage with the individual or family and create an environment where effective communication can be achieved. The importance of trust and cooperation has been discussed in Chapter 2.

Planning – The practitioner will need to agree with participants what information will be gathered and how this will be done. There is a danger that a rushed process will result in a poor-quality assessment, and an unnecessarily complex assessment will overwhelm participants. Seek to stage the assessment process to gather information at the most appropriate pace for the subject.

Framework specific – Each framework will have its own set of procedures, forms and time scales. Often, they will be based on equally important principles that will describe the overriding ethos of the approach. As an example, the recovery model in mental health is based on the principle that people can recover and should be allowed to take the lead in identifying a way forward. In following procedures, bear in mind the under-pinning principles which provide them with direction and clarity. Practitioners who fail to understand the core principles of an approach will be unlikely to achieve the desired outcomes.

Coordination – The completion of an *integrated* (or unified or single) *assessment system* that incorporates the information from a range of professionals and other stakeholders will require skilled inter-professional and inter-agency working. This collaborative approach is discussed further in Chapter 4.

Advocacy – Assessment and decision making involve collaborative gathering of information, but there may be occasions when the voice of the individual or family will not be heard without help. Social workers should strive to ensure that the needs and wishes of all participants are recognised and that their rights are upheld in any decision-making process.

Quality and fidelity – Two important aspects of any assessment framework are its quality and the way that is used. Before we use an assessment framework or tool, we need to ensure that it is appropriate for the specific task. It is possible to assess the quality of assessment tools in terms of:

- **validity** – does the tool assess what it says it will assess?
- **reliability** – would two professionals using the same assessment tool with the same client complete the assessment form the same way and reach the same decision?

- **usability** – how easy is the tool to use?
- **appropriateness** – is the tool appropriate and tested for use with this culture or type of clients?

Validity is difficult to demonstrate, because to do this properly one needs to know the outcomes of the assessment. For example, if the tool predicts that a particular child will be abused, is the child in fact abused?

Research Summary   'Fit for Purpose' (McIvor and Kemshall 2002)

McIvor and Kemshall reviewed existing literature to provide the following essential criteria for assessment tools used with serious violent and sexual offenders.

- Validated – at least one peer-reviewed publication on validation of the tool
- Validated against a relevant population
- Actuarially based and empirically grounded in risk factors
- Able to differentiate between high, medium and low risk
- Has reliability (all assessors will use the tool in the same way with the same result)
- User-friendly
- Resource lean
- 'Easy' to train staff to use appropriately.

Having a quality assessment framework does not always produce accurate results. The term fidelity refers to the ability and willingness of practitioners to use the framework as its authors intended. It is possible that errors in the assessment outcome are related to the process and not the instrument. Remember always that an assessment tool is just that – a tool for a job, to be used to assist the effective gathering of information.

Research Summary   Tool Compliance (Miller and Maloney 2013)

Miller and Maloney assessed the extent to which a group of American probation officers complied with the agency risk assessment tool. They found three broad approaches:

Substantive compliers: (47.7 per cent) completed the tool correctly and used the content to inform their decisions about risk.

Bureaucratic compliers: (39.8 per cent) completed the tool correctly but made their own decisions about risk.

Cynical compliers: (12.4 per cent) completed the tool carelessly or manipulated answers to achieve the result they wanted.

The authors suggested that compliance was linked to the practitioners' attitudes to risk assessment tools, the level of training and monitoring, and their perceptions of their employing agency.

The future? Decision support systems

A key challenge for social work assessment is the sheer volume of factors that may have a bearing on the case and therefore should be taken into account. Practitioners do not have the time or the resources to evaluate all potential options and as a result there will always be unexpected outcomes. Also, human beings will always have the potential for bias and errors. The widespread development of computerised analysis has created the possibility that large data sets and knowledge of risk factors could be used to flag concerning cases. Such systems are being used in some parts of America to support risk assessment in child protection cases. The Allegheny Family Screening Tool (AFST) analyses existing historical records from 21 sources to provide telephone hotline staff with an indication of potential risk rated between 1 and 20 (Chouldechova et al. 2018). Agencies using the tool claim it has increased the accuracy of call screening (Centre for Public Impact 2018), but in other evaluations machine learning approaches were shown to be much less effective (Clayton et al. 2020). Critics claim that algorithms perpetuate disadvantage and are 'antithetical to social justice' (Gillingham 2019, p277). To date, computerised systems have proved to be marginally more accurate than professionals in predicting future harm (whether re-offending, child abuse or an older person suffering a fall, for example) (Coulthard et al. 2020). However, there are many other aspects of assessment, and such algorithms can only ever be an aid to human judgement in a field such as social work (Coulthard and Taylor 2023). Government agencies are watching progress with interest and decision support systems may become part of the social work assessment process in the future.

Activity 3.2 Reflection

- Do you think computers are more or less likely to assess risk accurately?
- How would you feel about a computerised system to support your decision making?
- Should practitioners have the ability to override computerised prompts if they felt they were unsafe?

Theoretical underpinnings

In this chapter we discussed how frameworks and tools might support the assessment and decision-making process. Two theoretical perspectives that are of particular interest are:

- Human needs and development – Irrespective of the assessment that is being undertaken, the needs and rights of children, adults and families will form a central focus for information gathering.
- Reflection and reflexivity – When considering whether an assessment has achieved an accurate understanding of the situation, practitioners will need to engage in a reflective process that considers their role and the way that they interpreted the available information.

Knowledge and skills summary

- There is an increasing number of frameworks to support social workers in the assessment process.
- These are not a shortcut to quicker or better outcomes and the practitioner needs to have the relevant knowledge and skills to use them effectively.
- Available tools may be quantitative in nature, assisting the practitioner to measure risk, or qualitative in nature, assisting the gathering and structuring of meanings and perceptions.
- It is important to consider the quality of an assessment tool including its validity, reliability, usability and appropriateness.
- There is a growing interest in *decision support systems* although ethical and statistical issues have prevented their widespread use.

Further Reading

Wrench, K. (2018). *Creative ideas for assessing vulnerable children and families*. London: Jessica Kingsley.

As mentioned above, this book provides a range of creative tools that can be used with children or family members.

Basarab-Horwath, J.A. and Platt, D. (Eds) (2019). *The child's world: the essential guide to assessing vulnerable children, young people and their families* (Third edition). London: Jessica Kingsley.

This comprehensive book covers all aspects of assessment relating to the English assessment framework.

Parker, J. (2020). *Social work practice: assessment, planning, intervention and review* (Transforming Social Work Practice Series) (Sixth Edition). London: Sage.

This book provides a valuable overview of the assessment process. Chapter 3 includes a practical description of assessment tools like gemograms, ecomaps and culturalgrams.

4

Collaborating, communicating and managing conflict in making decisions

---

Achieving a Social Work Degree

This chapter will help you develop the following capabilities from the Professional Capabilities Framework (2018):

2. Values and ethics
5. Knowledge
6. Critical reflection and analysis
7. Skills and interventions
8. Contexts and organisations
9. Professional leadership

See Appendix 1 for the Professional Capabilities Framework Fan and a description of the nine domains.

(Continued)

(Continued)

It will also introduce you to the following standards as set out in the Social Work Subject Benchmark Statement (2019):

5.2   Knowledge of social work theory
5.5   The nature of social work practice
5.15 Communication skills

See Appendix 2 for a detailed description of these standards.

Introduction

This chapter focuses on partnership working across professions and organisations, as well as informal decision-making processes. For the purposes of this chapter, we use a definition of effective inter-professional collaboration adapted from that of the Robert Wood Johnson Foundation:

> *Effective inter-professional collaboration promotes the active participation of each discipline in patient and client care, where all disciplines are working together and fully engaging patients, clients and those who support them, and leadership on the team adapts based on patient, client and family needs. Effective interprofessional collaboration enhances client- and family-centered goals and values, provides mechanisms for continuous communication among caregivers, and optimizes participation in decision-making within and across disciplines. It fosters respect for the disciplinary contributions of all professionals.*

(2015, p1)

For the purposes of this chapter, we are considering inter-professional collaboration in relation to assessment processes; processes of assessing and **managing risk**; and making decisions. Chapter 2 explored the engagement of clients and families in assessment, risk-managing and decision processes.

The chapter includes principles for effective inter-professional communication about risk and multi-professional decision making. A greater understanding of the roles of other professionals and organisations is promoted, in the context of being clear about the social work role. The chapter discusses ways to facilitate multi-professional decision processes, including ensuring clear communication of concerns (risks); separating fact from opinion; framing the decision; working with conflict; and maintaining clarity of professional and organisational responsibilities within group processes. Ethical aspects are embodied through respect for the knowledge and skills of other professions; appropriate open communication about risks; and using appropriate processes for making decisions, particularly in conflict situations. There is reference to organisational and court work contexts for decision making and managing risk.

Increasingly, protocols, policies and procedures are being used to shape inter-agency working, particularly in relation to safeguarding work and social care of adults (Ambrose-Miller and Ashcroft 2016). There is no scope within this book to discuss the various assessment tools and processes used in different countries and regions in detail and, in any case, these change over time. Rather our focus is on the generalisable professional knowledge, skills and values that are required to engage in these processes effectively regardless of client group, setting or country.

For an extended treatment of the topics in this chapter suited to post-qualifying level, see Taylor (2017a). For current issues on the topics in this chapter see Section Two 'Assessment, Risk and Decision Processes' in Taylor et al. (2023). The personal safety of staff is beyond the scope of this book, and the interested reader is referred to a companion book by Sage (Taylor 2011). For a more in-depth discussion of interpersonal communication aspects of inter-professional collaboration, see Reder and Duncan (1999)

Collaboration

Collaboration (in various forms) in decision making is essential to:

- share knowledge and opinions so as to formulate a sufficiently comprehensive assessment 'picture';
- inform other professionals about services available in your domain;
- prevent services from 'pulling in different directions';
- ensure a consistent and cohesive message for clients and families; and
- reduce duplication of services and unnecessary costs.

In order to achieve effective multi-professional working, it is essential that each professional understands their own role, has some understanding of the knowledge base, skills, responsibilities and service configuration of other professions, and is open to disagreement and learning together. These topics are the focus of this chapter, which focuses on communication between professionals, particularly about risks and for the purpose of making decisions.

Collaborative decisions are often made in a group context, even if the group does not meet face to face. Our focus here includes multi-professional groups for such purposes as a child protection case conference; a hospital ward round to plan discharge; a strategy meeting or a panel to allocate resources such as a home care service; or admission to institutional care. The main focus of this chapter is on collaborative work with other professions and organisations. Chapter 2 discussed engaging and supporting clients and families in assessment, decision and risk processes. Legal aspects of risk communication and decision making in groups were considered in Chapter 3. This chapter looks at communication between professionals, although the principles apply to interactions with other social care workers (Taylor and Donnelly 2006b).

Barriers to collaboration may be due to a variety of factors including role confusion, ineffective communication, perceptions of group pressure, inefficient systems and differences in priorities between professions or between organisations. This textbook is designed for qualifying social work courses. Hence, our focus here will be on those aspects that the newly qualified social worker is likely to have most responsibility for or be able to influence most. For more in-depth discussion of other aspects of barriers and enablers to collaboration, see the companion book designed for post-qualifying studies in social work (Taylor 2017a). For further discussion of the need for consistency in assessment within the social work profession, see Sørensen (2023); for group processes and conflict in these see Lindsay (2011); and for organisational decision supports see Bastian and Schrödter (2023).

Role clarity

Being clear about your own role is essential to good multi-professional and multi-organisational decision making. For clients and families, a problem or issue may seem relevant to a wide range of organisations, and a referral may trigger a variety of responses from health, education, police and justice organisations as well as social care. A lack of coordination of services can be confusing, and uncoordinated services are likely to be less effective. Determining role in relation to client needs and perspectives is an essential part of the discussion during assessment. Clarity about role is commonly taught on social work qualifying courses as a foundational element in inter-personal helping skills (Shulman 2009), and we will give only an outline here as relevant to the focus of this book.

In safeguarding work, whether with children or adults, the social work role is essentially determined by statutes with their accompanying regulations and guidance as this role focuses on protecting people on behalf of society. Further detail will often be given in policies and procedures (increasingly including assessment tools) of the organisation. Within the international definition of social work (International Association of School of Social Work and International Federation of Social Workers 2014), the 'deemed competence' of the social work professional may be determined by the relevant national professional regulatory body (such as the Health and Care Professions Council for England, the Northern Ireland Social Care Council, the Scottish Social Services Council and Social Care Wales) and bodies with responsibility for regulating education and training of social workers (Quality Assurance Agency 2016). In Activity 4.1 there are some questions to prompt your thinking about defining the social work role in a particular situation.

The 'mission' or purpose of your particular social work team or voluntary sector organisation will be a key component in helping to clarify your role in relation to any particular client and family situation. If in doubt, your team leader or professional supervisor should provide the guidance that you need to define the scope and priorities of your role.

Activity 4.1   Role clarity

In order to think through the process of defining the social work role, reflect on a recent practice experience, such as on your placement:

- What was the focus or purpose of the referral from the referrer's perspective?
- How is the essential social work task defined from your employer's perspective?
- What are the challenges in defining clearly the social work task in this case?

Each profession must work within its 'deemed competence' (Taylor and Campbell 2011); that is, the tasks for which their qualifying training is intended to equip them. In assessment, we must clarify which client needs are relevant to the role of a social worker. Our role broadly relates to psycho-social needs, although there is some overlap with other health and social care professions at a basic level. As an example drawn from adult services to illustrate one possible configuration, the NISAT is designed to be used by all health and social care professionals for planning care of older people in the community. The overall design includes:

- Contact Screening (completed by a professional or a trained non-professional such as in a call centre or referral point);
- Core Assessment (completed by any health and social care professional);
- Complex Assessment (completed by any health and social care professional who is trained and supervised to undertake more complex work);
- Various tools to request and to provide a summary of specialist assessments.

Any health and social care profession might complete the Core Assessment with the older person if the needs are not complex. The domains of the Core Assessment are:

1. Physical health
2. Mental health and emotional well-being
3. Awareness and decision making skills
4. Management of medications
5. Communication and sensory functioning
6. Walking and movement
7. Personal care and daily tasks
8. Living arrangements and accommodation
9. Relationships
10. Work, finance and leisure.

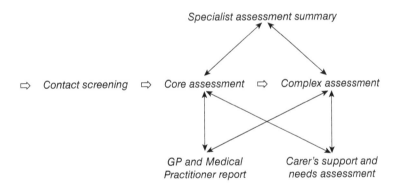

Figure 4.1 An illustration of communication channels using the example of an integrated assessment tool in adult services: The Northern Ireland Single Assessment Tool for the Health and Social Care of Older People (McCormack et al. 2008; see also Taylor 2012a)

Responsibilities in multi-professional and inter-organisational contexts

If the first principle for multi-professional working is to be clear about your own role, the second principle is to be clear about, and respectful of, the roles of other professions and organisations. Families and individuals facing multiple adversities and pressures (e.g. mental health problems, unemployment, drug and alcohol misuse, homelessness) need multi-professional and multi-agency assessment and support that is well coordinated (Fengler and Taylor 2019). We all use our understanding of human behaviour (whether articulated or not) by which to make sense of the situation that we must address. Becoming more aware of these mental models helps in understanding the communications of other professionals and in framing our communication with others (Sicora et al. 2021; Taylor 2021).

A key practice skill in inter-professional working is to respect the roles and responsibilities of others, and not to regard any other profession as lesser or to be feared. The role of the social worker is often to coordinate specialist contributions to decision making into a holistic, person-centred picture and to identify key issues to be addressed in a coordinated decision process, often involving explicit management of risks. This demands knowledge of the roles of other professions and organisations, and skills in managing the decision process. The essential approach is to respect the complementary contributions of each profession:

Inquiries show that too narrow a medical view of mental illness offers an inadequate framework for assessing and managing risk, while an over-reliance on social factors without sufficient attention to medical treatment and medication is potentially as unsafe.

(Reith 1998, p180).

Social workers may have a specialist assessment role in addition to a coordinating role (Mental Health Commission 2006).

Although multi-professional and inter-agency collaboration is to be encouraged (not least as good risk management), the responsibility of each profession and organisation is distinct. There may be a statutory or policy requirement for partnership and collaboration in specific areas of practice (Taylor 1999), but this does not mean taking on responsibilities of other professions or organisations! A useful working principle is to regard each profession as accountable for the decisions that fall within its deemed competence as determined by its training and registration. Similarly, each organisation is responsible for decisions that lie within its purpose, powers and duties. A group may have some formally defined powers. For example, in relation to child protection, a child protection case conference can usually decide whether a child requires a formal safeguarding plan (or registration, or similar system) or whether to cease one. Responsibilities of the group beyond this, other than to communicate reasonably as outlined briefly below, are usually very limited for legal reasons. You and your supervisor are responsible for your actions, not other professions or organisations. You must, however, take into account the facts available and opinions of others in forming your judgement, and must inform others of the decisions of your profession and organisation. And you must not, of course, sabotage the decisions of others to the deliberate detriment of the client. This provides an essential foundation for trust and robust group decision processes. For further discussion see Taylor (2017a) and *Wilsher v Essex Area Health Authority [1986] 3 all ER 801 (CA).*

Research Summary   Multi-professional child protection decision making

A systematic narrative literature review synthesised 30 studies (from six countries) on the implementation of multi-professional child protection decision making in community settings (Alfandari and Taylor 2022). Of particular interest were the contextual conditions upon which joint working is built (inputs), aspects of interactional functioning (mediators) and the results of working together (outputs). The analysis outlined key building blocks that form the structure for collaborative decision making and identified cognitive, relational and behavioural interactional properties that occur when making decisions together.

A second systematic narrative literature review synthesised 26 studies (from ten countries) on how a multi-professional approach to child protection decision making was implemented in hospital settings (Alfandari and Taylor 2023). In all the hospital-based settings studied, child protection decision-making tasks were assigned to a designated multi-professional team. However, there was remarkable diversity in models of team structure, regulation of workflow, structured procedures and standardised tools through which practice was carried out. Research focused on evaluating the teams' effectiveness in fulfilling their duties, which were, first and foremost, the identification of possible child maltreatment. The analysis identifies various systemic approaches and quality improvement methods to promote effective team-based decision-making processes in hospitals. The interactional aspect of collaborative team-based practice was generally missing from the published research.

Communication for decision making

Communication is an essential element of decision processes, including use of both formal processes and informal channels of communication. Everyday thoughtfulness – such as regarding a good time of day to telephone someone, or to hold a meeting – should not be forgotten. An aspect of communication which is not so 'everyday' is to consider consciously the appropriateness of the mode of communication: face-to-face, telephone, e-mail, other electronic communications, etc. In sensitive communications, a professional must weigh up issues such as level of formality, confidentiality, possible means of communication and planned scope for the discussion.

In professional life, there will also be consideration of the timeliness of communication. These relate to issues such as the urgency of making a particular decision; the availability of appropriate parties to participate in the decision; and the best sequence in which to exchange information with other stakeholders.

In all fields of social work the use of language must be precise enough to enable effective decision making. Open and honest, yet tactful, communication is essential to clarify issues and develop mutual understanding, trust and respect. It is important that participants in the decision are confident in the process and feel safe to raise their issues even if some disagreement may ensue. There is increasing recognition of the interface

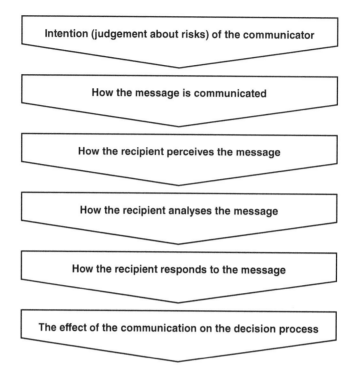

Figure 4.2   Communication stages in decision making processes

between communicating risk and decision-making processes (Taylor and Whittaker 2019; Whittaker and Taylor 2018).

Communicating risks

A critical issue in communication for decision making is the communication of 'concerns' or 'risks'. There may be different perceptions of 'risks' (Taylor and McKeown 2013). An important early step is to separate facts from opinions, and to clarify what is the agreed perspective of each profession involved. We conceptualise **risk communication** as the exchange of information between individuals receiving services, family members and professionals about possible harm and potential benefits in client situations and care options, in order to inform decision making about care (Stevenson, McDowell and Taylor 2018).

A starting point, building on earlier chapters, is to clarify whether the term 'risk' is being used to refer to the seriousness (value) of the harm that we are seeking to avoid, or to the likelihood of the harm. The term 'risk' is often replaced with terms such as 'concerns' or 'unanticipated events'. Social work by its nature is concerned with daily life, and the conceptualisation of 'risk taking' in daily life can be even more diverse than the use of the term 'risk' in terms of harms. People tend to focus on what they want to achieve or what they have always done, often without clearly articulating what risks they run in the process. The conceptualisation of 'risk' in social work needs to include at least:

- the types of possible harms ('risks') for your area of work;
- the social constructions of risk used by clients and families;
- a professional understanding of objective measures of the likelihood of identified possible harm occurring;
- approaches to dealing with risk including acceptable risk taking; and
- some understanding of how risk relates to making a judgement and decision-making processes (Stevenson, McDowell and Taylor 2018).

Research Summary   Conceptualising risk in community care

Data were gathered across five focus groups (35 health and social care professionals) covering concepts and perspectives on verbal, numeric and visual forms of communicating risk. Risks were primarily conceptualised as consequences (positive and negative) rather than as likelihood, and related to a wide range of domains. Perceptions were influenced by sociocultural factors including risk-assessment mechanisms and wider discourse relating to positive risk taking. The language of probability was used in a non-quantified, subjective manner. While professionals routinely received quantitative information, they did not typically communicate using numeric expressions. Verbal expressions of likelihood were widely preferred to numeric expressions of likelihood. When risks were presented in numeric formats, frequency presentation was seen as more comprehensible than percentages. Several participants saw potential in visual forms of risk communication. Bar charts were generally favoured to icon arrays as more easily understood. Good practice examples for risk communication were identified.

- How is risk conceptualised in your field of social work?
- How could you improve your communication about risk to clients, families and other professionals?

(Stevenson and Taylor (2017) Risk communication in dementia care: professional perspectives on consequences, likelihood, words and numbers: *British Journal of Social Work*, 47(7), 1940–1958. Reproduced with permission of Oxford University Press.)

Risks in terms of likelihood of harm are often communicated with words, but increasingly are communicated with numbers, and occasionally visually (Taylor, Stevenson and McDowell 2018). People understand risk in diverse ways depending on their life experiences, and on the focus of their thoughts when posed the question. The way in which risk information is communicated may shape the recipient's understanding of the facts of the situation. Words may be misunderstood by listeners but, on the other hand, numbers can sometimes have an unjustified air of authority about them. The presentation of information may be a particular issue in formal decision situations such as courts. There is little exploration yet in social work of communicating about probabilities with more visual means such as graphs or charts.

One approach is to use both words and numbers, perhaps along the lines of: 'Your honour, I would describe the likelihood as "..........", meaning about x% based on relevant research and the evidence available in this case...' (Carson and Bain 2008, p167). There are some initiatives to create a useful correspondence between numbers and words, but progress is limited in terms of findings of relevance to social work practice. As an example, the following has been proposed as terms to express likelihood of re-occurrence in sexual abuse cases:

- < 5% Very unlikely
- 5–20% Unlikely
- 20–40% Somewhat unlikely
- 40–60% Undetermined
- 60–80% Somewhat more likely than not
- 80–95% Likely
- > 95% Very likely (suggested by Wood 1996).

As the 'information age' moves forward (Schrödter et al. 2020), it will become increasingly important that professionals can use statistical information about risks and appraise its quality and usefulness (Taylor and Moorhead 2020).

Legal aspects of communicating risk

Giving information and advice to clients and to other professionals is part of a social worker's role. Legal aspects will vary according to the jurisdiction in which you are working. Only brief comments on legal aspects will be provided here, drawing on case law judgements regarded as applicable across the different jurisdictions within the UK, and which may be cited for reference in legal cases elsewhere even if not binding.

In *Coles -v- Reading and District Hospital Management Committee and Another [1963] 107 S.J. 115*, the House of Lords confirmed that a doctor was under a duty to disclose any substantial risk involving grave adverse consequences of following or not following the advice given. Precepts for this were clarified by *Montgomery (Appellant) v Lanarkshire Health Board (Respondent) (Scotland) [2015] UKSC 11 On appeal from: [2013] CSIH 3; [2010] CSIH 104*. The duty to communicate about risks should be regarded as whether a reasonable person in the position of this client would think that the risk of the proposed intervention was significant in terms of consequences or likelihoods. Risk communications must be personalised to the individual client or family, rather than simply being a matter of getting a document signed. In contentious or high-risk cases, consider agreeing what is adequate written advice with your line manager or professional supervisor, and consider what should be evidenced in contemporaneous records.

Case Study   Duty to Communicate about Risks

It is important that concern for confidentiality does not blind us to the need to share information that might reasonably be expected to help to prevent harm. For example,

W and Others v. Essex County Council and Another [2000] 2 All ER 237 reports how a local authority social services department placed Peter [pseudonym], a child who was known to have sexually abused other children, with a foster family. The social workers responsible for placing the child withheld this information from the foster carers. The foster child went on to sexually abuse the children of the foster parents. The court found the local authority negligent for failing to disclose this information about the foster child, as it was reasonably foreseeable that he or she might abuse (or try to abuse) members of the foster family.

Comment

- The dilemma in terms of what to tell to whom might usefully be considered in terms of responsibility towards each of the parties. Empathy with each party, and considering the seriousness of various risks, will assist in thinking about what they might reasonably expect in terms of communication.
- What is the responsibility of the authority towards Peter?
- What is the responsibility of the authority towards the host family?
- What is a reasonable professional decision in such a situation?
- What communication would be good professional practice with the parties?

Despite our general professional value of respecting confidentiality, there are situations where we face a dilemma when we know information *confidentially* which might protect someone from harm. You should be aware that you may have a duty of care to override confidentiality to inform identifiable third parties if there is a specific risk of violence to an identifiable individual (*Tarasoff v Regents of the University of California [1976] 551 P 2d 334 [USA]*; there does not seem to have been any clear confirmation or contradiction of this judgement in the UK courts). Even if a professional is employed privately by a client or by a solicitor on the client's behalf, he or she may still have a legal duty to protect the public from identifiable violence which may override the duty of confidentiality to the client (*W v Edgell [1990] All ER 835*). In particular, child and adult safeguarding systems may require passing of information without consent where this is justifiable, for example in terms of urgent action to protect someone from serious immediate harm. *This is a complex area and legal advice should be sought urgently if you are facing this type of situation.* The issue also needs to be considered in the context of the Data Protection Act 2018 (UK), and comparable legislation in other countries. The general points that we derive are that professionals should be educated on risk factors (see Chapter 8); should carry out competent assessment (see Chapters 3 and 5); and should communicate effectively with other professionals (this Chapter). For general education the interested reader is referred to Monahan (1993) and Kopels and Kagle (1993).

Facilitating group decision processes

Social workers often have a key role in facilitating group processes as part of decision-making procedures. This requires values such as respect for the knowledge and skills of other professionals; building trust; knowledge of the group mandate and relevant protocols; and ability to contribute to facilitating group processes. Some key tasks in facilitating decision processes include:

- focusing on the best interests of the client and family;
- taking account of relevant values, principles and protocols;
- ensuring that professional identities are not threatened;
- ensuring appropriate people are engaged at an appropriate stage in the process;
- managing an effective decision-making process if you have a coordinating role;
- ensuring that you are clear on your role and the powers and duties of your organisation, and that these are communicated clearly to others;
- ensure that roles of other participants are clarified;
- acting with integrity, building trust and respect in the group, and making appropriate use of social work skills such as conveying empathy and partialising issues;
- clarifying with stakeholders (client, family, professionals and organisations) what is expected of them and what they expect of you, for what purpose and within what time scale;
- giving all parties an opportunity (and sometimes support) to make effective, timely contributions, sharing facts and expressing their opinions appropriately;
- clarifying how the decision will be implemented;
- informing parties of the decision outcome.

(Adapted from: Ambrose-Miller and Ashcroft 2016; Lindsey 2011; Mitchell et al. 2011)

In decision processes, fact must be separated from opinion. And the client voice must be heard distinctly from the family views and the professional opinion. A group decision compared to an individual decision has the advantage of drawing on wider knowledge, skills, experience, resources and ideas. It may also generate 'ownership' of the decision. Communication in a group about risks and decisions may have the effect of challenging assumptions and requiring participants to clarify their language so as to reach a common understanding. Disadvantages of group decision making are the potential for conflicts of interests, perspectives, aims and values which may make consensus difficult to achieve. Engaging appropriate stakeholders may be a painful process.

Research Summary   Effectiveness of Inter-professional Working in Elder Care (Trivedi et al. 2013)

This literature review aimed to identify the models of inter-professional working (IPW) that provide the strongest evidence base for practice with community-dwelling older people. We searched electronic databases from 1 January 1990–31 March 2008, with findings updated in December 2010, and selected papers describing randomised controlled trials (RCTs) reporting user-relevant outcomes. Included studies were classified by IPW models (Case Management, Collaboration and Integrated Team) and assessed for risk of bias. A narrative synthesis was conducted of the evidence according to the type of care (interventions delivering acute, chronic, palliative and preventive care) identified within each model of IPW. We retrieved 3211 records and included 37 RCTs, which were mapped onto the IPW models. Overall, there is weak evidence of effectiveness and cost-effectiveness for IPW, although well-integrated and shared care models improved processes of care and have the potential to reduce hospital or nursing/care home use.

Study quality varied considerably, and high-quality studies are needed to identify the key components of effective IPW in relation to user-defined outcomes. Differences in local contexts raise questions about the applicability of the findings and their implications for practice. We need more information on the outcomes of the process of IPW and evaluations of the effectiveness of different organisational models of health and social care professionals for the care of community-dwelling older people.

Framing the decision in group decision processes

In collaborative decision-making situations, social workers need skills in framing the decision, articulating shared goals and working with conflict. The collaborative decision-making process may highlight the differing conceptualisations of risk as ways of framing the decision (Taylor 2006).

Placing the needs of the client and family at the centre can help to ensure an effective framing of the decision process (Anand et al. 2013; Killick et al. 2015; Stevenson et al. 2019; Taylor and Donnelly 2006a). In some contexts, it is important to separate the perspectives of the client from those of the family (Kirk et al. 2019; McGinn et al. 2016; Stevenson and Taylor 2016).

There is limited research on group decision processes involving social workers (Alfandari, Taylor, Enosh et al. 2023). While there may be a moral or procedural requirement or expectation to collaborate, there may also be diverse 'political' pressures involved (Przeperski and Taylor 2022). The work by Farmer and Owen (1995) on child protection case conferences illustrated how the process of **assessing risk** in such groups can sometimes lead to *accumulating concerns* and a disproportionate sense of impending harm, and thus to more *risk averse* group decisions than the judgements of individuals acting alone. This perhaps reflects the views of wider society which might choose less risky options than professionals. Their research highlighted how pressure can be experienced to conform to the majority view in the meeting. However, there is some evidence that child protection case conferences may sometimes assume a more extreme position than the average of the members individually, whether more *risk taking* or more *risk averse* (Kelly and Milner 1996), perhaps because of the need to make a clear decision with an explicit justification.

Some key dimensions of practice to consider in relation to collaborating and communicating across professions and organisations are illustrated in Figure 4.3. This figure structures considerations into three categories: (1) those that are primarily related to yourself; (2) those that primarily concern relationships with other individuals; and (3) those that relate primarily to organisational and inter-organisational aspects of collaborative working and communication.

Working with conflict in collaborative decision making

The benefits of inter-professional collaboration in decision making must not blind us to the challenges that can occur in reconciling competing objectives. We may need to challenge opinions on occasion as well as seeking compromises. *The training of social workers must equip them with the confidence to question the opinion of professionals in other agencies when conducting their own assessment of the needs of the child* (Laming 2003,

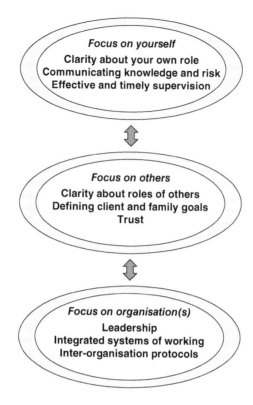

Figure 4.3 A diagram to illustrate some key aspects of communication and collaborative working

Recommendation 37). This questioning of the opinions of others must, of course, be done respectfully. We as social workers should also anticipate and accept our opinions being challenged.

As a newly qualified social worker, your responsibility is likely to be ensuring that you are an effective participant rather than leader of a multi-professional group. Nonetheless you will want to use some of the skills expected of a group facilitator, such as attending to the process (what is felt and experienced in a group meeting) as well as the content (what is said). You will want to be aware of emotions in groups, perhaps relating to self-disclosure, anxiety, sense of power or powerlessness, control, trust, fear, need to belong, or desire to see a particular outcome. You will then need to process these thoughts internally in relation to your role, in deciding what to say or not to say.

Research Summary   Overview of serious case reviews (Dickens et al. 2022)

Dickens et al. (2022) conducted an overview and analysis of 235 cases which led to serious case reviews (SCRs) in England between April 2017 and September 2019. The SCRs were because children or young people had died or suffered serious harm, and abuse or neglect was known or suspected (and, in the non-fatal cases, there was cause for concern as to the way in which agencies had worked together to safeguard the child). Findings and recommendations included (page 11):

* The exchange of information is necessary but not sufficient for effective communication. Professionals need opportunities to engage in discussion about cases and to 'translate' information for other professionals outside their discipline.
* Discussion and respectful challenge between professionals are key to robust decision making. Framing this as 'resolving professional differences' rather than 'escalation' may assist in creating opportunities for constructive inter-professional dialogue.

Formal decision settings

Social workers are often engaged in *contested decision making*, despite our best efforts to create collaborative partnership ways of working. Contested decisions are required where there are conflicts between rights, responsibilities and interests, such as where statutory safeguarding powers are being exercised. Courts and other formal settings require particular attention to rights, procedures and the rules of evidence within the decision processes.

There are particular issues where information is given anonymously or *in confidence*. Courts are a key mechanism in society to resolve such conflicts and have increasingly clear and stringent expectations of social work judgements. '*Expressions of opinion must be supported by detailed evidence and articulated reasoning*' (Munby J. in *Re M [Care Proceedings: Judicial Review]* [2003] 2 FLR 171 p183).

Safeguarding roles present many challenges for professionals in striving to engage clients and families in decision making and partnership working that will enable therapeutic change in relationships. In such collaborative working, we should strive towards such goals as *fairness* and *openness*, recognising that as professionals with safeguarding responsibilities we have been given powers and duties by society in order to protect the most vulnerable.

The most strongly contested decision-making processes are normally conducted in a court or similar formal setting. This is not to imply that a court setting is entirely negative. Jones (2006, p476) suggests that: *Courts can be therapeutic... and bring reluctant parents into a setting where change becomes a reality... The authority, thoroughness, fairness and neutrality of the court process seem to me to be ingredients that have the potential to be a foundation and driver for family change.*

As a social worker you may be in court on behalf of an organisation that is a party to the proceedings (such as a statutory authority bringing an action to protect children from abuse) or you may be in court as an expert witness (for example, providing a report in a private law dispute between separated parents about custody and access to their children). However, as you are appearing in your professional capacity even in the former case, the courts will generally treat you as an expert in relation to areas within your competence. It is essential to engage with your line management, professional supervisor and legal adviser as appropriate.

You may find it surprising, in view of the emphasis on collaborative and inter-disciplinary working, that in court you are not giving evidence as a member of a team, but as an individual. As an employee, you obviously have to follow the instructions of your managers; if, for example, it is decided in a case conference to recommend the initiation of care proceedings and you are instructed to take this forward, then you must do this. However once in court your primary duty is to the court, which requires you to give evidence of your personal knowledge and opinions, not those of anyone else... If the court wishes to hear from your team or service manager, or anyone else, then they can be called as a witness, and indeed should be if their views and decisions are important to the case.

(Seymour and Seymour 2007, p101)

Evidence in a court may include facts about the client, family and context. As a professional you are expected to be knowledgeable in relevant areas, such as (in child care proceedings) attachment and bonding, child development and parenting that inform your judgement. You have to articulate the context, issues, facts, opinions, concerns and strategies relevant to the case. A robust argument requires that there is evidence, including a proper analysis for and against the proposed course of action, and that there is an adequately reasoned professional judgement. This must include a proper balancing exercise and an analysis of the proportionality of what is being proposed in terms of compulsory protection measures and the seriousness of the harm to be avoided. You are required to provide a balanced overview of relevant research or theory, not a partisan selection of favourable studies. In such formal decision situations, you may be challenged on the facts of the case, on your credibility and on your competence. It is important to be clear on limits to your competence and to respect the competence domains of other professions.

The court needs to know how you formed your opinion so that it can fairly weigh up the arguments (Duffy et al. 2006). Courts in the UK are gradually formulating more explicitly their expectations regarding seeing essential information being weighed up in some rational manner within social work reports (Re B-S (Children) [2013] EWCA Civ 1146). Ensure that your opinions can be backed up by evidence. For further reading see Seymour and Seymour (2007).

Concluding comments

This chapter has outlined key concepts for engaging with other professionals in the various processes which may be involved in professional practice in relation to assessment, managing risk and making decisions in partnership with other professions and organisations. We have focused particularly on being clear about your role and that of others; on effective communication that is both clear and timely; and on beginning skills in facilitating multi-professional collaboration, as this role falls often to social workers. The reader interested in exploring further some of the complexities and issues in working in multi-professional teams and networks is referred to Alfandari, Przeperski, et al. (2023). For further discussion of the organisational context of assessment, risk and decision making, the reader is referred to Gregory (2023).

Theoretical underpinnings

This chapter draws on theoretical material and empirical studies relating to communication, conflict and group processes as they apply to social work practice situations involving assessment, managing risk and decision making. This includes material with roots primarily in:

- communication studies
- social psychology
- sociology, and
- legal studies.

Knowledge and skills summary

- The first principle of multi-professional and multi-organisational decision making is to be clear about your own role; the second principle is to be respectful and sufficiently knowledgeable of the roles and area of responsibility of other professions and organisations.
- Although multi-professional and inter-agency collaboration is encouraged, the responsibility of each profession and organisation is distinct and needs to be clear.
- Communication is an essential element of decision processes, including both use of protocols and formal processes, and an understanding and awareness of informal channels of communication.
- The timing and timeliness of communication are important aspects of group decision processes.
- Ensure good communication about risks, whether with words, numbers or visually.
- Social workers often have a key role in facilitating group processes as part of decision-making procedures. This requires values such as respect for the knowledge and skills of other professionals, and skills in facilitating group processes.
- In group decision processes, fact must be separated from opinion, and the client voice heard distinct from family views and professional opinion.
- Social workers need skills in framing the decision, articulating shared goals and working with conflict in collaborative decision-making situations.
- Courts and other formal settings require particular attention to rights, procedures and the rules of evidence within the decision processes.
- Multi-professional collaboration is a good risk-management principle, but remember that each profession remains responsible for decisions within its deemed competence.
- Being able to construct a rational, ethical argument underpinning a professional judgement is an essential area of knowledge and skills for social workers to contribute effectively to decision processes.

Further Reading

Seymour, C. and Seymour, R. (2011). *Courtroom and report writing skills for social workers* (Second edition). Exeter: Learning Matters.

This attractive textbook in the Sage Post-Qualifying Social Work Practice series includes useful chapters on legal aspects of contested decision making, and on values and principles relevant to collaborative decision processes.

Killick, C. and Taylor, B.J. (2023). Studying risk managing, decision making and assessment processes. In Taylor, B.J. Fluke, J.D., Graham, J.C., Keddell, E., Killick, C., Shlonsky, A. and Whittaker, A. (Eds), *The Sage handbook of decision making, assessment and risk in social work*. London: Sage.

This chapter, within a comprehensive reference work on the topics in the present book, provides an overview of research methods suited to studying processes of assessment, risk and decision making in social work.

Taylor, B.J. (Ed.) (2011). *Working with aggression and resistance in social work*. London: Sage.

This book in the Transforming Social Work Series addresses work in a range of situations of conflict. Although the focus is on work with clients and families, key principles are transferable to work with professionals where there is conflict, and the book includes a chapter on working with conflict in group situations.

Taylor, B.J. (2017). *Decision making, assessment and risk in social work* (Third edition). London: Sage.

This textbook, designed for qualified social workers, contains a chapter focusing on collaboration, communication and conflict in decision making. The book includes greater detail on the topics in this chapter.

5

Analysis in assessment

(Continued)

It will also introduce you to the following standards as set out in the Social Work Subject Benchmark Statement (2019):

5.2 Knowledge of social work theory
5.10 Problem-solving skills

See Appendix 2 for a detailed description of these standards.

Introduction

Chapter 1 discussed the way that knowledge can inform our assessment process and support our analysis of information. Analysis is one stage within the assessment and decision-making process, but an analytical approach should be present in all aspects of the social work role. Professional social work involves evaluating the available information to help us understand complex social situations, and explain how and why problems are arising. In this chapter we will consider in more depth the centrality of an analytical approach, and the ways in which it links to knowledge and critical practice. We will argue that analysis should not be seen as an added extra, but as a framework that will guide the entire process. Specific tools to encourage analytical assessments will be discussed.

The analytical approach to assessment

Social workers develop skills in engaging with people and gathering information, but sometimes we are less able to synthesise this in a way that explains the reality of the situation. It is possible that a social worker could gather and present a range of important facts and perspectives, but produce a report that fails to illustrate a meaningful overall picture of the subject's experience. Particularly in complex assessments, the meaning can easily be lost in the sheer quantity of data. Using an analytical approach prompts the practitioner to constantly question their impressions and perspectives.

Figure 5.1 illustrates stages in an analytical approach that processes information using existing knowledge, critical thinking, analysis and reflection. In Chapter 4 we discussed how a knowledge base or framework could help to identify the aspects of a case that are important and why. Our existing theory can provide a scaffolding or structure for information gathering. It is the underpinning knowledge that helps us to know what information will be important to our assessment.

Critical thinking is an ongoing process of weighing up the information that is available to us in order to establish its importance and credibility. This includes an evaluation of potential bias that might distort our own thinking or interpretation. (Bias is discussed further in Chapter 7.) Analysis is the stage of assessment when we review the available information and interpret its potential meaning. It is also an

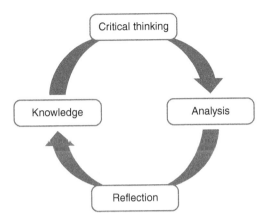

Figure 5.1 The Analytical Process

opportunity to weigh up a range of positive and negative factors and estimate their impact on a child or adult's well-being. Finally, reflection is the process of drawing learning from the work that has been undertaken. This allows the practitioner to fine-tune their knowledge base to accommodate new information or perspectives. It may be helpful to study each of the elements of analytical practice in more depth considering how they can be implemented in our practice.

Knowledge

Both 'formal' and 'informal' knowledge provide a framework that helps the social worker to understand the issues that they are facing and the role that they and others might play. When supporting families, we need to understand child development. If a child has a disability, we need to understand models of disability. In adult services we need to understand the social impact of mental illness or ageing. Our knowledge base will incorporate structural issues like poverty and discrimination as well as specific issues like health and nutrition. The 'big' theories learned in university must be blended and internalised through practice, to give us an understanding of the lived experience of individuals and families. Secker (1993) described how student social workers acquired the ability to use theory to make sense of their work. She identified three levels of ability:

1. an unquestioning approach where theory was only applied in hindsight;
2. a fragmented use of ready-made explanations; and
3. the ability to weave together fluently theory and other sources of understanding to produce 'custom-made theories'.

The ability to relate formal and experiential knowledge to practice is a key skill of the social work practitioner. Interestingly, Secker indicated that in her experience not all students had achieved this level of application at the point of graduation. The ability to relate knowledge to practice is one that can continue to develop over the course of a social work career. It is this practice knowledge that can assist in both planning assessments and making sense of information. It helps the practitioner to understand the purpose of the assessment so that they can gather and structure the appropriate information.

Trevithick (2008) has provided a valuable model that helps us understand the ways in which knowledge informs assessment. She identifies three overlapping forms of knowledge:

1. theoretical knowledge that explains the issues and the social work role;
2. factual knowledge that can be confirmed or refuted; and
3. practice knowledge that includes the subjective reality of the key stakeholders including ourselves.

Theoretical knowledge can be seen as a map (Milner et al 2015) that guides the journey of the assessment process. Often theory underpins the assessment framework, but it is essential that the practitioner has a firm grasp of these core concepts. Factual knowledge is essential in producing an objective explanation of events and consequences. This may be observed or reported behaviour but is drawn also from policy and research findings. The role of research evidence in assessment and decision making will be discussed further in Chapter 7. In social work, objective, factual knowledge is always contextualised with an understanding of subjective perspectives that explain the reality as perceived by the individuals involved. Practice knowledge includes the perceptions of each individual, as well as the knowledge that professionals have gained from previous work. Practice knowledge also includes the important element of intuition. This is a subconscious processing of information that has been described as instinct or 'gut feeling' (Sicora et al 2021). Research suggests that intuition has significant influence in social work decision making. Cook (2017) investigated social workers' decision making during initial home visits. She described a 'sense making toolkit' that included formal information, intuition and emotions. In discussion some elements of intuition could be linked to observable factors. Staff were attuned to the openness of parents, the coherence of their statements, and their emotional state. They noticed if parents focused on the needs of the child and took responsibility for the situation. Other aspects of intuition were not easily explained using conscious logic. One respondent stated '*I just got a feeling she was telling the truth*' (Cook 2017, p438).

Decisions, particularly within social work, include an element of 'irreducible uncertainty', and the practitioner may use a combination of intuition (based on past experience) and analysis to form a **judgement**. The approach to decision making can be influenced by the personality of the practitioner, the nature of the decision and the time available, although the process can often be unconscious and at times practitioners struggle to explain the methods that they use (Duffy et al 2006).

Case Study   Ajiza Abadi (age 17) – part one

Ajiza moved from Syria to Scotland with her parents and older brothers six years ago. She is bright, hard-working and popular with her peers. Today she is refusing to return home because she says her father and brothers mistreat her. She says they refuse to allow her to go out with friends or wear the clothes she likes. In particular they will not allow her to meet her boyfriend, Kenny. During an argument before school Ajiza's brothers threatened her with violence if she continued to disobey her parents.

- What knowledge will help us understand the issues in this case?
- What policy and factual information are relevant?
- How could we assess the perceptions of key participants?

Critical thinking

A key social work skill is the ability to evaluate each source of evidence to establish its credibility. This is because we can rarely be certain of our information, and there is always the potential to misunderstand or to be misled. Critical thinking describes a purposeful engagement with all information to ensure that it is accurate and meaningful (Rutter and Brown 2020). Social workers use professional curiosity to interrogate sources of knowledge rather than taking them at face value. Criticality can be applied to all aspects of the assessment including our own assumptions and interpretation.

Aspinwall-Roberts (2012) describes a dialectic mindset with which we can interrogate our mental processing. Some examples of critical thinking questions have been provided in Activity 5.1. The questioning of our assumptions allows us to be open to wider possibilities. It can be replicated by asking a colleague or manager to look at the information with a fresh set of eyes and question our reasoning. The role of supervision in assessment and decision making is discussed further in Chapter 10. Critical thinking is central to assessment because it informs the process as well as the outcome. It will not make the process infallible, but it will be more defensible as the practitioner will be able to show how and why they came to their decisions.

Activity 5.1 Critical Thinking

The below questions help us explore and synthesise the meaning from the information that is available to us. Perhaps you could use these to review a recent case you have been involved in.

- What did she/he mean by that comment?
- Why do these two accounts differ?
- Which account deserves more weight and why?
- Is any information missing?
- Is this information, assumption or interpretation supported by the evidence?
- Are there other possible explanations?

Analysis

We have already argued that an analytical approach should be threaded through the assessment process planning, contextualising, justifying and interpreting the information that we gather. There also needs to be an explicit stage within an assessment process where the practitioner draws together the information and endeavours to explain what it means. It is hoped that a professional curiosity during the information-gathering process and the explicit analysis of the material will result in a report that clearly articulates the reality experienced by the key individuals. Decisions based on an accurate assessment are more likely to be fair and just (Platt and Turney 2018). Research suggests that this analysis stage of assessment is not easy. Where deficits are identified in assessment, the quality of analysis is often a factor.

It is clear from the studies we reviewed that the analysis of information has continued to be problematic in practice so attention needs to be focused on strengthening this crucial aspect of the assessment process.

(Turney et al 2011, p7)

Lack of analysis and blind adherence to procedure are vital flaws in more complex, confusing cases.

(Brandon et al 2005, p172)

Assessments are of a variable quality and do not routinely inform plans for children. The majority are detailed and updated on time but often lack analysis, professional curiosity and the voice of children and their families.

(Ofsted 2019, p2)

When dealing with complexity and disagreement, social workers can find it difficult to identify the most important issues and express their professional opinion. It is often easier to simply describe what we saw and heard, but a synthesis of the information is essential to make a reasoned decision and is part of our professional role. Analytical assessment writing is a skill, and like other skills it is improved through coaching and practice. Practitioners learn to write analytically through experience, with feedback from peers and professional supervisors. Hopefully analytical skills are learned on placement and during the first months of employment, but the honing of the skill is a lifelong task.

There are a number of helpful guides that illustrate analysis. These have been designed for child protection, but are equally useful in other programmes of care. For example, Bentovim et al (2009) describe a 'How and Why mindset' that prompts the writer to include context and meaning into their reports. The mindset asks two questions:

- What needs of the child are being met … and how?
- What needs of the child are not being met … and why?

Figure 5.2 The How and Why mindset

Case Study   Ajiza Abadi (age 17) – part two

We previously discussed the way that knowledge might inform this case. It is possible that the How and Why mindset will assist us in planning an assessment and analysing our findings.

What needs are being met?

Ajiza tells us that her family provides for her physical needs. She is well looked after and until recently she has felt loved and nurtured.

How?

Ajiza's parents both work. They tell us that they are aware of her physical and emotional needs and that they make every effort to support her growth and development.

What needs are not being met?

Ajiza says that does not feel safe living at home. Her brothers have threatened violence and she believes they are serious.

Why?

There has recently been increasing tension in the family home over Ajiza's friends and behaviour. Ajiza is spending time with schoolfriends including her new boyfriend Kenny. She does not see why this is unacceptable. Her parents feel her behaviour is disobedient and disrespectful. They accept that Ajiza is fearful about her safety.

You can see how the above analysis tries to focus in on the key issues and explain what is going on. It also raises further questions that would provide more insight into the specific areas of concern:

- Why is Ajiza's behaviour causing concern?
- Why were threats of violence not addressed?

In a resource pack for Research in Practice, Brown et al (2014) provide a five-question framework for analytical thinking. The questions are:

1. What is the assessment for?
2. What is the story?
3. What does the story mean?
4. What needs to happen?
5. How will we know if we are making progress?

Framing the assessment as a story is more likely to produce a holistic narrative that explains the reality of the person at the centre.

Case Study   Ajiza Abadi (age 17) – part three

Ajiza's story is one of a culture clash, parental expectations and growing independence. She recognises her parents' support but values her friendship group. She believes she has a right to make choices and have these respected.

The story of her parents may be one of struggle to retain traditional values in a new setting. They believe that they are acting in Ajiza's best interests and are concerned that her actions will shame her and the family.

The ability to articulate each of these stories helps us to understand the motivations of key characters and the factors that promote conflict. Asking 'what needs to happen?' focuses our attention on Ajiza's well-being and prompts us to imagine an outcome where her needs are met.

The final question identifies measurable indicators of progress relating to the most significant issues. These will be useful in agreeing a direction of travel that all agencies and individuals can work towards.

Five 'whats?'

Both of the above models have the potential to draw together material gathered during an assessment with a client and family in order to make sense of it, formulate a **professional judgement** and present this coherently. Elements of both models have been incorporated into the five 'what?' questions below. Such tools will never be exhaustive, so be prepared to add additional questions as your experience grows.

Figure 5.3   Five 'Whats'

1. What aspects of the case have we identified as **important** and why?
2. What **evidence** is available and how credible is it?
3. What are the hopes and **wishes** of the person at the centre of the process?
4. What **strengths** have been identified and to what extent do they reduce concerns?
5. What needs to **change** and what would progress look like?

Below (Table 5.1) is an extract from a child's needs assessment. The practitioner has provided a list of positive and negative aspects of the family lifestyle, but we have little understanding of the child's world. Similarly, there is no indication of the primary concerns or why they may be occurring. Statements like 'Danny does not get much exercise' suggest there is a reason for concern but don't indicate how severe this is or what harm might occur. It will be difficult to make decisions based on this report. It is also unclear what action needs to be taken.

Case Study   Child's Needs Assessment Form (part one)

Table 5.1   Child's Needs Assessment Form

Section 7a: Child or Young Person's Needs	Name: Danny Shaw (7)
Health and Development	
All immunisations up to date.	
Attends dentist and GP as necessary.	
No behavioural problems at home or at school.	
No identified issues with sleep.	
Danny does not get much exercise.	
Poor diet. Danny eats processed foods and not fresh fruit or vegetables.	
Danny's parents smoke in the house.	

The revised version (Table 5.2) tells us more about the important issues in Danny's life. The practitioner has tried to focus in on the key needs and explain why there are concerns. The wishes of Danny and his parents have been included, as have the healthy aspects of family life. There is some indication why these issues may be arising and some suggestion of what might need to change. This report is more likely to inform a decision-making process. If Danny and his parents are present, they should be more aware of the need for change and the actions that will promote progress.

Case Study   Child's Needs Assessment Form (part two)

Table 5.2   Child's Needs Assessment Form Revised

Section 7a: Child or Young Person's Needs	Name: Danny Shaw (7)

Health and Development

Mr and Mrs Shaw are aware of Danny's health and development needs, and they have taken active steps to address this including immunisations, GP contact and dental care. In general Danny's development is normal for a child of his age but two areas of concern need to be highlighted.

Mr and Mrs Shaw have found it difficult to get Danny to eat a varied diet that includes fresh fruit and vegetables. The attached food diary shows that Danny's current diet is dangerously high in fat, sugar and salt and he is already somewhat overweight. A consistently poor diet could result in physical and emotional health problems. Danny accepts that eating healthy food is important, but he will need ongoing encouragement to make this change so that he improves his physical and emotional health. It should be recognised that financial constraints are a factor, but Mr and Mrs Shaw would value support addressing the issue of diet.

Dr Kennedy has stated that Danny's asthma is being exacerbated by Mr and Mrs Shaw smoking in the house. Danny's asthma attacks have become more frequent and severe despite a recent increase in the strength of his medication. Danny reports that breathlessness is preventing him from playing football. Mrs Shaw does not agree that smoke is a contributing factor, and she does not wish to consider stopping. However, she and her husband have agreed not to smoke in the house and a smoke-free home could have health benefits for all family members.

Analytical thinking and writing involve bringing all forms of information together and making sense of the whole rather than the individual elements. Do the different accounts that I have heard agree? Are the opinions supported by facts? How do strengths mitigate against potential harm? The third of the 'what?' questions is particularly important. Research suggests that the voices of children and vulnerable adults can be easily lost among the perceptions of more vocal adults. Holland (2001) found that children's progress was more likely to be included in an assessment than their views and wishes. Often information about children was gained from parents. When the views of children were sought there was the potential that they could be influenced by parents. It is sometimes possible to obtain the perceptions of even very young children, but this can be time-consuming.

Case Study   Involving People in the Analysis of Information

Maggs

Alice is a single parent who has significant mental health issues. She recently started a relationship with Arnie, who is described as having a violent temper. Her daughter Maggs is 6 years old. Maggs is described as very quiet and withdrawn.

Rachael

Dr and Mrs Evans have a 22-year-old daughter called Rachael who has a severe learning disability. The family has recently moved from London, and they are keen for Rachael to get a day care placement. Rachael is described as very quiet and withdrawn.

- How important is it that we include the views and perceptions of Maggs or Rachael in an assessment?
- What approaches might you use to maximise their input to the process?
- What might hinder us in gaining their participation?

As we analyse the information that we have gathered, our central focus should be the child, the older person or adult who has disabilities. Often the views and wishes of parents, carers and professionals dominate the process. They can be given undue weighting and therefore be over-represented in the final report. It is the responsibility of the assessor to ensure that the world of the child or adult is clearly presented, and this is best achieved with their collaboration as we make sense of the information.

Ethics of analysis

The ability to frame the issues and tell the story within an assessment puts the practitioner in a position of power. They will decide what is important and what is not. They will attribute meaning and interpret the actions of key players. As with other aspects of professional social work, it is important that ethical standards guide this important process. The following principles are particularly relevant to the assessment process.

1. Integrity – We need to be honest with all parties. People may not like what we have to say but they should trust that it is an accurate account.
2. Equality – We should constantly be alert to the potential for conscious and unconscious discrimination. Our critical thinking and analysis must recognise prejudice or bias in ourselves or others.
3. Empowerment – Assessments work best when everybody plays a part. This will require us to proactively promote participation and choice.
4. Clarity – To fully participate, everybody needs to understand the available information. Material should be presented in an accessible manner with reasonable adjustments made for those who cannot read or who do not have English as a first language.

Recommendations

Part of the analysis process may be to suggest a course of action that will help to achieve positive change. Often this will be done in collaboration with a senior social worker or manager. The final 'what?' question is 'What needs to change and what would progress look like?', so it is not unreasonable to recommend practical steps that might support change. Aijza and her family may benefit from a facilitated dialogue relating to her needs and wishes. Mr and Mrs Shaw might value the support of a dietitian as they encourage Danny to eat a healthier range of food. Including this within the analysis allows us to consider how effective it is likely to be. In Chapter 2 we considered the cycle of change which helps us tailor our recommendations to the individual's readiness to change. Too often assessment processes recommend actions that are unachievable, therefore setting the family up to fail.

Critical reflection

Critical reflection is an important safeguard within analysis as it allows us to check the judgements we have made. In a world of uncertainty and complexity, critical reflection provides the opportunity to step back from the turmoil in an effort to gain some objectivity. In social work it is not always possible to use a logical linear thinking process, as much of our practice exists in what Schön (1983) describes as:

> *The swampy lowlands, where situations are confusing messes incapable of technical solution and usually involve problems of greatest human concern.*

(p42)

Schön argues that reflection during and after interventions allows the practitioner to make sense of their work. Reflection acts as a counterbalance to intuition, allowing us to review our assumptions, our interpretation and our conclusions. Practitioners often engage in informal reflection as they process their experiences, but it is important that opportunities for formal reflection are also supported. The introduction to Stan Houston's model for reflection identifies four reasons why we should promote reflection:

- *To avoid bias or distorted thinking;*
- *To ensure we don't reproduce or perpetuate oppression;*
- *To connect with service users and the meaning in their lives; and*
- *To enhance insight into risk and need and how to safeguard and protect service users in a better way*

(Houston 2015a, p7)

There are various models for reflection that help the practitioner to review their interactions and learn from their experience. Formal opportunities to reflect are not always provided and practitioners may not wish to revisit painful experiences (Ferguson 2018). However there are three reasons why some form of reflection can help the assessment process.

1. To ensure that the story we are telling is accurate – It is entirely possible that we have misread the situation or given undue weighting to one point of view. We may have been deliberately misled or we may have misinterpreted the cues.
2. To challenge assumptions – There is a danger that our assessment and conclusions will be influenced by the 'dominant discourse' or the accepted way of seeing things. Examples of dominant discourses are provided below.

- 'We do not provide older people with assistance with cleaning.'
- 'If people are actively abusing substances they cannot avail of services.'
- 'Residential childcare should only be used as a last resort.'

Whether these are formal policies or unspoken agreements, they will have a significant impact on the assessment process. Fook (2016) suggests a process of deconstructing these discourses so that the assumptions can be made explicit and, if necessary, challenged.

3. To review how our experience relates to our knowledge base – it is through reflection that we develop experiential knowledge. With each experience we adjust our understanding of social issues and the social work role. Our learning allows us to develop our knowledge skills and values and apply them to new situations.

Knowledge and skills summary

- This chapter stresses the importance of an analytical approach that will help to inform the assessment process and the synthesis of information.
- An analytical approach scratches beneath the surface to draw out the meaning of the information.
- Analytical thinking and writing are difficult, but they are skills that can be learned and developed.
- Some basic 'What?' questions can support this process.
- Knowledge forms the scaffolding understanding to which additional information will be added.
- Critical thinking encourages us to question every source of data to ensure that it is credible and relevant.
- During the analysis stage the practitioner draws out the most important issues and explains what they mean.
- The opportunity to reflect on the process and outcome enables us to reconsider the story that we have constructed, including the underlying assumptions and conclusions.

Theoretical underpinnings

In this chapter we discuss how knowledge and critical reflection can support analytical thinking and writing in assessment reports, which includes the challenging of assumptions. A theoretical model of particular interest is social constructionism, which recognises the subjective and contextualised nature of aspects of people's lives and experience. It encourages practitioners to challenge assumptions and aspects of society that have previously been taken for granted (Tunmore 2017).

The precepts of 'Plain English' and concise, clear writing are valuable guides to communicating clearly your understanding and perspective to clients, families, other professionals and courts.

Further Reading

Aspinwall-Roberts, E. (2012). *Assessments in social work with adults*. Maidenhead: McGraw-Hill Education.

This text is strong on the skills and values relating to assessments of adults.

Brown, L., Moore, S. and Turney, D. (2014). *Analysis and critical thinking in assessment*. Research in Practice.

This short guide produced for Research in Practice helps practitioners to conduct assessments in an analytical way.

Frith, L. and Martin, R. (2021). *Professional writing skills for social workers* (Second edition). New York: McGraw-Hill Education (UK).

This very readable book includes a chapter on critical analysis in professional writing.

Part Two

Application to practice

6

Legal and ethical aspects of assessment, risk and decisions

Achieving a Social Work Degree

This chapter will help you develop the following capabilities from the Professional Capabilities Framework (2018):

2. Values and ethics
4. Rights, justice and economic wellbeing
5. Knowledge
7. Skills and interventions
8. Contexts and organisations

See Appendix 1 for the Professional Capabilities Framework Fan and a description of the 9 domains.

(Continued)

(Continued)

It will also introduce you to the following standards as set out in the Social Work Subject Benchmark Statement (2019):

5.3   Values and ethics
5.16 Skills in working with others

See Appendix 2 for a detailed description of these standards.

Introduction

Following introductory material on the context of law and professional regulation, this chapter outlines key legal aspects of undertaking assessments; working with risk and uncertainty; making professional judgements; and engaging in decision processes. The law is viewed as supporting reasoned, reasonable risk taking as something inherent in the professional task. The law provides a framework for the foundational ethical principles underpinning a democratic society and social work practice. The reader interested in a discussion of the relationship between the law, ethics and rights in relation to social work is referred to Preston-Shoot (2023).

The principles for making reasonable, reasoned judgements are extended from a legal context to other situations of scrutiny such as inquiries, judicial reviews, political and media challenges. Duty of care (in terms of the Bolam test), and the need for a research or theoretical basis for decisions (as in the Bolitho judgment) are outlined, as well as the duty to communicate about risks. Principles underpinning standards of care in negligence illustrate the embodiment of ethical principles in practice. Responsibility for decisions in groups is discussed. Case law is viewed in the context of the codification of some principles in the Human Rights Act 1998. Emergencies and dilemmas (where no option is risk-free) are outlined briefly. Our basic approach is to help you to be a competent, confident, caring professional through a fuller appreciation of how the law supports reasonable, reasoned decision making. Our aim is to promote defensible, rather than defensive, decision making.

Legal aspects of multi-professional team working and communicating risk were discussed in Chapter 4; legal aspects of predicting harm are discussed in Chapter 8. It is beyond the scope of this chapter to cover considerations arising from statutes in particular jurisdictions. See Further Reading and, for an illustration of the range of statutory provision for a topic such as adult safeguarding, see Montgomery et al. (2016). All topics in this chapter are explored in greater depth in the companion post-qualifying volume (Taylor 2017a). For a fuller discussion of legal aspects of risk assessment and evidence in situations that are less certain and more open to legal challenge, the reader is referred to Bross and Plum (2023); for legal aspects of decisional capacity, to Brown et al. (2015); for consideration of gross negligence, to Carson and Bain (2008); for accountability of social workers, to Carson and Mullineux (2023); for writing court reports, to Seymour and Seymour (2007); and for ('emergency') decisions made under time pressure, to Taylor (2017a).

This chapter is intended only as an introductory guide to legal aspects of reasoned, reasonable professional judgement in a context of risk. Do not rely upon this book as a substitute for legal advice on any individual set of circumstances. This chapter aims to inform you about general principles and issues so that you are more able to identify when legal advice needs to be sought, and enable you to better understand and discuss the issues. This book does not aim to address the detailed legal requirements in any particular jurisdiction, but to educate on general principles underpinning reasonable professional practice that are common in democratic countries. Case law examples are for illustration, and to emphasise key points. It is beyond the scope of this book to provide a comprehensive analysis of all relevant case law.

Context: legal aspects of risk and decision making

The basis of law

What avenues for redress should you have as a citizen if you think that a public body or licensed professional has made a wrong decision relating to some service provision? Conversely, what protections do you think that you as a professional and employee should have from complaints about your decisions, complaints which may be malicious or badly informed? There are various remedies in democratic societies for those who are aggrieved, and for applying sanctions, pressure or penalties to those who make decisions that are regarded as inadequate. In our society these include such channels as inquiries, child safeguarding practice reviews, safeguarding adult reviews, serious case reviews, inspections, reports by commissions and actions by politicians and the media. The law is a primary mechanism for accountability and that is our focus here, although the principles apply in other contexts where professional decisions are challenged. Common law is formed by the decisions of courts in decided cases. Case law precedent is the basis for most of our consideration here of professional negligence and standards of care, although gradually the Human Rights Act 1998 is codifying key principles.

Regulation of professionals

One mechanism in democratic societies for ensuring quality of services (including assessments and decisions) is registration of professions and employment groups. Registration normally requires the attainment of qualifying training that meets specified standards (at graduate level for a profession); a register (independent of employers) from which individuals can be struck off for bad practice; and some provision for making it a crime for someone to pass themselves off as a qualified worker (with intention to deceive) if they are not appropriately qualified. In the European Union such standards apply to registration of professions; social work in all parts of the United Kingdom now meets these EU standards for regulating professions. Professional regulatory bodies have quasi-legal mechanisms to determine whether a professional is fit to continue practising. The main focus of this chapter is on the expectation that professionals make reasoned, reasonable and lawful decisions as applied to social work.

Case Study   Expectations of Professional Judgement

A profoundly disabled young man, Tomas [pseudonym], was living with his mother and two siblings. He was considered under the relevant social welfare statute (the Chronically Sick and Disabled Persons Act 1970 and the 'direct payments for care' regulations in England) for publicly funded services. The court criticised the social worker for reporting that a certain level of care was needed while failing to indicate that he or she thought that this level of care was required. The court also criticised the social worker for failing to explain why Tomas required this level of care. It was not acceptable for a professional simply to reiterate the views of the family.

R (on the application of KM) (by his mother and litigation friend JM) v Cambridgeshire County Council [2012] UKSC 23 (also at: 1218–1236 All England Law Reports [2012] 3 All ER)

The law and making reasonable decisions

Key points in decisions being regarded as reasonable are:

- Legality: decisions must take into account relevant criteria and not irrelevant considerations.
- Rationality: the purpose of legislation must be respected.
- Procedural propriety: the rules of natural justice must be observed.
- Proportionality: the action should be the least necessary to achieve the aim.

(Lord Diplock: Council of Civil Service Unions v Minister for the Civil Service [1985] AC 374)

Not only must decisions themselves be fair, but also the manner in which a decision is made must be fair. Decisions about care and support plans must be reasonably designed to meet needs but also take account of overall resources for services, and the courts generally recognise this. However, where resources for a service are being reduced, it is not acceptable simply to reduce the service for individual clients without a re-assessment of their needs. For further detail on these points see Preston-Shoot (2019).

The following pointers from administrative law may be useful to guide practice.

- Identify the correct basis in law, regulations, guidance, standards, policy and procedures and follow any statutory criteria (for example, in the application of terms used or in any procedural requirements).
- Know the relevant powers and duties; do not go beyond them and use them for their intended purpose.
- Take into account only relevant considerations (including avoiding discrimination).
- Follow the requirements of natural justice (for example: letting people have their say; not making up rules after the event; hearing 'both sides'; avoiding bias).
- Make use of mandated assessment processes and employer procedures to gather appropriate information.
- Reach decisions that link to the evidence and knowledge available.
- Be able to demonstrate the basis for your views and the communication with the client before reaching your conclusions.

- Act in good faith and with fairness.
- Apply appropriate statutory safeguards, avoiding 'heavy-handedness'.
- Act reasonably, with a rational argument for your decision (see Bolitho judgement, below).

(cf. Bingham 2011; Taylor et al. 2015; White et al. 2009, p101)

Making a rational and ethical argument

Contested decision making requires us to have rational and explicit approaches to arguing a case, often as we work through an assessment process. *Effective clinical reasoning requires skill in developing arguments, establishing the relevance of information to an argument, and evaluating the plausibility of assertions or claims* (Osmo and Landau 2001, p489). The work of Stephen Toulmin and colleagues (1958) on ethical decision making offers one structured approach to constructing a rational argument, and the practice example illustrates another.

Practice Example   One Way Of Outlining A Rational Decision Process

- *My starting point was concern about risk(s) [A] communicated to me by professional [B]. I am aware of other potential starting points in terms of risks, needs and decisions, and I have borne these in mind as the assessment proceeded.*
- *I took the following actions to ensure immediate safety of the child/vulnerable adult while I gathered sufficient relevant information for a fuller assessment. I endeavoured to avoid actions that would prejudice future decisions by [C].*
- *The assessment was informed by the following sources [D] and professionals [E].*
- *I formed the judgement that the evident and underlying issues causing concern in the case included elements [F]. My view on the available evidence was that in these circumstances the main concern was [G].*
- *I therefore developed the following proposed strategy to intervene, manage and reduce the risks and meet client and family needs: [H] which is being presented to my supervisor/practice teacher/team manager for discussion on [J].*

To add to subsequent reports on the case:

- *The situation has changed in terms of [K], based on my observations [L] and reports from other professionals [M]. The outcomes of the strategies seem to be [N].*
- *In summary, the concerns identified have changed in the following ways [P]. The main type and level of risk to the child/vulnerable adult would now seem to be [Q].*

(adapted from Hollows 2008, p58)

Explicit ethical argument prompts clearer engagement with values, knowledge, assumptions, feelings and experiences in arriving at the rationale for pursuing or refraining from a course of action. This model can be seen as a way to assist in guarding against arbitrariness and inflexibility in decision making when balancing the rights of the various individuals involved. See Duffy et al. (2006) for an example of an application in social work.

The Human Rights Act

The European Convention on Human Rights (1950) (ECHR) was created under the auspices of the Council of Europe and ratified by the UK in 1951. It seeks to put into effect the Universal Declaration of Human Rights proclaimed by the general Assembly of the United Nations in 1948, in the aftermath of the Second World War. This international agreement pre-dates and is independent of the European Union. The Convention focuses on identifying and protecting certain fundamental rights and freedoms such as the right to life; the right to a fair trial; freedom of thought, conscience and religion; and freedom of expression. The Human Rights Act 1998 (HRA) came into force in the UK in October 2000, requiring all courts to take into account the ECHR. Some rights relate to actions of public authorities; others relate to the broader culture which governments have agreed should be created within society. Actions or inactions of public sector social workers and their employers, and failure to comply with these 'human rights', may be subject to challenge in court.

A key issue for social work decision making and management of risk in signatory countries is Article 8 of the ECHR, whereby everyone has the right to *respect for his private and family life, home and correspondence*. This right is a qualified right; that is, it is subject to restriction clauses that enable a consideration of the balance between the rights of the individual and the public interest: *There shall be no interference by a public authority with the exercise of this right except such as in accordance with the law and is necessary in a democratic society in the interests of... public safety,... for the prevention of crime and disorder, for the protection of health or morals, or for the protection of the rights and freedoms of others.*

Articles 2 and 3 of the ECHR are also relevant to practice decisions. The Convention rights impose positive obligations to promote and protect, such as responding to alleged abuse, as well as negative obligations not to interfere.

Potential impacts of the Human Rights Act relevant to the focus of this book are:

* delays in assessment of individuals for domiciliary care services;
* retraction of services already being provided;
* failure to take account of the client's views;
* failure to respect confidentiality; and
* failure to meet an assessed need within a reasonable time.

Human rights principles should inform and be an explicit part of the thinking and records of decision-making processes. Decision makers should:

* Involve those affected in the decision-making process. Note that this does not give clients a veto over decisions that are a responsibility of the professional or organisation.
* Expressly consider the individual rights of each person involved.
* Consider the risks (to the vulnerable person) of any proposed action.
* Consider the least intrusive measure that would achieve the desired objective.
* Consider the options available and the risks inherent in each (see Chapter 8).
* Balance the rights and freedoms of affected parties with the risks to the vulnerable person.

The Human Rights Act provides a framework that is leading to codification of key legal points relevant to decision making in social work. For further discussion of the above points see Preston-Shoot (2019). The fundamental framework in the UK is based on case-law judgements, which we discuss next. This chapter provides a summary on these points; for further discussion see Taylor (2017a).

Duties and standards of care

In democratic countries, an individual may take civil proceedings against another for compensation for loss or personal injury. Our focus is on the tort of negligence, which may be considered as *failure to take such care as the law requires*, where the plaintiff must prove that:

- the defendant owed the plaintiff a legal duty of care;
- the legal duty of care was breached; and
- damage was suffered as a consequence.

In this chapter we consider two key questions for a professional defending a claim for negligence.

- Was there a duty of care?
- Did I breach the relevant standard of care?

For further detail see Carson and Bain (2008) and Taylor (2017a).

Who has a duty of care?

One question that the court service in democratic countries is likely to consider is: *Is it fair, just and reasonable to impose a duty of care on professionals carrying out a public service role?* Would imposing a duty of care deter or prevent social workers from carrying out essential public functions effectively? This is akin to the debates about the level of criminal activity (for example drug-taking) which a professional, such as a social worker, nurse or youth worker, should be obliged to disclose to the police if they become aware of it, in order to avoid committing an offence themselves. Would imposing a duty of care make the professional task of trying to help people in these situations impossible or ineffective?

Courts generally draw a distinction between the liability of professionals and organisations in relation to children who are in the care of the state and situations of investigating (assessing) situations of alleged abuse where sufficient powers and freedom from hindrance are required in order that the task may be carried out effectively. The House of Lords decided that professionals had a duty of care in relation to a child who had been in statutory care from a few months old, about matters arising while in care (*Barrett v Enfield London Borough Council [2001] 2 AC 550, [1999] 3 All ER 193*). Conversely in *D v. Bury Metropolitan Borough Council [2006] EWCA Civ 1*, a four-month-old baby was found to have fractured ribs and it was thought that these had been caused by a non-accidental injury. The local authority social services department obtained an Interim Care Order which permitted it to remove the baby from the parents. It was later discovered that the baby in fact had brittle bone disease, and the injuries were indeed accidental. The baby was returned to the parents and care proceedings against the parents terminated. The parents then sued the local authority in negligence for the psychological harm that they had suffered as a result of the unsubstantiated allegations against them and the removal of their baby. Despite acknowledgement by the court that the parents were entirely innocent of committing any abuse and had indeed suffered psychological harm as a consequence of the allegations, the case was held to be not actionable in negligence. In other words, social workers were held not to owe a duty of care to the parents and therefore could not be sued. It would not be possible for professionals such as social workers to carry out effectively their responsibilities in areas such as protecting children from abuse if they could be found liable for decisions that had been carried out in good faith, using appropriate processes and using the best knowledge available at the time. The UK Supreme Court judgement in CN & GN v Poole Borough Council gives a valuable overview of key issues: *'It was held that a duty of care would arise in social welfare cases when the authority created the source of danger or had assumed responsibility to protect the claimant from harm, unless the imposition of such a duty would be inconsistent with the statutory framework within which the authority was operating'* (1 Crown Office Row, 2019). A key point to remember is that the scope of a duty *to* care depends on professional values and your personal beliefs, whereas a legal duty *of* care is a more precise concept defining who might be sued when a plaintiff alleges negligence.

Standards of care

The next question to consider is whether the standard of care is acceptable. It is a defence that the professional acted in a way that would be considered reasonable by a responsible body of professional opinion, widely referred to as 'the Bolam test' (*Bolam v Friern Hospital Management Committee [1957] 1 WLR 582, [1957] 2 All ER 118*). The standard of care required is not the best possible practice, nor what the majority recommend, nor what most practitioners would do. The question is whether a responsible body of co-professional opinion would have supported the decision, at the date of the event and in the circumstances of the case. In other words, pioneering treatments and changes in care services and practices are not prevented, but there must be a level of professional support for the approach taken. In Scotland an equivalent test is that a practitioner *'has been proved to be guilty of such failure as no practitioner of ordinary skill would be guilty of if acting with ordinary care'* (*Hunter v Hanley [1955], s.200*).

The courts will seek to ascertain, as a matter of fact, professional standards of practice at the time of the event. It is normally a decision of the appropriate professional body to set standards of care for practice. However, the courts retain the right to be the final arbiter of a professional standard.

The Bolam test must be viewed in the light of the judgement in *Bolitho v City & Hackney Health Authority [1998] House of Lords AC232*. This case, involving a paediatrician in a hospital, concluded that professionals must be able to give a rationale such as research evidence or a theoretical basis for their views that an approach was justifiable in the circumstances (Mulheron 2010). This emphasises the essential place of *evidence-based practice* – using the best available knowledge to inform decisions (Taylor et al. 2015). We discuss this further in Chapters 5 and 7.

The Bolitho judgement is also helpful in clarifying the evidence that might be expected in explaining the reasonableness of risk taking within decisions:

In particular, in cases involving, as they so often do, the weighing of risks against benefits, the judge, before accepting a body of opinion as being responsible, reasonable or respectable, will need to be satisfied that, in forming their views, the experts have directed their minds to the question of comparative risks and benefits, and have reached a defensible conclusion on the matter.

(Lord Browne Wilkinson, in *Bolitho v City & Hackney Health Authority* 1998, p1159)

Case Study Standards of Care and Reasonable Risk Taking

Aquila is 58 years old with a learning disability. She is deaf, has epilepsy and no speech. She was discharged four years ago to a small (24 bed) residential unit from a long-stay hospital. Staff were keen that she developed self-care skills and an agreed care plan was developed. They knew that she enjoyed baths. Over time she developed skills to take baths on her own, eventually locking others out. For three years there was no problem. Then one day staff had to break open the bathroom door. She had experienced an epileptic fit, slipped down in the bath and drowned. The case was referred to the coroner.

- What do you need to know to judge whether this was a sound care plan?
- What standards of care might apply in this situation?
- How would you ensure that the care plan was seen as sound even if a tragedy or harm ensued?
- Did the staff have legal power to stop Aquila bathing on her own?

Comment

This case illustrates the importance of the organisation having statements, such as relating to 'normalisation', which form a rationale and hence justification for reasonable risk taking within care plans. (See *R v HM Coroner for Reading ex parte West Berkshire Housing Consortium Ltd [1995] CO/2994/94*.)

Emergencies and dilemmas

A situation might be considered as an 'emergency' if you are acting under tight time pressure and with unavoidably limited information. The law acknowledges emergencies where a lower standard of decision-making may be acceptable because of pressures such as time and lack of harm-free options (dilemmas) (Carson and Bain 2008, p320). If you regard a situation as an 'emergency', you need to consider how you would answer questions such as:

- *Why was this emergency not foreseen?*
- *Why could more time not be taken to make the decision?*
- *Why could more information not reasonably be sought before making the decision?*

A dilemma is a decision where there is a lack of harm-free options. Many social work decisions might be framed this way. Dilemmas are not easy emotionally, but it is important to agonise over some dilemmas and to retain a *healthy scepticism*. If a tragedy ensues, what is important is that you record – as near the time as possible – the context of the decision making, making time and resource pressures clear. In recording and report-writing, explain the options that are available and the anticipated dangers of each option, bearing in mind how it might look with hindsight.

Case Study   Ambula's Walk

Ambula (pseudonym) was a 17-year-old autistic child living in a residential unit who was taken for a walk by a care worker. Ambula became agitated when she saw Mrs Partington walking towards her and lashed out at her before the care worker could stop her. Mrs Partington sued for damages on the grounds of negligence on the part of the local authority that ran the residential unit, regarding their lack of care and control of Ambula (see text for citation to legal judgement).

Activity 6.1   Ambula's Walk

Review the Case Study about Ambula and consider the following questions:

- Do you think that the authority or the worker is liable for damages?
- What do you want to know to reach a reasonable judgement?
- What law or regulations are relevant if this situation arose now?
- Is it relevant that Mrs Partington has a red and white stick to indicate her visual and hearing impairment and taps this on the pavement as she walks?
- In what circumstances would the care worker or the organisation have a right to prevent Ambula from taking a walk? (See Dimond 1997, re: trespass to the person.)

In this case the court held that the local authority was not liable, as Mrs Partington had not shown that Ambula was improperly supervised: '*What the duty [of care] involved varied from person to person and, perhaps, from day to day, depending on the handicapped person's mood.... The problem was to balance what was best for the handicapped person with the interests of the rest of the world.*' (*Partington v London Borough of Wandsworth [1990] Fam Law 468*; see *The Independent, 8 Nov 1989*.) As in this case, it is most often the employer who is sued on the basis of vicarious liability, although individuals may be sued also.

An aspect of emergencies and dilemmas not often addressed in textbooks are situations where you are considering the need to enter locked premises (for example to ascertain whether an elderly person has fallen and is unable to summon help). The interested reader is referred to Dimond (1997) for this aspect of practice. This is a good source also in relation to considering what constitutes 'trespass to the person' in the context of personal care-giving.

Legal dimensions of client involvement in decisions

Client consent and risk-taking decisions

A competent adult who acknowledges and accepts a foreseeable risk would not be successful in suing for negligence. Client consent is a full defence to a claim in negligence, hence the importance of ensuring that this is evidenced in records in any risk-taking situation.

An individual who has the mental capacity to make a decision, and chooses voluntarily to live with a level of risk, is entitled to do so. The law will treat that person as having consented to the risk and so there will be no breach of the duty of care by professionals or public authorities.

(Department of Health 2007, p22, para 2.26)

However statutory authorities remain accountable for the use of their funds, which must not be used for inappropriate purposes: '*Ultimately the... authority has a statutory duty of care and a responsibility not to agree to support a care plan if there are serious concerns that it will not meet an individual's needs or if it places an individual in a dangerous situation*' (Department of Health 2007, Executive Summary, para 7).

Activity 6.2   Consent to Take Risks

Identify a situation where your social work judgement might be challenged.

- What is the most likely threat to your judgement?
- How would you prepare to discuss the issue effectively with your supervisor?
- What recording would you make of the decision process?

It is generally regarded as your responsibility to ensure that your client is capable of giving consent to whatever care or treatment you are proposing. In multi-professional teams it is common to look to specific professions to undertake particular tasks so as to create more cooperative working. However, this is not an excuse for a professional abdicating their responsibility for their own care planning with the client and family.

Decisional capacity

In some jurisdictions (including England and Wales) there are mandatory procedures for ascertaining capacity to make decisions through mental capacity legislation. The same principles of good practice apply generally where there is not a specified process.

- *A person must be assumed to have capacity unless it is established that he lacks capacity.*
- *A person is not to be treated as unable to make a decision unless all practicable steps to help him to do so have been taken without success.*

- *A person is not to be treated as unable to make a decision merely because he makes an unwise decision.*

    (see Mental Capacity Act 2005 [England and Wales] Part 1, Section 1: The Principles)

Detailed consideration in relation to client capacity to make decisions is beyond the scope of this book, and the reader is referred to more specialised materials such as Brown et al. (2015).

Competence of children to make decisions

In relation to children the courts have taken the approach that children who have competence should be able to consent to treatment (*Gillick v West Norfolk and Wisbech Area Health Authority [1985] 3 All ER 402 (HL); R (on the application of Axon) v Secretary of State for Health (Family Planning Association intervening) [2006] EWHC 37 (Admin)*). The Gillick case arose in relation to whether there was a duty of a doctor to tell the parents if he or she was providing contraceptives to a child under the age of consent (16 years), contraception being classified as a medical treatment. This approach has been applied by professionals dealing with children and young people in other areas where consent is necessary. When it comes to refusing treatment, the courts do not seem to have applied this rule; instead they tend to allow parents to override refusal. Nonetheless, there are examples where *Gillick competence* seems to be used as a practice principle also in terms of refusing consent, such as in the case of Hannah, a terminally ill 13-year-old who was interviewed by a child protection social worker as part of a process whereby she persuaded a hospital to withdraw a High Court action that would have forced her to have a risky heart transplant against her will (Barkham 2008).

Challenges and supports

Conflict, confidence and being sued

This chapter clarifies legal aspects of decision making in lay language. Uncertainty about rights and responsibilities in relation to the law can inhibit robust, reasoned, reasonable approaches to supporting choice and managing care risks (see Glossary: **Direct Care Risks and Indirect Care Risks**). The place of knowledge as supporting sound judgement is developed in Chapter 7. There is, of course, nothing to stop someone commencing an action for negligence against any individual, including a professional. The claim itself may be without merit, but answering such a claim can be stressful. Thankfully it is rare that a social worker is sued, and extremely rare that a social worker is sued successfully! However, you might have to fight a case, which can create much anxiety. A particular aspect that may cause stress is that the loser of the action may have to pay the legal costs of both parties as well as damages. Even though a case against a social worker may be successfully defended, despite 'winning' you may be responsible for some or all of your own costs. Therefore it is essential that you have professional indemnity insurance, through a professional body such as the British Association of Social Workers.

Organisational support

Challenges to your social work practice that may have legal implications are situations that you should discuss with your line manager (and professional supervisor if your line manager is not a social worker). The degree of urgency with which you seek supervisory advice should reflect the seriousness and time frame of the situation. It is not possible in a textbook such as this to address detailed consideration of the threshold at which supervisory support should be sought. In any case this will vary according to country, organisations and policies. Learning to seek advice from your supervisor when it is appropriate, but not bothering your supervisor when it is not necessary, is a key part of the learning journey in the first year or two of practice as a newly qualified social worker. This aspect of managing risks and decisions is covered in more depth in the companion volume designed for newly qualified social workers (Taylor, 2017a).

Theoretical underpinnings

The knowledge base for this chapter relies heavily on case law judgements in the UK, for which there may be similar precedents in other jurisdictions. This is particularly in relation to the tort of negligence, as the focus of the chapter is on generalisable principles that are reasonably enduring over time and across many democratic countries. It is beyond the scope of this chapter to attempt to clarify the application of a particular statute in a particular jurisdiction. The foundation in case law judgements is linked to a broader knowledge base drawn from practice at the interface between law and social work, relating to:

- standards of care;
- decisional capacity; and
- reasoned and reasonable judgements.

Knowledge and skills summary

- As social workers we are accountable to society, through the law and professional regulatory mechanisms, for our judgements and decisions.
- The law supports reasoned, reasonable risk-taking decision making as something inherent in the professional task.
- As well as case law, the Human Rights Act; social welfare statutes with their accompanying regulations and guidance are key frameworks for considering legal and ethical aspects of managing risks, making judgements and participating in decision making.
- Other than in protection situations where you have a clear statutory authority through your employing organisation, you must ensure that a client has the capacity to consent to the proposed care or treatment, including risk-taking steps towards rehabilitation, independence or better quality of life.
- The law provides principles that help you to articulate reasoned, reasonable decision making in the face of challenges such as from inquiries, complaints, politicians or the media.
- If your decision comes under scrutiny, a key point is whether your practice is likely to be judged reasonable by other social workers respected in that field.

- Record evidence of assessment and decision-making processes in sufficient detail in case of challenge.
- Seek timely legal advice, through the arrangements in your employing organisation, when you are facing high risk or very contentious decisions.
- Ensure that you have professional indemnity insurance through your professional organisation.

Further Reading

Carson, D. and Bain, A. (2008). *Professional risk and working with people: decision-making in health, social care and criminal justice.* London: Jessica Kingsley.

This textbook on legal aspects of risk and decision making explores the way the law supports as well as challenges decision making by professionals.

Dyke, C. (2019). *Writing analytic assessments in social work* (Second edition). St Albans: Critical Publishing.

This book provides helpful detail on chronology and analysis in writing social work assessments, including for reporting under child care and mental health legislation in England and Wales.

Hothersall, S.J. (2014). *Social work with children, young people and their families in Scotland* (Third edition). London: Sage.

This book outlines the legal framework for social work with children and families in Scotland and provides a good guide for practice there.

Mackay, K. (2008). The Scottish adult support and protection legal framework. *Journal of Adult Protection*, 10(4): 25–36.

This article provides a useful review of the legal framework for adult protection in Scotland.

Preston-Shoot, M. (2019). *Making good decisions* (Second edition). Basingstoke, Hampshire: Palgrave Macmillan.

This concise and readable book, in a series on aspects of law for social workers, is richly illustrated with case law examples.

White, C. (2020). *Northern Ireland social work law* (Second edition). London: Bloomsbury Professional.

This is the main textbook for social workers on relevant aspects of the law in Northern Ireland.

White, R., Broadbent, G. and Brown, K. (2009). *Law and the social work practitioner* (Second edition). Exeter: Learning Matters.

This textbook gives an overview of practice in relation to the main social welfare statutes in England and Wales, and contains useful chapters on the Human Rights Act and aspects of decision making.

The British and Irish Legal Information Institute website – **www.bailii.org** – provides access to freely available British and Irish legal information.

7

Professional judgement and using knowledge in practice

(Continued)

5.2   Knowledge of social work theory
5.5   The nature of social work practice

See Appendix 2 for a detailed description of these standards.

Introduction

This chapter focuses on the use of knowledge in forming an individual, professional judgement, which may then inform collaborative decision-making processes (see Chapter 4). The chapter highlights the importance of having a clear conceptual understanding as an underpinning to assessment and working with **uncertainty** (risk) in making professional judgements and contributing to care, support, safeguarding, service eligibility and intervention decisions. There is consideration of discretion, objectivity, subjectivity, framing and common cognitive biases. Further discussion of these topics is in Taylor (2017a). This chapter outlines types of research questions which provide knowledge for social work, and appropriate research designs for these types of questions. The basic stages of identifying, appraising and synthesising best evidence for practice are outlined. Ethical issues are incorporated in terms of the responsibility of professionals to avoid bias; to use the best available evidence in decision making; and to reflect on their own judgement processes (including through supervision as appropriate). Two particular types of professional judgement are considered further in Chapter 8 (judgements against a threshold, such as for safeguarding or service eligibility) and in Chapter 9 (balancing benefits against harms such as in choosing care or support options). An overview on using research within social work is in Taylor (2020b), and more detail (suitable particularly for final year undergraduates and post-qualifying study) is in Taylor et al. (2015). The responsibilities of organisations to support their staff in the use of research evidence to inform practice is discussed in McGlade (2023).

Using knowledge in forming a professional judgement

How do you make a decision in a situation of uncertainty? Do you seek the least risky option – perhaps when selecting a walking route in an unknown city? Do you balance the pros and cons – perhaps when choosing a holiday? Or do you take the first 'good enough' option that you find – perhaps when buying a second-hand car? Do you identify the most important features and focus on those? Do you pray for guidance? Do you follow 'the rules' and hope that you do not need to make a personal judgement call? Do you just 'go along with' the views of others?

We have already seen (Bolitho case law judgement: see Chapter 6) that it is not acceptable for a professional simply to reiterate the views that they hear from others. When you form your own judgement, you need to be able to justify your opinion. Knowledge derived from research and theory – as well as information about the client and context – must be used to inform your recommendation about a plan for care or a safeguarding intervention or hospital discharge or re-ablement or recovery in the community. These are some of the issues discussed in this chapter, which focuses on your individual cognitive processes in forming a judgement prior to or while engaging in assessment and decision processes with your client, family and organisation (Fengler and Taylor 2019). This chapter goes a step further and broader than the consideration of analysis in assessment discussed in Chapter 5, to consider the use of knowledge in forming a professional judgement.

Although experience is a valuable source of knowledge, social workers who rely solely on personal experiences to inform their practice run the risk of bias (McCafferty and Taylor 2022). We need to use sound professional knowledge in our judgement in order to be transparent and fair in our decision processes, and so as to achieve the best outcomes for clients. This has come to be known in recent decades as evidence-based practice, although the essential principles are not new. The origins of social work in Western democracies might be viewed as rooted in efforts to apply the question 'what works?' to the endeavours of Christian and socialist charitable activities in the nineteenth century. Evidence-based practice is about consciously identifying, understanding and using the best available relevant knowledge to inform practice decisions. It involves having skills such as being able to appraise the quality of research rather than treating something as completely authoritative when it lacks rigour; being able to consciously apply research and theory to practice; and for social workers in appropriate roles to contribute to the development of the profession's knowledge base through well-designed research on priority topics.

Ethical aspects of using the best available evidence

Quite apart from the legal requirement to use best available knowledge, there are ethical considerations underpinning evidence-based practice. Knowledge helps us to identify the right support for those who need it, and helps us to use scarce public and charitable resources most effectively for those who need help. It can be argued that vulnerable people have the right not to be the 'victims' of untested and possibly harmful interventions, however well-intentioned. As a client or family member you would almost certainly expect professionals to use the best knowledge available to inform their influential judgements (Duffy et al. 2006). Of course, there may be competing values to be considered, such as between the individual of concern and family members in some adult safeguarding cases.

Social workers, like other professionals, must use the best available knowledge to inform their judgements. This is important for public credibility for the profession as well as for the legal reasons discussed in Chapter 6 and the ethical issues discussed here. We expect recognition as equals among other professions, and respect their domains of knowledge and skill. Organisations have a responsibility for good governance (Taylor and Campbell 2011), which includes supporting staff in making decisions in complex risk situations that embody ethical issues.

Conceptual understandings in assessment

The conceptualisation of people who use our services, as expressed through their views, are important in assessment (see Chapter 2) and in forming professional judgement. An interesting finding in a study of the perceptions of older people as to what constitutes elder abuse (Taylor et al. 2014) was that older people regarded the *intention* of the potential perpetrator to be paramount. For example, an adult daughter locking her elderly mother with dementia in the house for an hour while she went for essential shopping was not regarded as abusive if this was done to keep the elderly person out of institutional care, regardless of concerns raised by professionals consulting their policy documents. The perceptions of individuals and families can be used to shape assessment processes and hence inform professional judgement. For example, the perceptions of people with physical disabilities about risks and risk taking may be used to design a simple assessment tool for everyday social work practice (Taylor and McKeown 2013) and thereby influence professional judgement and the decision process.

The way that you frame a situation is key to the judgements that you make. Theoretical conceptualisations may include, for example, information about how professionals understand 'risk' in terms of consequences and likelihoods of harm (Stevenson and Taylor 2017). Sometimes theoretical conceptualisations can develop into models which can be visualised in diagrammatic form (Taylor and Donnelly 2006a). Professional conceptualisations may also be considered to be heuristics, i.e. mental shortcuts to using large quantities of information efficiently and effectively (Taylor 2017b).

Research Summary   Paradigms for Conceptualising Risk

Data from 19 focus groups and nine semi-structured interviews (99 staff in total) were used to explore perspectives on risk and decision making regarding the long-term care of older people. Focus group participants and interviewees comprised social workers, care managers, consultant geriatricians, general medical practitioners, community nurses, occupational therapists, home care managers and hospital discharge support staff. Health and social care professionals conceptualised risk and its management according to six paradigms: (1) Identifying and Meeting Needs, (2) Minimising Situational Hazards, (3) Protecting this Individual and Others, (4) Balancing Benefits and Harms, (5) Accounting for Resources and Priorities, and (6) Wariness of Lurking Conflict. Professionals tended to use one paradigm predominantly when asked about 'risk', but switched to one or two other paradigms when faced with different issues. The task of translating risk management into practice needs to address the complex issues facing health and social care professionals.

(Taylor 2006)

Bias, subjectivity and objectivity

People like to have a public image conveying that their decisions are rational, although reality may not be quite so logical! Selwyn Hughes (2005, p33) suggests: '*We arrive at some of the greatest decisions of our lives based not so much on reason or logic but what is going on deep within us – in our hearts – and then we look for logical reasons to support our feelings.*'

Some bias (or 'error') in any human decision might be attributable to tiredness or emotional exhaustion or other sources of bias, such as reluctance to change one's mind (Munro 1999). Another example is judging what is normal child development or the normal ageing process by one's own experience, disregarding variation within society.

Table 7.1 Some Common Biases

Anchoring bias	Judging new situations in relation to an 'anchor' point which may not be typical of the wider society.
Availability heuristic	The ease with which a problem or situation may be conceptualised or imagined may influence the judgement.
Confirmation bias	We may search for and interpret information consistent with our beliefs, knowledge, experience and information.
Hindsight bias	A tendency to view past events as being more predictable than they were at the time.
Illusion of control	We may underestimate uncertainty because we believe we have more control over events than we really do.
Loss aversion	A tendency to want to avoid the possibility of loss and pain more than seeking the possibilities of benefit and gain.
Over-confidence	We have a tendency to be over-confident about the extent and accuracy of our personal knowledge.
Prejudice	Bias from conscious or unconscious stereotyping.
Repetition bias	A willingness to believe what we have been told most often and by the greatest number of different sources.
Wariness of lurking conflict	Anxiety in case of assault, complaint, being sued or criticised by inquiries, the media or politicians, etc.

(simplified from Taylor [2017a], which contains further examples and detail of sources)

Case Study   Avoiding Potential Bias

Carl (aged 15) is under social work supervision for stealing a car. My role is to advise and assist him with a view to reducing the likelihood of him re-offending, and also to assess the risk that he presents to others so as to protect society. In seeking to help Carl, I am aware that I need to understand his world. My own upbringing was very different from his: he has no father at home; he is living on a housing estate with a high crime rate; and he is under pressure to conform and has received threats from peers and adult criminals. At each point where I am seeking to help him to take positive steps forward, I seek to avoid the bias of my own upbringing.

- What expectations do you have from your own upbringing and life in terms of how to respond to social pressures, threats or bullying?
- How can you tune in most effectively to Carl's circumstances?
- How can you most effectively convey hope and potential for change to Carl?
- How would you balance your responsibilities to Carl, his family and wider society?

Inevitably there is a subjectivity about professional judgements, and robust research can help to identify issues relating to risk and decision making (Putnam Hornstein et al. 2013) and provide evidence to inform good practice. Self-awareness, such as about cultural issues, can help us to avoid bias. It is important that the practitioner has an awareness of how the client and family culture, and their own culture, influences understandings of 'risk'. A 'respectful curiosity' can be a useful attribute of a social worker engaging in a multicultural context (Tedam 2023). The journey that we are on as professionals and as individuals is to strengthen the knowledge base in order to bring greater objectivity to our judgement and decision processes.

Discretion and decision framing

Discretion is an intrinsic part of professional responsibility. No set of procedures will ever address every detail of the varied and complex situations that are encountered by professionals. At the same time, professional judgements are increasingly being challenged in Westernised societies, so it is increasingly necessary that professionals can articulate the basis for their judgements. Being clear about the scope of discretion that is permitted in relation to a particular type of decision is essential, and this may be a useful discussion topic with your professional supervisor.

Research Summary   Family Involvement in Adult Safeguarding

The review of previous research which formed the foundation for the study by Carole Kirk and colleagues (Kirk, Killick, McAllister and Taylor 2019) highlighted the need to see the individual 'vulnerable' adult at risk of abuse as part of broader family and community systems. Such dimensions were important so as not to lose sight of aspects such as access to services (where a person might need informal support to contact a professional) and connecting with networks of people who might assist in prevention. Defining the role of the social worker in adult safeguarding only in terms of procedures for investigating the harm to an individual provided an insufficient foundation for effective intervention.

The factors that we take into account in order to make sense of a complex, changing mosaic of information may be described as *framing the decision* or *framing the risks*. The narrative by which we construct meaning out of our observations and other client information is an essential component of the 'context' of the judgement (Hodge 2013). Framing factors to consider include:

- the problem and who is facing what decision;
- services available and function of your organisation;
- needs, issues and strengths in the individual and family;

- past events, present situation and prospects;
- your role and the aim of the social work intervention;
- law, regulations, policies and procedures;
- religious, spiritual and other cultural aspects of the person's life;
- family, friends, neighbours and community who may help or hinder progress;
- values, standards and principles of the service and the profession;
- response to and effectiveness of previous services provided; and
- relevant knowledge, research, theory and skills.

Working with uncertainty (risk) in making decisions

Making decisions in uncertainty is an essential component of any professional task, whether for an engineer building a bridge, a surgeon conducting a medical operation or a social worker. Certainty means that we know that something will occur; impossibility means that it never does. In many situations we are 'uncertain', meaning that the likelihood of something occurring ranges from about 1 occasion in 100 situations to 99 occasions out of 100 situations. Logically, working in situations of uncertainty (risk) means that harm – as well as benefit – must occur from action on some occasions. We cannot eliminate the undesirable, harmful events; we can do our best to manage the 'risks' given the state of knowledge.

The challenge is that we do not know the particular situations in which the harmful outcome will occur. We only know that within some defined population we expect a certain number of undesirable outcomes. For example, we accept on the basis of reliable data that young drivers are more likely to have accidents, and have estimates of how much more their car accidents cost on average compared to the average accident. On this basis, society accepts young drivers being charged higher car insurance premiums, even though not all young drivers have accidents, and some older drivers do have accidents. Expecting social workers to predict which families will abuse or kill their child (or any other harmful outcome) is like expecting an insurance company to predict exactly which young drivers will have accidents. Far more research is required on risk factors relevant to social work (Taylor 2017a).

The dimensions of systems and organisations are largely ignored in inquiries into social tragedies (Carson and Bain 2008), even though these are key features examined when an aircraft crashes or a problem arises in a manufacturing business. However, inquiries into child homicides, suicides and other similar tragedies tend to focus almost entirely on the presenting needs and the capacity of individual professionals to predict the undesirable outcome (Carson 2012). Systemic factors, such as excessive staff vacancies, over-bureaucratic documentation or lack of investment in training and knowledge transfer are rarely investigated. A more proactive approach to professional 'risk taking' is required (Carson and Bain 2008), based on an approach to reasoned, reasonable decisions as outlined in this book. For social work of the future, it is important the profession develops an understanding of probabilistic risk factors and their use, as well as understanding organisational dimensions in efforts to prevent social tragedies.

Case Study Reflections   Using Research and Theory to Understand Professional Decision Making

Philip Gillingham and Andrew Whittaker (2023) used an anonymised case study of a child death inquiry to analyse the decision-making processes of child protection practitioners using a range of theory and research. Firstly, extracts of data from the inquiry were analysed to identify main themes and sub-themes. Secondly, thematic analysis was undertaken using a framework from a previous study that drew widely on the field of heuristics and biases, and on decision making in organisational contexts. Some key findings and reflections were:

- that it is necessary to understand both psychological aspects of those making the decisions and features of the decision environment to understand the decision processes;
- that 'an approach to analysing practice that is grounded in theory and research is more constructive than one based on an atheoretical legalistic or technical-rational materialist ideology' (op cit, p17);
- that professionals' perceptions of a parent may be biased due to a narrative of 'victimhood' or a sense of relief that he or she is engaging well with services;
- that the child may be 'invisible', despite policy statements to the effect that the child should be central; and
- that cognitive biases such as the 'halo effect', the 'rule of optimism' and 'accepting information at face value' may hinder professionals from recognising parental deception and disguised compliance.

For further discussion of biases see Cook (2023), Kettle (2023) and Spratt (2023). The authors know of no evidence that bias is any bigger issue among professional social workers than among medical doctors, psychologists, nurses and comparable human service professions. What concerns there are about bias must lead us towards greater use of robust knowledge to inform our cognitive judgements and decision processes, as well as to ensuring that we use effective reflective practice processes (see Chapter 10). This leads us on to a brief consideration of effective ways to use knowledge within professional judgement and decision process.

Types of practice questions to inform decisions

Increasingly, statistical information, about risk factors and the effectiveness of services which can be used to support social work and related human service decision makers, is becoming available. This is in line with the recommendation of the Croisdale-Appleby Report (2014) on social work in England, which recommended that a social worker must be seen as a social scientist as well as a practitioner and professional.

Research is the key to building a knowledge base for social work. Before considering possible research methods, it is important to consider the types of question that are of interest.

- People's experience of this issue – which informs teaching and tuning-in in preparation for meetings.
- The typical causes of these types of problems – which informs our understanding of the causes of social problems.
- Experiences of receiving services – which informs our planning and delivery of services.
- Experience of providing services – which informs our training and mechanisms for delivering services, and ways to support staff in their roles.
- The extent of social problems – which informs the strategic planning of services.
- The effectiveness of particular interventions – which informs our choice of interventions and services for a particular client or family situation.

For any topic, there is a diversity of types of question. For example, in relation to stress among social workers, we might ask:

- How common is stress among social workers?
- Does social worker stress vary with age or client group?
- What is the experience of stress among social workers?
- Does intervention X reduce stress in social workers?

Each of these is a distinctly different question, suited to being addressed by a different type of research design.

Types of research design for types of practice questions

The approach in this book is that the selection of an appropriate research design depends on the type of question. Quantitative approaches (using numbers) emphasise objectivity, rational argument and measurement to enable comparison. Qualitative approaches (using words) emphasise the uniqueness of perceptions, variety of experiences and social constructions of the meaning of facts.

Qualitative studies explore experiences and perceptions (of people who use services, family carers or providers of services) in their own words, and are appropriate for building our understanding of the experience of problems and needs; and the experience of receiving or providing services. Typically interviews or focus groups are used to gather in-depth insights from respondents.

Surveys are suited to measuring prevalence (such as how widespread this issue is) and correlations (i.e. what factors this problem correlates with). For an example of a survey see Hamilton et al. (2015), where case files were used to identify the risk factors correlating with suicidal ideation and behaviour among young people leaving state care. Typically, a survey questionnaire is distributed (by post, e-mail or by giving access to a web page) or similar information might be extracted from files (paper or digital) at a point in time.

Research that is experimental and quasi-experimental (similar to 'experimental' in purpose) is suitable for measuring the effectiveness of a planned intervention. In essence the effectiveness is measured by comparing the outcome measures for a group of people receiving the service with a group that does not. Measures at the start and finish of the process enable differences to be used to identify change during the period of the intervention. For an example of a randomised controlled trial carried out by a social worker, see Duffy et al. (2007), where the effectiveness of cognitive behavioural therapy for post-traumatic stress disorder arising from civil conflict was measured using individuals on the waiting list as a control group. Note that when we say 'it works', we do *not* mean that everyone who undertakes the intervention being studied becomes perfectly and instantly well every time. The essential criterion for the effectiveness of psychosocial interventions – as for appraising the 'effectiveness' of medicines – is that the experimental group improves 'statistically significantly' more than the control group. Consider the parallel situation with medicines for headaches, where an international consensus that a particular medicine 'works' does not mean that it works for every person on every occasion. The principle is the same in social work as for health care. For more diverse, 'holistic' social work interventions, more complex research designs are required (e.g. Furlong 2018).

The effectiveness of interventions is appropriately, and essentially, measured in terms of outcomes to clients or families receiving the service (Darragh and Taylor 2008; Taylor 2012b). However, it should be noted that the quality of decisions must be based on an appraisal of the processes used, rather than outcomes, as will become increasingly apparent through reading this book (see also Carson and Bain 2008). For further information about research designs see Campbell et al. (2016).

Identifying relevant research to inform practice

A number of research studies that confirm each other provides better evidence than a single study. A *systematic review* of research (Rutter 2013; Taylor et al. 2015) is of more value than an individual study. A *systematic review* embraces:

- an explicit process to retrieve relevant research (Taylor et al. 2003; Taylor, Wylie et al. 2007; McFadden et al. 2012; McGinn, Taylor, McColgan and McQuilkin 2016; Stevenson et al. 2016);
- an explicit process of deciding which studies to include in terms of quality (Taylor, Dempster et al. 2007); and
- an explicit process for synthesising the studies to produce a unified message to inform practice (Taylor et al. 2015).

Detail on how to undertake the above processes is beyond the scope of this book. The interested reader is referred to Taylor et al. (2015). Creating a systematic review that synthesises all relevant, high-quality research on a particular topic is a time-consuming and skilled job requiring collaboration between professionals and information scientists. There is increasing use of web search engines as well as bibliographic databases to identify relevant research (Bates et al. 2017).

Appraising and synthesising research quality

Once relevant studies have been identified for a practice evidence question, the quality of the research should be appraised before synthesising the key findings. When considering the usefulness of knowledge to inform our practice, there are two key questions.

- How robust or rigorous is the knowledge in its own right?
- How relevant is the knowledge to this client situation?

One source is to use articles about individual studies (e.g. Duffy et al. 2007). More rigorously, however, following appraisal of quality, findings of a number of studies may be synthesised. This may be done in a number of ways. Where the effect sizes of studies of interventions are combined statistically, this is termed meta-analysis. This is the process used for the systematic reviews conducted by the Cochrane Collaboration and the Campbell Collaboration (see Further Reading). Some examples are given in the Research Summary box. More commonly, the conclusions of studies are combined into a narrative that makes sense of the assembled findings, thus creating a *narrative synthesis*. A narrative synthesis that is based on a rigorous process for identifying relevant studies is termed a *systematic narrative review*. Some examples of systematic narrative reviews in social work are:

- older people's conceptualisation of elder abuse (Killick et al. 2015);
- resilience of child care social workers (McFadden et al. 2015);
- preventing loneliness among older people (Hagan et al. 2014);
- survivor perspectives on intimate partner violence interventions (McGinn, Taylor and McColgan 2019); and
- professional perspectives on decision making on elder abuse (Killick and Taylor 2009).

Research Summary   Evidence of Effectiveness of Interventions

The *Cochrane Collaboration* library contains about 100 systematic reviews of the effectiveness of interventions that might be carried out by social workers (some requiring post-qualifying training), including individual, family, group and programme interventions for problems such as:

Family and child care

- child and adolescent conduct disorders and delinquency;
- women who experience intimate partner abuse;
- attention-deficit disorder or attention-deficit/hyperactivity disorder;
- parenting programmes for physical child abuse and neglect;
- kinship care for children removed from home due to maltreatment;
- assisting foster carers in the management of difficult behaviour; and
- improving outcomes for young people leaving the care system.

Mental health, dementia and addictions

- deliberate self-harm; depression; post-traumatic stress disorder;
- anorexia nervosa, bulimia nervosa and binging; eating disorders;
- cocaine and psycho-stimulant amphetamine-related disorders;
- learning-disabled sex offenders; and
- cognitive ability and wandering in dementia.

Older people

- preventing falls, discharge planning from hospital to home; and
- smart home technologies for health and social care support.

Use of knowledge from big data

The use of big data is becoming increasingly prevalent within contemporary society, as an extension of the use of statistical methods for estimating the likelihood of future events such as the weather. This raises a range of philosophical issues (Horvat et al. 2022). In the context of our topic, this development is particularly relevant in relation to the use of computers to analyse large data sets to give estimates of the **probability** of some harmful event occurring (Søbjerg et al. 2020). There are many aspects to the debates over the value and pitfalls in the use of 'big data' and 'predictive analytics'. It has been argued that the use of computer algorithms – if the limitations of the data and analysis are clearly explained – is fairer to clients and families than a 'professional judgement' for which only a limited rationale is available for the predictions of harm which underpin the decision making (Coulthard et al. 2020). Others are more cautious about their use, particularly in relation to ethical issues (Gillingham 2020). The general way forward requires increased attention to the interface between human abilities and the contribution that can be made by statistical and machine-learning methods (Shlonsky and Wagner 2005). It is beyond the scope of this book to explore this topic in depth, not least because the profession has not yet reached sufficient knowledge and consensus for the inclusion of clear helpful guidance in a textbook written for students on qualifying training. There is further material on prediction of harm generally in Chapter 8. The reader interested in further exploration of big data issues is referred to Coulthard and Taylor (2022, 2023), Cuccaro-Alamin et al. (2017), Keddell (2023) and Putnam-Hornstein (2011).

Reflective learning about risk and decision making

As social workers we are not infallible or all-knowing; we learn by using research, concepts, theories and models to aid us in reflecting on our practice so as to improve our professional judgements (Taylor and Whittaker 2019). As knowledge and skills become increasingly internalised with experience, decisions may become less conscious and might be described as more 'intuitive', at least in the sense that we may be less aware of the cognitive (analytic) process of reaching the judgement (Sicora et al. 2021). We need to understand the processes of forming a judgement so that we can most effectively learn from experience, build on the best practice of ourselves and others and teach those newer to the profession. We need to become conscious of the application of our knowledge base – including communication studies, law, psychology, human growth and development, mental health, illness, disability, criminology, sociology and social policy – so that we can minimise bias in the way that we apply it to the unique features of a particular decision and can explain our judgement process to those to whom we are accountable and to those who might learn from us. No professional can 'know everything'; the more important requirement is to recognise that you need to know, and to know how to find out what you need to know. Social work inherently requires 'thinking on one's feet' and continually creating new understandings, as each unique client and family situation is addressed in the light of the knowledge base that is developing for the profession.

An important part of the reflective learning process for social workers is through supervision, as well as through peer-learning, whether within a social work team or with professionals from other disciplines. This is an essential element in improving professional judgement, and is explored further in Chapter 10.

As a student social worker, thorough preparation will help you to make the most of your time on placement. Table 7.2 is an adapted version of Table 1.2 in Chapter 1 and highlights some avenues to explore once you know something about your placement or new work setting.

Table 7.2 Tuning in to the placement or work setting (based on Taylor and Devine (1993))

The Context

What are typical outcomes that are sought for clients?
What does this work demand of clients and their families?
What knowledge and skills are required of social workers?

The People

What are people and families like who come for help?
What positive change is sought, and what harms avoided?
What are the main features of the social culture?

The Work Team

What are the aims of the team?
What is the team culture like in terms of 'risk'?
What knowledge and skills are required for this work?

My self

What knowledge and skills do I bring?
What anxieties do I have about what might go wrong?
What knowledge and skills do I plan to develop?

Theoretical underpinnings

This chapter has drawn on theoretical material and empirical studies from:

- cognitive psychology in relation to bias in decision making;
- sociology in relation to the exercise of professional discretion;

- philosophy regarding the conceptualisation of 'risk'; and
- ethics such as possible misuse of predictive analytics for predicting harm.

Knowledge and skills summary

- Social workers, like other professionals, must use the best available knowledge to inform their judgements.
- Ethically, as well as legally, professionals must keep themselves informed on relevant knowledge for their work.
- Like many other professions, social work is both an art (involving engaging with a diverse range of citizens) and a science (involving use of a reliable knowledge base to inform our judgements and decisions).
- The profession, politicians and the public need a deeper understanding of risk in terms of causal 'risk factors' being probabilistic (rather than absolute causes) even though we regard them as 'true' indicators of possible harm.
- Practitioners need to be able to understand and use the steadily increasing quantity and quality of research relevant to social work and social care.
- As a profession we need systematic approaches to identifying, appraising, synthesising and applying research knowledge to inform practice and policy. This will involve increasingly information scientists, librarians and social workers with a particular role focus in championing getting evidence into practice.
- Commitment by individual professionals and by employers of professionals is required for effective transfer of knowledge into practice; both have responsibilities.
- Reflective practice, including use of supervision and peer-learning, is an essential part of continuing professional development, and assists in reducing bias, understanding cultural aspects, and developing a sound frame of reference for managing risks and participating in assessment and decision processes.

Further Reading

Taylor, B.J., Killick, C. and McGlade, A. (2015). *Understanding and using research in social work*. London: Sage.

This textbook focuses on practical skills in shaping an answerable practice question; identifying relevant research; appraising quality; and synthesising findings to inform practice. It contains extensive material on the main research designs outlined in this chapter: qualitative, surveys and (quasi-)experimental studies, as well as material on mixed-methods and co-production in social care research. It is the ideal 'next stage' to build on the material in this chapter.

Gibbs, L. (2003). *Evidence-based practice for the helping professions: a practical guide with electronic aids*. Pacific Grove, CA: Brooks/Cole.

This book, with accompanying web-based learning materials, aims to support practitioners to adopt a process of lifelong learning involving posing specific questions of direct practical importance to clients, searching objectively and efficiently for the current best evidence related to the question, and taking appropriate action guided by knowledge.

Gambrill, E. (2012). *Critical thinking in clinical practice: improving the quality of judgments and decisions* (Third edition). Hoboken, NJ: Wiley.

This thorough book addresses aspects of applying knowledge to practice judgements. Note that the word 'clinical' as applied to social work is used here, as is common in North America and Australasia, to indicate therapeutic or helping practice with individuals and families (as opposed, for example, to safeguarding, case management or community development activities).

Nosowska, G. and Series, L. (2013). *Good decision-making: practitioners' handbook.* Dartington, Devon: Research in Practice for Adults.

This attractively presented book is in effect a 'trainers' toolkit' conveying in diagrammatic form a wide array of useful ideas for reflecting on decision making in social work.

Organisation resources: websites

Campbell Collaboration (www.campbellcollaboration.org) members undertake systematic reviews of the effectiveness of interventions in disability, education, international development, justice and social welfare.

Cochrane Collaboration (www.cochrane.org) members undertake systematic reviews of the effectiveness of health and social care interventions.

Community Care Inform (www.ccinform.co.uk): *Community Care Inform Children* and *Community Care Inform Adults* provide online resources for social workers and other social care workers, focusing on England and Wales. Community Care Inform is typically purchased via an organisational subscription.

North-South Child Protection Hub (http://members.nscph.com) enhances and shares child protection knowledge by providing access to:

- local, national and international research on child protection;
- British and Irish national policy documents and guidance;
- reports of child protection inspections and inquiries;
- executive summaries of serious case reviews; and
- coverage of child protection news and events.

The focus is primarily on British and Irish materials, and membership is required.

Research in Practice (www.researchinpractice.org.uk) supports evidence-informed practice with children and families, young people and adults.

Safeguarding Adults Collection (https://digital.nhs.uk/data-and-information/data-tools-and-services/data-services/adult-social-care-data-hub/dashboards/safeguarding-adults-collection) is a dashboard that gives users the ability to interact with aspects of safeguarding activity at national, regional and local levels relating to England.

Safeguarding Adults at Risk Information Hub (www.saarih.com/) is an online central information resource for practitioners, managers, researchers, educators and policy makers with an interest in adult safeguarding and protection. The focus is primarily on British and Irish materials.

Social Care Institute for Excellence (www.scie.org.uk) is a UK organisation that seeks to improve the lives of people of all ages by co-producing, sharing and supporting the use of the best available knowledge and evidence about what works in social care and social work.

What Works Centre for Children's Social Care (https://whatworks-csc.org.uk) seeks to improve the lives of children and families through setting standards in research and generating the best evidence into what works in children's social care.

8

Safeguarding, protecting and eligibility for services

Achieving a Social Work Degree

This chapter will help you develop the following capabilities from the Professional Capabilities Framework (2018):

2. Values and ethics
6. Critical reflection and analysis
7. Skills and interventions

See Appendix 1 for the Professional Capabilities Framework Fan and a description of the 9 domains.

It will also introduce you to the following standards as set out in the Social Work Subject Benchmark Statement (2019):

(Continued)

(Continued)

5.2 Knowledge of social work theory
5.3 Values and ethics
5.18 Use of technology and numerical skills

See Appendix 2 for a detailed description of these standards.

Introduction

This chapter focuses on decisions about eligibility for services and safeguarding interventions where the level of risk of future harm must be judged against a 'threshold' or criterion in order to decide what protection (if any) should be provided to this individual or family members. This includes mental health and justice settings as well as child safeguarding (e.g. Working Together to Safeguard Children, updated 2022) and adult safeguarding (e.g. Care Act 2014). Early social workers conceptualised their role as focused primarily on 'meeting need' with an allied concern in some cases to 'protect the vulnerable from harm' (Taylor and Devine 1993). This second dimension has gained increasing prominence within professional activity, with 'protecting from harm' being extended increasingly to the whole of society. During the past 25 years, within many countries the tension between 'care' and 'control' in the provision of social care services has increased. This has happened in parallel with growing 'risk awareness' and 'risk aversion' in relation to many aspects of life in society – from home, farm and industrial accidents to mobile phone masts and infectious diseases. During this time the conceptual understanding of 'risk' has expanded to include more clearly: the communication of risk; distinguishing between severity and probability of harm; growing attention to managing as well as to assessing risk; and developing connections between assessment, risk and decision making (Alfandari, Taylor and Baginsky et al. 2023). During this time, some countries have developed a range of legislation to seek to protect identifiable groups within society who are particularly vulnerable (Hothersall and Maas-Lowit 2010, Chapter 3).

In this chapter, the potential and pitfalls of statistical models for predicting a harmful outcome will be outlined, including reference to static, dynamic and mitigating (strength) factors. Safeguarding and service eligibility decisions are normally based on an appraisal of the likelihood and seriousness of future harm so as to inform decisions about protecting the vulnerable individual or family. This chapter provides more in-depth material for understanding approaches to predicting harm, providing underpinning knowledge for the chapters on assessment and professional judgement. A general explanation and critique of statistical (actuarial) and intuitive (clinical) approaches to predicting harm provides a foundation for understanding this important area of development in social work. The chapter outlines psycho-social rationality models for structuring professional judgement, which could be considered as lying in the middle-ground on a continuum between statistical and intuitive models of professional judgement. Ethical issues implicit in professional endeavours to predict harm are discussed, such as the implications for feeling stigma due to 'labelling'. This chapter builds particularly on Chapter 5 on analysis in assessment, and on Chapter 7, which considered the use of evidence within diverse types of professional judgements and decision processes.

As society becomes more 'risk-averse', social workers find themselves increasingly in the role of seeking to predict and prevent future harm, rather than simply addressing presenting needs. The appraisal of future harm relates to practice issues such as protecting children from abuse and neglect; deciding on whether or not to support proposed steps towards independence by people with a disability; decisions about hospital or psychiatric hospital discharge in relation to safety on return home; and efforts to prevent re-offending. The purpose of this chapter is to develop an understanding of general principles of predicting harm.

Judgement against a threshold (1): safeguarding decisions

Ever since Henry Kempe's identification of the 'battered child syndrome' (Kempe et al. 1962), the issue of 'risk' has become increasingly prominent for social work practice and organisations. Social workers engaged with a range of client groups increasingly have to address questions such as: 'Is the risk (seriousness and likelihood of harm) high enough to warrant <intervention X or service Y> in order to protect this individual?' An example would be: 'Is this family situation safe enough for this child to remain at home?' or 'Is this person's recovery or progress sufficient to make it safe enough to return from hospital to live at home?' A focus on the likelihood of possible harm is prominent in the areas of child protection (abuse and neglect), mental health (violence and suicide) and criminal justice (preventing re-offending), although protection of vulnerable adults from abuse and intimate partner ('domestic') violence are receiving increasing attention.

Threshold judgements and decisions

Judgements about whether or not a situation requires a safeguarding (protective) intervention and judgements about whether or not a situation is eligible for a particular service, as discussed above, can both be considered as examples of a '**threshold judgement**' or a 'threshold decision'.

A 'threshold decision' is a dichotomous (two-option) decision that depends on whether a result is above or below a particular line or level on a (conceptual or actual) measurement scale. The threshold may relate, for example, to an aspect of compulsory intervention on behalf of society or to eligibility for a particular service.

(Taylor et al. 2023, Glossary)

Judgements about whether a situation is above or below some threshold of risk or need may form the basis for choosing between 'care' and 'control' as a focus of action (Alfandari, Taylor and Baginsky et al. 2023). Although the decision may sometimes be framed seemingly simplistically as, for example, 'significant harm', the process of determining how a particular individual or family situation fits with a given threshold is often complex.

Neglect (of children or of adults) presents particular challenges by comparison with situations where, for example, there is clear evidence of assault or criminal activity such as theft. Sometimes it is a particular incident which provides a 'catapult' or 'trigger' that becomes a justification for action (Dickens 2007; Taylor and Donnelly 2006a). Platt and Turney (2014) found that threshold judgements were influenced by a range of factors including the nature of the concerns about the child, and the policy and organisational context of the social workers. They concluded that 'sense-making' within teams was a central aspect of meaningful and effective practice, even though this might appear to be 'intuitive' rather than purely 'rational'. This is discussed further in the next section of this chapter.

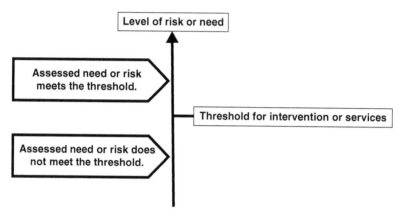

Figure 8.1   Diagram to illustrate assessment in relation to a threshold

Although social workers are as prone to bias as any other human service worker (Benbenishty et al. 2015), social workers may be surprisingly consistent in their judgements as to what constitutes abuse (Jent et al. 2011). We must be continually vigilant and use systems (such as supervision) to minimise bias. The knowledge and skills balance in social work between practice and policy, law and therapeutic helping is fundamental to effective work in threshold decision making.

Research Summary   A Threshold For Child Protection Referrals

This study of decision making focused on a hospital-based child protection team considering whether to report a case to the community child protective services (CPS). The study involved analysis of case files using a structured questionnaire for data extraction. The sample included all referrals of children aged from birth to 9 years who arrived at the hospital from 1991 to 2006. Of the 915 cases studied, 54 per cent were reported to CPS, the decision being predicted well (82 per cent accurate) by case factors studied. Reporting was predicted by some socio-demographic factors: single-parent and poor families were reported more frequently. Physical signs, and children's and parents' negative reactions to the investigation, predicted reporting. Child protection teams in the hospital seemed to use systematic decision processes that reflected current knowledge in this area, although biases may also have played a part.

(Benbenishty et al. 2011)

In these types of decisions, the task is to distinguish between situations requiring safeguarding interventions and those that do not, usually using a statutory framework, regulations, guidance and threshold criteria. In some jurisdictions the threshold in relating to protecting children is framed in terms of 'significant harm' (Hothersall 2014; Munro 2008). In relation to the mental health of adults, provision commonly relates to those with a diagnosed mental disorder and those who at the time of assessment lack the ability to make decisions (Brown 2019). In the criminal justice field, social workers are more often considering broader concepts of 'managing risk' (Home Office 2005). In all these contexts, the essence of assessing risk is to inform a decision to be made about whether or how to intervene to protect someone or some people from an identified harm. What must be clearly understood, however, is that there will always be a degree of error in any prediction about the future well-being of a client or family, whether the prediction is by a human service professional, a statistical model or a machine-learning system. Social workers and their managers, and other decision-making bodies such as courts, can but act in the best interests of the client or family as they perceive it, based on the information and knowledge available.

Since risk assessment is, by definition, making judgements under conditions of uncertainty, there is an unavoidable chance of error. It is impossible to identify infallibly those ... who are in serious danger ... Professionals can only make fallible judgements of the probability...

(Munro 2011, p40)

Judgement against a threshold (2): service eligibility decisions

Social workers are asked frequently to address questions about whether the needs of an individual are above the threshold for receiving a particular service that is funded publicly or by charitable giving. Examples would be family support services, mental health programmes, and services for older people and those with disabilities. In some countries similar assessments are required for 'direct payment' schemes, where an individual receives a publicly funded payment related to their needs, which is then used by that individual to buy services. In general terms, the justification for providing services is increasingly conceptualised in terms of *risk* rather than *need*. This requires the knowledge base used by social workers to have a greater focus on understanding risk in order to prevent harm and allocate services as appropriately as possible to those at greatest risk. Chapter 6 includes a discussion of the legal aspects of responsibility for what the organisation provides or advises, as distinct from what the client decides to do independently of the services, equipment or advice offered.

Case Study   Meeting Service Eligibility Criteria

Mrs A is a lady of 87 years living at home with her husband, who has dementia. Their three children live at a considerable distance from them. Mrs A fell, sustaining a fractured neck of femur. She was admitted to hospital and the hospital social work service was alerted. Mr A was found to be very confused; unsafe if left for long periods on his own; and unable to manage his medication or make meals.

- What are the main risks in terms of outcomes for the clients?
- What are the main areas where social care services might be provided?
- How do the needs of this client relate to the service eligibility criteria under which your local social care services operate (including under the Care Act 2014 if you are practising in England or Wales)?

The developing systems for social care governance, parallel to the development of clinical governance in medicine, require stronger social work approaches to managing risk (Taylor and Campbell 2011), particularly where decisions have to be made about compulsory intervention or eligibility for services. Among other things, this requires a professional workforce that has a greater understanding of the potential and challenges in seeking to predict future harm in making threshold judgements, as discussed in this chapter. The reader interested in a more detailed discussion on threshold decisions is referred to the companion post-qualifying textbook (Taylor 2017) and to the Sage Handbook (Taylor et al. 2023) for a cutting-edge overview.

Intuitive approaches to predicting harm

An increasingly central aspect of safeguarding and service-eligibility decisions in social work is predicting future harm in seeking to protect vulnerable individuals and families. This section considers what are called 'intuitive' or 'clinical' approaches to predicting harm. Later sections in this chapter consider the principles of statistical approaches and psycho-social rationality models.

How can professionals predict harm? How can anyone predict future behaviour? The 'normal' human approach, without using any statistical method based on research, might be called *intuitive*. This is likely to be based on life experience, perhaps subconscious, as a child and as an adult. With professional training we more consciously draw on a knowledge base that includes such areas as communication skills, human growth and development, health and ill-health, psychology and sociology. With practice experience we draw increasingly on our experience of similar cases, transferring learning to new situations. We also draw on the knowledge and experience of colleagues. This type of process of forming an opinion based on a wide-ranging, useful but ill-defined body of practice knowledge and experience is known in the literature as a *clinical* approach to prediction.

There are several challenges in attempting to predict some undesirable event (for example, violence or abuse) using a *clinical* or *intuitive* approach.

- Judgements often rely too much on self-report of the person being assessed.
- Professionals may be exposed to a non-representative range of clients.
- Professional perceptions may be subject to bias such as more recent or more dramatic events (for themselves or in the team) having undue impact.
- Professionals may be subject to bias from economic considerations, political or media pressure, and personal and societal prejudice.

In addition, professionals often get limited feedback on the outcomes of their interventions or non-intervention, and our knowledge of the effectiveness of interventions is limited at present (see Chapter 7). This adds to the complexity of making decisions about which services to offer.

Research Summary   Clinical (Intuitive) Approaches to Predicting Harm

Psychiatrists and psychologists were accurate in no more than one out of three predictions of violent behaviour over a several-year period among institutionalised populations that have both committed violence in the past (and thus had high base rates for it [so prediction should be more accurate than with a general population]) and who were diagnosed as mentally ill.

(Monahan 1981, p48)

Social workers are not alone in the inaccuracy of their intuitive or clinical professional judgements. Although there are some studies of the accuracy of social work judgements (Davidson-Arad and Benbenishty 2016), most studies are of medical doctors and psychologists, and show similar inaccuracy in unaided human judgement across a range of health and social care situations (Grove and Meehl 1996).

Research Summary   Cultural And Organisational Aspects of Predicting Harm

A total of 828 social workers in four countries (Israel, the Netherlands, Northern Ireland and Spain) were presented with a vignette of an alleged child maltreatment case and were asked to determine whether maltreatment was substantiated, to assess risk and to recommend an intervention. Practitioners' child welfare attitudes and the different protective system context across countries correlated significantly with the judgements of respondents. Awareness of the impact of one's own attitudes and of the organisational culture are essential to reduce bias in social work judgements and decision making.

(Benbenishty et al. 2015)

Statistical approaches to predicting harm

So how can we improve on intuitive and clinical approaches to predicting harm? A key aim is to reduce the variability of human judgements, which may be due to human bias through emotion and stress, as well as learning effectively from the experience of others facing similar situations (Schrödter et al. 2020). The main 'logical' approach is to look at what outcomes have occurred in the past in situations with similar features. We could then ask what factors (**risk factors**) correlate with harm occurring. If we knew that, we might look out for such factors in future situations. This is a *statistical* approach, sometimes called an *actuarial* approach as it is the approach used by actuaries in calculating insurance premiums. The aim is to calculate the probability of harm in the situation on the basis of the presence of risk factors that were predictive of harm in many previous situations. For example, a parent having a mental health problem may be predictive of child abuse if a (statistically) significantly greater proportion of parents who abuse their children have mental health problems than among parents in general.

This statistical approach does not claim, of course, that the presence of the risk factors will always indicate a situation where harm will occur. Rather, the understanding has to be simply that there is an increased likelihood that this will occur. There are obvious comparisons that can be drawn with the accepted 'truth' that smoking causes lung cancer, although not every smoker gets lung cancer and some people die of lung cancer who have never smoked (Horvat et al. 2022).

Research Summary

Social workers in criminal justice provide reports to courts, including assessments of the likelihood of reoffending, which are used to assist in judicial decisions. This study presented true-to-life vignettes to 93 social workers employed as Probation Officers in Northern Ireland in a factorial survey design to measure factors influencing their judgement of the risk of reoffending. Analysis using regression and ANOVA showed that judgements about the likelihood of reoffending were influenced by dynamic factors (such as substance misuse, support networks, level of responsibility taken for offending behaviour and cooperation with probation supervision) as well as more widely tested static risk factors (such as previous convictions and age). This study highlights a range of dynamic factors that might inform review of criminal justice social work assessment tools which typically incorporate the better-tested static factors. The findings will contribute to current thinking in social work education, which is starting to address issues of risk and decision making more explicitly in the curriculum at both qualifying and post-qualifying stages. The more nuanced assessment of factors considered by experienced criminal justice social workers will complement the evidence from more strongly evidenced static risk factors to inform teaching about professional judgements. As we seek to incorporate statistical knowledge into the human processes of social work assessment, Brunswik's Lens Model and other psycho-social rationality models – which bridge between analytic and descriptive models of human judgement – may be useful conceptualisations of the professional judgement process in social work.

(Mullineux et al. 2020).

The majority of studies show that actuarial prediction is generally slightly more accurate than clinical prediction in predicting human behaviour, including the types of situations of interest to social work (Meehl 1954; Dawes et al. 1989). There are a number of reasons why this is common sense:

1. Factors that are studied and refined for statistical prediction are those identified by those practising in the field as being the most value to study.
2. As further factors are identified by professionals, research is undertaken to determine whether or not this factor does influence the outcome.
3. If they are shown to have a statistically significant correlation, these risk factors become accepted as valid.

Further developed actuarial approaches in social welfare work are in the prediction of re-offending (e.g. Hood et al. 2002; Maung and Hammond 2000; Raynor et al. 2000), homicide and violence by people with mental illness (e.g. Monahan et al. 2001) and suicide (e.g. Gunnell and Frankel 1994). There is little development in relation to child abuse (e.g. Johnson et al. 2015) or in relation to people with disabilities. This knowledge can be used to inform professional practice, for example through the design of assessment tools as discussed in Chapter 5.

Research Summary   Predicting Child Homicide

Pritchard et al. (2013) undertook two rigorous studies of factors correlating with child homicide. Firstly, the correlation between child homicide (children under 14 years) and relative poverty (using four validated scales) was studied using World Health Organization data. There was no correlation between child homicide and relative poverty. Secondly, data from a range of public services relating to 4 per cent of the UK population was used to identify the risk factors that correlated with the 22 homicides that occurred in that region over a ten-year period. The largest number of child homicides (8) correlated with mothers having mental health problems, and the next largest numbers correlated with fathers having mental health problems (4) and situations where there was a stepfather in the family network with previous convictions for violence (4). This data was then compared with the prevalence of these situations (such as the number of women of childbearing age having mental health problems in the whole region). With this analysis, a stepfather in the family network with previous convictions for violence was the largest risk factor, approximately five times larger than mothers with mental health problems.

Questions: If, by current standards, this is viewed as a robust study for its purpose:

*   Do you think that poverty might be a risk factor for other domains of child abuse or neglect even if not for child homicide, and if so why?
*   What challenges might there be in using the findings of the second study in practice? (Pritchard et al. 2013).

Issues in predicting harm

There are various issues in developing expertise in predicting harm in a field such as social work (Schrödter et al. 2020). Purely intuitive (clinical) approaches can create a sense of a mystique owned by professionals that is beyond the ability of 'ordinary mortals'. On the other hand, the numbers in statistical approaches might convey an aura of false confidence if incorrectly understood. What is clear and agreed in the profession (and is in accord with case-law judgements in the UK) is that the best available evidence should be used in making decisions, and that professionals and their employers have a responsibility (within available resources) to take reasonable steps to develop their knowledge base on an ongoing basis. We will consider here issues in predicting harm, by whatever method, under the domains of technical, ethical, legal, organisational and professional.

Technical issues

A major challenge in social work practice is the apparent expectation of some media and politicians that social workers and other professionals should be able to precisely predict harm that may be caused to a human being, whether by another (violence, abuse) or by themselves (self-harm, self-neglect, avoidable accidents) and be able to protect them from that harm. However, completely accurate human prediction about the behaviour of other human beings is impossible to achieve. All we can hope to achieve is steadily improving accuracy via research implemented through systems (such as assessment tools) and professional training courses. On the best evidence available, statistical methods could improve the prediction of harmful events. This is likely to be a major area of development in the future. Whatever approach to predicting harm is used, there will always be false positives (situations predicted as likely to lead to a particular harm, which in the end does not occur) and false negatives (situations predicted as safe, but harm does occur) as well as the true positives (situations correctly judged as risky) and true negatives (situations correctly regarded as not risky).

> ### Research Summary   Intuitive Versus Statistical Prediction
>
> *The review team studied published research on how clinical (intuitive) predictions about harm made by mental health practitioners compared with predictions using statistical approaches. Sixty-seven studies were identified spanning 56 years of research. Overall there was a somewhat greater accuracy for statistical methods. The most robust studies indicated 13% greater accuracy using statistical over intuitive methods. The accuracy of prediction varied with type of prediction; the setting in which data were gathered; the type of statistical analysis; and the amount of information available to the professionals.*
>
> (Ægisdóttir et al. 2006).

Ethical issues

One challenge, as methods of predicting harm become more accepted and more widely used, is the stigma of labelling. Whatever approach to predicting harm is used (and professionals are doing this every day, even if there is no formal structure to their approach), there will inevitably be some individuals who are incorrectly regarded ('labelled') as 'at risk' or 'a danger'. Social workers are typically trained to be well aware of issues of stigma, and develop interpersonal skills in addressing this.

In contemporary society, a major issue now is media coverage, which can distort information given to the public, and thereby makes the exercise of sound, reasonable judgement by front-line social workers and their managers more difficult. As an example, although the child homicide rate in the UK is fairly steady at about one per week (reflecting the approximately one-per-million rate across most of the Westernised world – see Pritchard and Williams 2009), the media coverage of such events seems to bear little relationship to educating the public or learning from what has occurred.

It should not be concluded from the above that social work services have no effect on child homicide rates. For example, there is evidence that over a 25-year period, the improvement in child protection services in reducing child-abuse-related deaths in England and Wales is comparable to the reduction in child deaths from illnesses (attributable primarily to health services) and in the reduction in child deaths from accidents (attributable primarily to health and safety initiatives) (Pritchard and Sharples 2008). Also, the effectiveness of social work services in child protection is likely to be even greater in relation to the range of types of abuse and neglect, than on the rare (and therefore less predictable) incidents of child homicide.

Legal issues

It might be assumed that courts would appreciate more rigorous approaches to an issue as important as knowledge to underpin assessments of future harm in situations such as child protection hearings. The reality is that courts tend to like to use experts whose opinion can be trusted, and do not seem to relish the prospect of appraising the quality of statistical argument. The implication is that those professionals providing evidence in such contested situations need to be competent in (among other things) current knowledge and skills in using statistical data about risks, including their strengths and limitations. The points in Chapter 6 regarding legal aspects of communicating about risks applies whatever approach the professional is using in judging the likelihood of future harm.

One useful point to consider, derived from the law, is the distinction between criminal cases, where the standard of proof is 'beyond reasonable doubt', and civil cases, where the standard is 'on the balance of probabilities'. Family law hearings in the UK fall within civil, rather than criminal, law. Thus it seems reasonable to conclude that decision processes leading up to court hearings or equivalent – such as case reviews in child protection and equivalent in relation to protecting the affairs of vulnerable adults – should be based essentially on the same standard of 'the balance of probabilities' when there are 'threshold decisions' to be made (Platt and Turney 2014). In social work, we often have to work with less than 'all possible information that might be relevant'. Sometimes decisions must be made with a degree of urgency, and thus have to be made on the basis of the best information available at the time. As discussed in Chapter 4, there should still be a reasoned and reasonable basis for the judgement or decision.

Organisational issues

One problem faced by organisations is that social work decisions are increasingly framed as 'yes/no' judgements, such as in the safeguarding and service eligibility contexts which are the focus of this chapter. Even with as much improvement in statistical prediction that we could envisage, framing the likelihood of particular human behaviour in this way will inevitably lead to some situations being wrongly classified. This is an inherent feature of any attempt to predict human behaviour, and one which service managers and regulators need to incorporate into their thinking. For organisations, some broader framework of principles for managing risk is required (Carson 2016), as well as investment in research to identify, conceptualise and measure risk factors. For the profession and employers, the challenge is in making the results of research available to staff (Taylor et al. 2015).

Professional issues

In good social work practice, the starting point is to engage as far as possible and appropriate with all relevant parties (Olaison and Donnelly 2023). The professional must also recognise, however, that he or she has access to (and training in) a wider knowledge base on the type of issues than most clients and families (e.g. Pritchard and Williams 2023). And in some mental health situations (e.g. Campbell and Campbell 2023), as well as in child protection, it is necessary sometimes to act without client consent in order to carry out safeguarding responsibilities. Assessment tools and decision support systems to assist the professional in these challenging tasks are developing steadily even if slowly. The interested reader is referred to sources such as Graham and Fluke (2023) and Sørensen (2023).

In situations of irresponsible political and media pressure, there are dangers that the profession focuses so much on the rare (and therefore hard to predict) most undesirable outcomes that the good that social workers can do for vulnerable people in general is ignored. This is not so much a criticism of professional practice, as of the 'blame culture' which seems to be growing in Westernised societies. It is important that the profession and employers develop ways to educate and communicate more clearly to the public about risk issues and the role of social work.

Psycho-social rationality approaches to professional judgement

Relying on unstructured intuitive prediction is becoming increasingly unacceptable ethically and legally (see Chapter 6). Conversely, there are pitfalls in ignoring the limitations of statistical methods, quite apart from our limited knowledge base at the present time. In the context of human beings being unable to compute large amounts of statistical data (Miller 1956), a number of *psycho-social rationality* models of human judgement have developed (Taylor 2017b; Taylor 2021). These models lie in the middle ground between purely descriptive (narrative) models which seek to describe the decision situation, and purely statistical models. These models structure information more than narrative approaches (such as the Social Enquiry Reports of an earlier generation of social workers) but do not attempt detailed statistical analysis. Some examples of psycho-social rationality models are listed below (adapted from Taylor 2017b).

- Models which classify types of risk factors – such as static, dynamic and mitigating factors – as concepts for human use rather than for statistical computation (Harris 2006; Taylor 2017a).
- Models, such as ecological models, which seek to locate relevant dimensions of the decision environment (organisational, societal, legal) which influence or inform individual judgement (Baumann et al. 2014).
- Models which assist in conceptualising the relationship between risk factors, such as Paul Brearley's (1982) model of vulnerabilities ('predisposing factors'), triggers ('precipitating factors') and strengths ('mitigating factors').
- Models which seek to conceptualise how the human brain works in particular contexts, such as heuristic models based on simple rules such as about searching for information, deciding when there is enough information and how that information is used (Taylor 2017b).

Two illustrative examples are provided below, although it is beyond the scope of this book to provide detail on each of these models. The interested reader is referred to Taylor (2017a).

Case Study   Static, Dynamic and Mitigating Factors

Jakob (16 years old) is just being discharged from a young offenders' establishment. His previous criminal record (*static risk factor*) includes X. He has begun to form a relationship with his estranged father in the past two years (*mitigating factor*), which may help to reduce the likelihood of him re-offending. Having work or an educational programme (*dynamic risk factor*) seems likely to be the focus of my work with Jakob.

Research Summary   Factors that Reduce the Risk of Suicide

1. willingness to talk about issues, thoughts, feelings
2. capacity for expressing emotion
3. having a key person in whom to confide
4. other important attachments
5. having regular contact with a counsellor or social worker
6. support of family, friends, community
7. involvement in activities and hobbies
8. sports or other physical activity
9. successful strategies for coping
10. an agreed crisis plan.

(Reeves 2015, p44, based on an international study on the effect of unemployment and financial indebtedness on suicide)

Prospects for developments in predicting harm

In our 'knowledge society' there is an increasing need for health and social care professionals to be skilled in using statistical data (Stevenson and Taylor 2017; Teater et al. 2017). However, much more research on risk factors (and on mitigating factors and strengths) relevant to social work is required before their use becomes widespread.

It must be borne in mind that any statistical prediction is based on establishing a correlation for situations where this type of risk factor has occurred in the past. Prediction of human behaviour will always be far less than 100 per cent accurate, even though statistical methods, once developed, are likely to be slightly more accurate than unaided human judgement.

> *Research therefore cautions us that [in mental health] as in other fields such as medicine and child protection there is no such thing as a 'risk free' assessment... There are no criteria which enable us to place individuals into sharply defined, once-and-for-all categories of 'dangerous' or 'not dangerous' [or at risk of a particular harm, etc.]. Rather there is a continuum of statistical risk with uncomfortably limited predictive capacity.*

(Perry and Sheldon 1995, p18)

Our knowledge of risk factors relevant to decision making in social work is growing gradually (Bartelink et al. 2015), although there is little substantial investment in research (Kirkman and Melrose 2014). With developments in information technology, statistical and machine learning approaches to identifying and measuring risk factors are likely to increase in the future. Professionals need training to use statistical information confidently within a broader understanding of the tasks involved in assessment and decision making in risk contexts (Regehr et al. 2010; Schwalbe 2004; Fengler and Taylor 2019). As decision aids are invented, they need to be developed in ways that are compatible with human cognition (de Bortoli and Dolan 2015), bearing in mind learning from psycho-social rationality models of judgement.

Practice Activity   Identifying Risks Facing Clients

It is beyond the scope of this book to attempt to provide analyses of risks faced by clients and families, because of:

a.   limited professional consensus of definitions of risk factors;
b.   varying levels of research-based rigour in our knowledge of risk factors;
c.   the range of factors across client groups relevant to social work in general; and
d.   the fact that a publication in book form would become dated as new research is published.

A valuable task in preparation for a practice placement (internship or practice learning experience), or during induction, is to:

1. identify major risk factors for the client group and sub-groups within it; and
2. find best research-based estimates of the likelihood of the most common harms occurring.

The material in Chapter 7 will be helpful, and your university librarian may be able to assist you in going about this task.

Theoretical underpinnings

This chapter draws particularly from theoretical material and empirical studies in:

- decision sciences regarding heuristics (including psycho-social rationality) and thresholds;
- risk sciences and epidemiology in terms of identifying and measuring risk factors; and
- legal studies of case law in relation to what constitutes a reasonable, reasoned decision.

The chapter is grounded in ethical principles derived from beliefs, philosophy and social work practice. The chapter is informed by developments in systems, policies and assessment processes in social care organisations as they seek to manage risks and to ensure reasonable and accountable decision making in practice.

Knowledge and skills summary

- Safeguarding and service eligibility decisions are often concerned with the likelihood of harm in the future as much as with the presenting needs.
- Making a safeguarding judgement (for example in relation to abuse, neglect, self-harm or criminal action) against criteria and determining eligibility for services are termed 'threshold judgements'.
- Most societies, through the law, have developed frameworks that seek to ensure reasonable and effective processes, within which social workers are often key players, to protect the most vulnerable. An awareness of societal and organisational culture helps in informing the use of such frameworks.
- We need to learn to use statistical information to inform care decisions, bearing in mind that no method of predicting human behaviour, whether 'intuitive' (clinical), statistical or through machine learning, will ever be 100 per cent accurate.
- *Risk factors* give an estimate of how much more likely this individual is to come to harm, or cause harm, than an average member of the population. Most research (typically in medicine and psychology) shows that statistical methods of predicting human behaviour using risk factors are more accurate than unaided professional judgement, although the knowledge base of risk factors relevant to social work is limited at present.
- Static factors (which we cannot change) are often stronger predictors of future behaviour than dynamic factors (which are amenable to influence or change), although understanding dynamic factors is central to planning effective interventions.
- In practice, human service professionals often use broader concepts drawn from *psycho-social rationality* or *structured decision making*, using concepts such as vulnerabilities, triggers and strengths.

- In Europe it is common for assessment tools based on professional consensus to be used to support judgements about the likelihood of future harm, although in North America statistical tools are more common.
- Over the next decade there is likely to be substantial progress in developing more robust statistical models for predicting social harms that social workers seek to help people avoid.
- Machine learning developments in computer science are likely to bring a step change in the development of predictive models to support professional judgement about predicting harm.

Further Reading

Barry, M. (2007). *Effective approaches to risk assessment in social work: an international literature review*. Edinburgh, Scotland: Scottish Executive.

This review of approaches to risk assessment is a valuable resource for the reader wanting to explore that topic further.

Brearley, P. (1982). *Risk in social work*. London: Routledge & Kegan Paul.

This classic text was one of the forerunners in exploring the concept of risk as applied to social work. Paul Brearley pioneered the concepts (using different terminology) of **vulnerability**, **trigger factors**, strengths and mitigating factors in social work decisions.

Gigerenzer, G. (2014). *Risk savvy: how to make good decisions*. New York: Penguin.

This popular book highlights the dilemmas and common misunderstandings about risk and uncertainty, for example regarding the meaning of terms such as 'likelihood of success' or 'likelihood of rain'.

Monahan, J., Steadman, H.J., Silver, E., Appelbaum, P.S., Robbins, P.C., Mulvey, E.P., Roth, L.H., Grisso, T. and Banks, S. (2001). *Rethinking risk assessment: the MacArthur study of mental disorder and violence*. Oxford: Oxford University Press.

This is a detailed book which helpfully outlines some of the detailed thinking required to undertake rigorous approaches to predicting harmful events, in this case in relation to violence by people with a mental disorder.

Taylor, B.J. (2017). *Decision making, assessment and risk in social work* (Third edition). London: Sage.

This textbook for post-qualifying social work studies goes into greater depth on all the topics in this book, including on the use of statistical methods to predicting harm. In particular it includes lists of readily available risk factors in relation to common situations where social workers are seeking to avoid harm occurring.

9

Managing risk and positive risk taking in planning care

(Continued)

It will also introduce you to the following standards as set out in the Social Work Subject Benchmark Statement (2019):

5.3   Values and ethics
5.14 Intervention and evaluation

See Appendix 2 for a detailed description of these standards.

Introduction

This chapter focuses on identifying and choosing between options such as in care planning, including in supportive, re-ablement and recovery models of care. A particular focus is that care planning normally takes place in a context of uncertainty where risks must be appraised as part of the planning process. In this chapter, responsibility under Health and Safety legislation to 'take reasonable steps to avoid harm' is put in the broader context of the reasoned and reasonable positive 'risk taking' which is an essential part of the role of professionals. This of course includes supporting clients to take reasonable, reasoned risks as an intrinsic part of the process. Values will be considered in terms of 'rights versus risks', the principles for providing services enshrined in social welfare legislation, and within decision models. The chapter outlines four contemporary approaches to analysis and choosing between options in care-planning decision making:

- understanding patterns of risk;
- balancing benefits and harms;
- decision trees; and
- risk-managing decision making.

Risk and uncertainty pervade all of life, and occupy a key place in our social discourse and public policy debates. Is it ever appropriate to *take risks*? Should we, morally or legally, seek always to *avoid risks*? For example, would you stop using online banking because of the risk of identity theft? Or would you avoid using medicines because of the documented likelihood of certain side effects (Taylor and Moorhead 2020)? How can we justify risk taking in decisions, for example, a business making a *risky* investment decision or a health and social care authority supporting a *risky* patient or client care plan? Risk taking might be regarded as foolhardy and reckless disregard for safety, cultural norms and the welfare of oneself and others. Risk taking may also be viewed as a positive attribute in society, for example bravery in battle; courage and tenacity in facing a challenging natural environment; the witness of martyrs. It has been argued that we live in a *risk society* (Beck 1992) because risk has a different significance than in previous historical eras.

This chapter focuses on the core concepts and issues involved in planning care, involving choosing between care (or intervention) options or advising others on these. Inevitably this decision task involves 'taking risks', in the positive sense that all of life involves 'risk taking' in order to survive and thrive. Chapter 4 explores in more detail collaborative processes in relation to such risk-taking decision-making processes. The reader interested in more general aspects of care planning is referred to Chapters 4 and 5 in Parker (2020).

Activity 9.1   Taking Risk in Everyday Life

- Should people who play sports and get injured be regarded as having self-inflicted injuries?
- Does your sense of blame depend on the sport?
- What might justify taking the risks inherent in the sport?

Care planning: identifying and choosing between options

This chapter focuses on the sort of decision making required in care planning. The term *care plan* (and similarly *care planning*) is used in this book as a generic term to include variations such as 'case plan', 'support plan', 'home care services plan', 'hospital discharge plan', 'prison discharge plan', 'protection plan', 'safeguarding plan', 'individual risk management plan', etc.

In essence, for the purposes of the topic of this book, *care planning* is about choosing between options. The process of choosing will involve clients and families as far as is possible and appropriate, and may also involve other professionals, other organisations and decision-making bodies such as meetings and courts. Collaborative aspects are discussed in Chapters 2 and 4 particularly. This chapter focuses on the challenge for individual social workers in supporting clients and families in reasonable, reasoned risk taking, and when they are charged with taking reasonable, reasoned risks in the interests of clients and families. Legal aspects are discussed in Chapter 6. As social work organisations develop and adopt assessment tools, there is also some development of tools to guide care planning (Taylor 2012a). However, care-planning tools are generally less detailed than assessment tools, and are more dependent on local services.

Our main focus in this chapter is on the cognitive aspect of the social work role in shaping care plans in relation to risk issues. For more general aspects of 'care planning' the reader is referred to Parker (2020). There are newer conceptualisations of services emerging using terminology such as 'recovery model', 're-ablement', 'care and support', etc. In essence these models involve the same basic challenges that are the focus of this chapter in identifying and choosing between available options where some element of risk taking is required. As possible care options are identified and considered, it will become clearer that there are risk aspects to each option. We will consider the perspective in relation to health and safety legislation before going on to discuss issues for professionals in reasonable risk taking.

Responsibility under Health and Safety legislation

A **hazard** may be defined as something that might cause harm (Health and Safety Executive 2009). Examples might be a slippery floor mat in the home of an older person or poor hygiene by someone with a learning disability. A *risk* is considered as the likelihood (probability) that somebody could be harmed in the situation and an indication of how serious that harm could be.

Table 9.1   Health and Safety Law in the UK: What You Need to Know

What you must do as an employer

1   Decide what could harm you in your job and the precautions to stop it. This is part of risk assessment.

2   In a way you can understand, explain how risks will be controlled and tell you who is responsible for this.

4   Free of charge, give you the health and safety training you need to do your job.

5   Free of charge, provide you with any equipment and protective clothing you need, and ensure it is properly looked after.

10   Work with any other employers or contractors sharing the workplace or providing employees (such as agency workers), so that everyone's health and safety is protected.

What you must do as an employee

1   Follow the training you have received when using any work items your employer has given you.
2   Take reasonable care of your own and other people's health and safety.
3   Co-operate with your employer on health and safety.
4   Tell someone (your employer, supervisor or health and safety representative) if you think the work or inadequate precautions are putting anyone's health and safety at serious risk.

(Health and Safety Executive [UK] 2009, extract)

Once a hazard has been identified, 'laws in European Union countries [and in the UK post-Brexit] require employers to do everything reasonably practicable to protect people from harm' (Health and Safety Executive [UK] 2009), and employees also have a role in relation to this. The general approach is that employers and those who create risk are responsible for managing it, and that employees have a right to protection but also a duty to care for themselves and others. In our context *others* might include staff in your own or other organisations, and visitors to work premises, including people who use our services.

Activity 9.2   Risks in Your Work Role

- What types of risks are involved in your work?
- What are the harms that you are trying to help clients to avoid?
- What are the most serious risks?

This approach might be described as *minimising situational hazards* (Taylor 2006). When there are hazards inherent in an activity, whether for a client or a colleague, we must consider how possible harm can be avoided. Such activities may be part of a detailed care plan for an individual or a group activity in, for example, a day centre or residential facility.

Reasonable and reasoned positive 'risk taking'

Health and safety legislation in European Union countries has been of tremendous value in reducing deaths, injuries and illness in workplaces. However, for social workers the principles underpinning the legislation need to be understood in the context of health and social care services. The focus of the legislation is on workplace health and safety; what is less clear is the definition of *a place of work* in social care contexts. Is the home of foster parents a *place of work*? Does a client's home become a *place of work* for the purposes of health and safety legislation if home care services are provided (Taylor and Donnelly 2006b)? There are implications if legislation designed for factories, mines and building sites is extended into people's own homes, and at present neither guidance nor case law in the UK has clarified the situation.

A second aspect is that there are dilemmas in health and social care contexts about what constitutes a *reasonably practicable step* to protect people from harm. When it comes to personal care tasks in somebody's own home, it may not be obvious what constitutes *reasonableness*. For example, to what extent do we accept a person's normal lifestyle arrangements as *given* and work around these if they are regarded as unsafe? This can be a particular issue in relation to providing home care services. To what extent do we insist on change (i.e. withdraw services in the last resort) if persuasion is not effective (Taylor and Donnelly 2006b)? There is particularly a tension between the principles of health and safety at work legislation to take *reasonable steps to protect others from harm*, where we are the gatekeepers for providing social care services.

More generally, we have to balance the requirements of health and safety legislation to protect people from serious harm as well as fulfilling the role and responsibility of health and social care professionals to take reasoned, reasonable risks and to support clients in taking reasoned, reasonable risks to further care plan goals such as independence and interdependence within society, motivation, quality of life and re-uniting families (Carson 2012). A reasonable decision is made to achieve some sort of benefit – interpreted broadly to include such things as good health, financial gain, social independence or moral integrity – with some reasoning process that could be explained to others if necessary. Taking reasonable, reasoned risk is intrinsic to human decision making, and hence to social work practice in advising and supporting clients to make decisions.

Case Study   Balancing Benefits and Harms

Paul is 19 years of age and has a moderate learning disability. He is due to go on a respite holiday where the provider has facilities for outdoor activities, including a rope traverse across a river. Paul has heard about rope traversing from his (non-disabled) brother and is very keen to do this.

- How would you justify supporting Paul in undertaking this activity?
- What safeguards against possible harm would you want to see in place?
- Does the suitability of the activity for other young people with similar physical ability but no learning disability have any relevance?
- How could you weigh up the possible benefits against the possible harm?
- What would you want to do to ensure that the decision was seen as sound if an accident did occur?

Balancing rights and risks

Social work clients sometimes make spontaneous decisions which have more serious consequences than expected. Examples might be a young person in residential care being led astray by a friend while on a social activity with peers, or a frail elderly person standing on a chair to change a light bulb rather than asking for help. Risks taken by a client as part of employment, social or recreational activities (for example, while a resident in a home, member of a day centre or in receipt of home care or family support services) will often involve an element of *risk* yet might not be considered as unacceptably *risky* by many people. The level of the dangers might range from crossing the road to get on a bus to go to work or the cinema, through taking the risk of getting mugged while visiting friends or shopping, to undertaking something more adventurous (*risky*) such as playing football or mountain walking. Where do individuals in society draw the line? To what extent should our support for clients' choices reflect our own values, our profession's values, society's values or the values of the client's sub-group within society? Where clients have impaired capacity, such as those with dementia, the responsibility on others to make decisions about risk – and by implication also *risk taking* – increases. For further consideration of issues of decisional capacity the reader is referred to Brown et al. (2015). Engaging with the challenges of these types of decisions is also part of the social work role, as well as more considered judgements such as safeguarding and long-term care decisions.

Balancing this tension between rights and risk taking is a core area of knowledge and skill in social work practice. Government policy in the UK is beginning to recognise this and provide some support for proactive rather than defensive approaches to managing risk through supporting reasoned and reasonable client decision making:

> *There will often be some risk, and... trying to remove it altogether can outweigh the quality of life benefits for the person.*

> (DoH 2007, p9)

> *The Health and Safety Executive endorses a sensible approach to risk, which seeks to address these concerns. Health and Safety legislation should not block reasonable activity. Through the care planning process risk assessments are undertaken which should also fulfil the requirement under health and safety legislation, providing the risk to both the person using the service and their family carer are considered...*

> (Department of Health 2007, p26, para 2.35)

Case Study   Re-ablement and Recovery Model of Care

Jim is a single man in his fifties. For many years he lived with his elderly mother, who looked after his benefit income and managed the household. He was first diagnosed as mentally ill when he was 35 years old. He became suspicious of his workmates in the transport depot in which he worked as a cleaner. Jim accused them of talking behind his back and plotting against him. Jim believed his supervisor was withdrawing money from his wage packet and threatened him.

Jim was admitted to hospital and diagnosed as suffering from paranoid schizophrenia. He was prescribed a depot injection once a month and has been on this medication ever since. After three weeks in hospital, Jim was discharged and has never been readmitted. He attends an out-patient clinic once every six months and was visited by the community nurse but never returned to work. Jim began to attend the local sheltered workshop and became one of their most reliable workers.

Everything changed when his mother died. Jim was left on his own. Alcohol was Jim's other big problem. He always liked a drink, but when his mother was alive his drinking money was controlled. After her death his drinking escalated, and his attendance at the workshop became spasmodic. He was seen on benefit days singing in the street. Jim enjoyed gambling on horses, and spent increasing amounts of time in the bookies. Between alcohol and horses his weekly incapacity benefit is spent within a few days and he has nothing to live on for the rest of the week.

Without his mother, Jim's flat is undecorated and the furniture is in need of repair. His neighbours know him and 'keep an eye out for him'. One offers to take him shopping and to look after some money for him; another sends over a meal when her children are not at home; other neighbours give him gifts of clothes. They are loyal to the memory of his mother and their support has helped to prevent hospital readmission.

Now, however, the situation is in crisis and there are demands from some neighbours that something must be done about Jim.

- What are the risks that require a social work response?
- In which situations are community supports such as described here sufficient?
- What are the threshold criteria for deciding that action is required?

Childhood development and risk

Another aspect of our 'risk society' is that children are protected from many more risks than in previous generations, perhaps to the neglect of being taught how to handle risks. Accidents are regarded increasingly as preventable, with implications for social work judgements when we must make 'reasonable' recommendations about diverse matters including child-rearing practices and what is 'safe enough' care at home. The paradox is that we need to take risks to progress as individuals and as a society, but are becoming more risk-averse, fearful of being blamed if an undesirable outcome ensues. Sometimes there may be a tension between the need for children to learn to handle risks in preparation for adult life and the 'avoiding harm' ethos of health and safety regulations, although there are signs that the apparently diverse approaches are coming closer together. The concern about over-protection in relation to good child-rearing has been recognised by the Health and Safety Executive for the UK:

The Health and Safety Executive has become concerned at the possibility of over-protection of children and their lack of risk experience. A degree of managed risk is necessary for children's development... Sensible risk management is NOT about stopping well-managed recreation and learning.

(HSE 2019)

Activity 9.3

- Write down an example that you regard as irresponsible parenting in terms of managing a child's recreational activities.
- Write down an example that you regard as responsible parenting that nevertheless involves the child in some risk taking.
- What are your criteria for distinguishing between these?
- (For further discussion of risk-related learning in childhood, see Thom et al. 2007)

Supporting clients to take reasonable, reasoned risks

When faced with choosing between two or more alternatives, people often start by listing (at least mentally) the desirable and undesirable aspects of each option. For an everyday example, consider the choice you face regarding going on holiday or buying a car. The positive and negative aspects of each option may be compared. In relation to care decisions, the same model might be used although the issues are likely to be of greater importance for the individual's future well-being. The outcomes in everyday decisions might be evaluated in terms of the gain or loss of money or pleasure as well as more basic needs of life such as health and security. In care decisions the priority is more often about benefits to health and social well-being, and possible harm whether from other people or accidents, so the terms *benefit* and *harm* are used here (Taylor 2012b). This model of *balancing benefits and harms* is adapted from a well-established judgement model known as **expected utility** (Baron 2008). This approach is based on the premise that the decision maker maximises the expected value of the outcome of the decision. That is to say, you choose the option which seems to offer, on balance, the greatest beneficial outcome when you weigh up the benefits (potential desirable outcomes) against the harms (possible undesirable outcomes).

It is important to be clear that supporting clients to take reasoned, reasonable risks is not *gambling*. Decisions about health and social care are important matters to patients, clients and their families. *Gambling* would imply that the process itself is undertaken for enjoyment rather than because the outcome is important. We support people to achieve *worthwhile* life goals in the context of their wishes, professional values, the purpose of the organisation by which we are employed (i.e. care-related goals in a broad sense) and the laws of our society. This is the answer to any accusation that we are *gambling with clients' lives* in appropriate reasoned, reasonable, professional risk taking.

In all domains of social work, we have to seek the best ways that we can to engage clients and families in assessment and decision processes, and the tasks involved in managing risks. We cannot abdicate the responsibilities placed on us by virtue of our professional role, particularly where this involves safeguarding or responsibility for allocation of public- or charitably-funded resources. The reader interested in exploring these challenges further is referred to Davidson et al. (2023) in relation to individual adults in general, and Kemshall (2023) for the criminal justice context in particular; Campbell and Campbell (2023) in relation to mental health social work; Fengler and Schrödter (2023) and López López et al. (2023) in relation to engaging children and young people; Montgomery et al. (2023) in relation to engaging families; and Olaison and Donnelly (2023) in relation to shared decision-making models, particularly in relation to older people and those with disability.

Understanding patterns of risk

There are two main components to understanding risk: the severity (value) placed on the unwanted harm, and the likelihood (probability) of harm. The usual statistical way to combine these is to multiply them to give an overall weighting of the risk. This is the approach often used for appraising risk within organisations as a whole, increasingly considered within systems for social care governance (Taylor and Campbell 2011).

Table 9.2 illustrates how the pattern of occurrence, severity and probability of the undesirable harmful event may be considered simply in a qualitative sense. However as the professional knowledge base develops and we have some clearer estimates as to how one risk compares to another, we can start to scale the risks relative to each other. In this table, the aspects of risk (pattern of occurrence, severity and probability) are compared on four-point scales.

Activity 9.4   Patterns, Severity and Probability of Risks

Table 9.2   Patterns, Severity and Probability of Risks

Risk identified	Pattern of risk	Severity of risk	Probability of risk
Identified risk	1 Isolated	1 Mild	1 Unlikely
	2 Occasional occurrence	2 Moderate	2 Likely (expected)
	3 Repeated occurrence	3 Serious	3 Highly probable
	4 Established pattern	4 Fatal	4 Certain

Consider the risks in a client situation on placement using these dimensions.

- How does this framework help you to put into words the level of risks?
- For what types of risks is it most useful?

Balancing benefits and harms in relation to care options

To support social workers in these complex risk-taking decisions, the Department of Health (London) acknowledge[s] 'that there will often be some risk, and that trying to remove it altogether can outweigh the quality of life benefits for the person' (Department of Health 2007, p9). The task is not simply judging how much of the likelihood or consequences of possible harm should be removed. Rather, the decision may be essentially about justifying the possibility of harm by evaluating the possible benefits of the course of action.

By taking account of the benefits in terms of independence, well-being and choice, it should be possible for a person to have a support plan which enables them to manage identified risks.

(Department of Health 2007, p10).

This process of *balancing benefits and harms* entails verbalising with clients, and recording potential gains from the decision as well as possible harms that might ensue. A critical issue will be helping the client to identify and clarify the value that they place on a particular benefit or harm. This is making explicit what is often considered implicitly in making a judgement about whether or not to *take the risk*. Potential gains might include dimensions such as:

- Rehabilitation
- Skills development
- Self-esteem
- Self-control
- Independence
- Quality of life
- Motivation
- Cooperation in treatment and care
- Participation in family life
- Participation in society.

Some of these 'possible gains' are connected to provisions under the Human Rights Act 1998. For further discussion, the reader is referred to Preston-Shoot (2019).

Case Study   Potential Benefits and Harms: Example of a Reasoned, Reasonable Approach To Creating A Care Plan

Maria is 37 years old and has been a patient in a psychiatric hospital for six months. She has been expressing suicidal thoughts throughout her stay, having been admitted when she intended to commit suicide. The decision is whether to permit a period of home leave. I found it helpful to articulate some of the benefits of a period of home leave or a day pass, to bear in mind alongside the more frequent consideration of the possibility of Maria harming herself.

- Reduce the growing dependency on the hospital staff and environment.
- Reduce detachment from her home community.
- Promote Maria's own coping skills and independence.
- Develop support in the community from her father.
- Taking a step forward, in discussion with Maria, that begins to move more responsibility back to her when she is ready.
- Begin the process of Maria using community rather than hospital supports, with support from her family and a counselling service.

Using decision trees

Decision trees are a visual way of showing our understanding of connections between key elements in a decision that is to be made. The main aspects of each possible option being considered may be identified and shown as joined by lines on a chart. This may be useful, for example, in areas or aspects of social work that are less tightly defined by procedures and eligibility criteria for services. Decision trees may be used simply as an aid to help to structure one's thinking about the main elements of the decision. In this respect, decision trees may be helpful in highlighting the framework being used for the decision, and thereby prompting reflective self-awareness and discussion with your supervisor about the options and the issues involved in each.

Decision trees may also include numeric data for the likelihood and seriousness of risks, with calculations to show the overall risk level for that option. This book does not use that detailed level of decision trees as, in our view, their use in social work has not yet been sufficiently researched and tested for useful inclusion in a textbook designed for qualifying courses. There is some further exploration in Luan et al. (2011), and in relation to social work specifically in Munro et al. (2016, especially pp 112–113) and in the companion post-qualifying book to this one (Taylor 2017).

Practice Activity   Identifying Risk In Decision-Making Situations

It is beyond the scope of this book to attempt to provide analyses of risk inherent in judgements and recommendations regarding the care of particular clients and families because:

1. the large range of types of decision situations across varying client groups;
2. the large number of benefits and harms that might be relevant; and
3. a publication in book form would become dated as new research is published.

A valuable task in preparation for a practice placement (internship or practice learning experience), or during induction, is to:

4. identify the types of aims which are commonly sought for these clients;
5. identify the particular potential benefits which are sought; and
6. identify the particular possible harms that the team seeks to avoid.

The material in Chapter 7 will be helpful, and your university librarian may be able to assist you in going about this task.

A contemporary approach to risk-managing decision making

Most models for understanding decision making (such as those above) frame the decision as being based on the risks that are present at the time the decision is made (Taylor 2012b). The way that this is done might use the *balancing benefits and harms* or the *decision tree* models above. However, in real life it may be that an individual weighs up some possible harm that may ensue with a course of action, but which might be modified or changed. In relation to social work, each care plan option may entail the possibility of some harm ('risk'), but it may be that ways can be envisaged to manage those possible harms. Thus this decision model embodies the management, not just the assessment of risk (Bär and Huber 2008). Here are some examples of understanding decisions and risks using this model.

- Where a family situation gives cause for concern about child neglect, what options for **monitoring** the situation are available, such as through family-aide or health visitor services, quite apart from considering family support interventions?
- The field social worker thinks that day-care services would be very helpful for a young man with a learning disability given the home situation, but the day-care staff are concerned about his aggressive behaviour. Could knowledge and skills specific to the type of outburst anticipated be taught to the day-care staff?
- Where a family member has a mental health problem, could family members be taught how to manage the most likely presenting risks?
- An elderly person is reluctant to take a new medicine just prescribed because the warning about side effects includes the possibility of having to go to the toilet more often, and the annual outing of the supported housing scheme is the day after tomorrow. How might this 'risk' be best managed?

Research Summary   Integrating Risk with Decision Making

'Making decisions' and 'working with risk' need to be integrated into a workable way of thinking that is useful for practice. *Expected utility* models of decision making usually treat risk only as measurable *likelihood*, although there are also dimensions such as *trust* and *risk perceptions* to consider. The expectations of society for more transparent approaches to decision making require an understanding of risk as well as of cognitive professional judgements and of decision processes.

(adapted from: Taylor et al. 2017)

- In your practice experiences, how are 'risk' and 'decision making' connected?
- Which aspects of risk link most clearly with decision making?

Theoretical underpinnings

This chapter draws on theoretical material and empirical studies relating to:

- social work practice in assessment and planning care (including re-ablement models);
- organisation studies relevant to social care services;
- health and safety material based on study of accidental deaths and harm;
- statutes relevant to social welfare and negligence;
- understandings of human growth and development;
- social policy considerations regarding welfare services; and
- legal concepts of reasoned, reasonable risk taking in balancing potential benefits and possible harms in decisions about future care or intervention.

The integration of decision making with how risks are managed is an innovative area at the interface between decision science (which draws particularly from learning in psychology, medicine and military studies) and risk (which draws particularly from learning in sociology, economics and business studies).

Knowledge and skills summary

- Care planning follows on directly from professional assessment, and in essence involves working with the client (and family as appropriate) to choose between care options. This normally involves contributing to or advising on how to balance, in some way, the potential benefits against the possible harms in the care options.
- Organisational dimensions relevant to delivering services must be considered in the care-planning process.
- Reasoned, reasonable risk taking decision making is an intrinsic function of the professional role in care planning to enable clients and families to achieve worthwhile care-related life goals.
- Health and safety at work legislation in European Union countries (and generally continuing in the UK after leaving the EU) has been very effective in reducing harm and disease in our society. As employees we are required to take reasonably practicable steps to avoid death, injury and illness in social care workplaces.
- There are some tensions between the principles of health and safety legislation and the professional responsibility to support clients in taking reasonable, reasoned risks to further care plan goals such as greater independence, rehabilitation, motivation and quality of life.
- Identifying patterns of risk may be a useful way to understand and analyse presenting behaviour and attitudes.
- A model of balancing benefits and harms may be useful on occasions to conceptualise the decision process.
- A decision tree may be a useful model to conceptualise this process of balancing benefits and harms, and facilitating communication with the client involved in the decision, even if statistical aspects are not used.
- Considering how risks apparent in care plan options might be managed if that option is chosen leads to a helpful conceptualisation of risk-managing decision making.
- The models presented in this chapter are aids to support your reflective practice, informing your understanding of care planning tasks and processes.

Further Reading

Carson, D. and Bain, A. (2008). *Professional risk and working with people*. London: Jessica Kingsley Publications.

This authoritative, engaging and practical book focuses on legal aspects of the tasks facing a range of human service professionals, such as social workers, who work with people in challenging situations.

Hothersall, S.J. and Maas-Lowit, M. (2010). *Need, risk and protection in social work practice*. London: Sage.

This book addresses some similar issues as our book in relation to risk, but with greater focus on needs, vulnerability and mental capacity, and less focus on the relationship with assessment processes and decision making.

Parker, J. (2020). *Social work practice: assessment, planning, intervention and review* (Sixth edition). London: Sage.

This book is in a similar practical style to the present book. It addresses broader aspects of assessment and care planning, rather than focusing on risk and decision-making aspects, which are our focus.

Taylor, B.J. (2017). *Decision making, assessment and risk in social work* (Third edition). London: Sage (Post-qualifying social work series).

This book in the Sage post-qualifying social work series is in a similar style to this one, and contains more depth and detail on the topics addressed in this book.

Health and Safety Executives were established in Great Britain by the Health and Safety at Work Act 1974, and in Northern Ireland the Health and Safety at Work (NI) Order 1978. The Health and Safety Executives established by this statute aim to *prevent death, injury and ill health in workplaces* (HSE 2009). They are the enforcing authorities for health and safety across the countries of the UK in a range of work situations including district councils, government departments, hospitals and care homes. The websites below provide a wealth of attractive materials including details of legislation and current policy issues. Topics covered include trips at work, stress at work, violence at work and working alone in safety.

Health and Safety Executive in England

www.hse.gov.uk/index.htm

Health and Safety Executive in Wales

www.hse.gov.uk/welsh/

Health and Safety Executive in Scotland

www.hse.gov.uk/scotland/

Health and Safety Executive for Northern Ireland

www.hseni.gov.uk/

10

Reflecting on your professional practice

(Continued)

It will also introduce you to the following standards as set out in the Social Work Subject Benchmark Statement (2019):

5.3 Values and ethics
5.5 The nature of social work practice
5.17 Skills in personal and professional development

See Appendix 2 for a detailed description of these standards.

Introduction

This final chapter considers the wider professional context within which assessments are undertaken. In previous chapters we have discussed the central role of supervision in supporting critical reflection and efforts to avoid bias and incorporate the best available evidence. This chapter will look at the organisational context in more depth to establish how good practice can be supported. It will examine the ongoing development of knowledge, values and skills related to assessment, working with risk, making professional judgements and making decisions. The impact of organisational culture on social work practice will be discussed, as will the need to articulate the social work role in multi-professional settings. The pressures of assessment and decision making in a complex contested arena will be considered, as will the implications of a blame culture. The human impact of engaging with stressful and distressing situations will be highlighted and some guidelines for promoting professional well-being will be suggested.

Professional support

A rigorous assessment is not something that you should be doing without supportive supervision. The social work role is complex and challenging, and our procedures presume that practitioners will be provided with organisational support. Much of this support function will be provided through regular formal supervision with an identified line manager or professional supervisor. This is usually a face-to-face meeting with an experienced social worker who understands your area of work. It is however possible that a different approach (like group supervision) will be used. It is also possible that your line manager will have a different professional background than yourself, in which case you should also have access to a professional supervisor who is a social worker. It is important to recognise that formal supervision is not the only form of support. Figure 10.1 provides examples of the forms of support that a practitioner requires (Westheimer 1977) and some sources where this support might be provided.

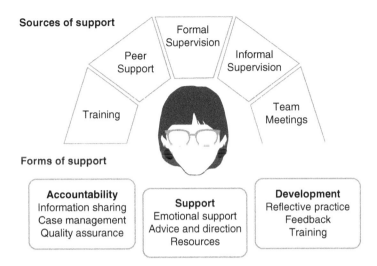

Figure 10.1 Sources and Elements of Professional Support (adapted from Westheimer 1977)

It is entirely possible that some emotional support is available from peers and some advice can be provided through informal supervision. There is however a real danger that with so many needs and so many potential sources of support, some of the support needs may fall into the gaps. A key challenge for line managers is to make sure that all support functions are covered in formal supervision if they are not being provided elsewhere. It may be helpful to consider each of the forms of support as they relate to the assessment process.

Accountability

It is important for the practitioner and the agency that assessments are undertaken correctly. We want our interventions to be as good as they can be, and research suggests that there is a relationship between the quality of practice and the quality of supervision (Bostock et al 2019). It will probably be in supervision that you can discuss your role and the purpose of the assessment. You will want to check out various aspects of the process and your employer will have expectations such as time frames. Often the line manager takes a role in agreeing recommendations or making decisions. Before doing this, they will want to critically evaluate the gathered information just as the practitioner has done. On occasions your professional supervisor or line manager will be acting as the gatekeeper. They will need to be convinced that a service or intervention is justified in the face of financial constraints. There may be times when this accountability function feels more like surveillance than support (Davys and Beddoe 2020), but a well-managed assessment process is more likely to meet the needs of the agency, the practitioner and most importantly the individual or family being assessed. Practitioners have indicated that good, regular supervision helps to keep their work organised and less-experienced staff value a directive approach to supervision (Saltiel 2017).

It is the role of the professional supervisor to set the standard and promote the principles of good assessment practice. Throughout this book we have discussed the aspects of process that will be most helpful to the participants. Overseeing the various stages, the manager will be able to promote a person-centred collaborative approach.

Supporting the practitioner

Undertaking assessments of adults or children is a complex, challenging and often distressing role. Just as the social worker endeavours to support the family, the supervisor endeavours to support the social worker. This may involve advice and direction on the best way to undertake the task. Support also involves practical issues such as workload and sick leave. However, a key aspect of supervisory support relates to the well-being of the individual. Research suggests that organisational factors such as line management can mitigate against compassion fatigue and burnout.

> We have found this may be achieved by making organisational-level adjustments to ensure social workers are supported to manage the challenges of the job. We know that having a realistic work-load and organisational supports such as a positive manager and co-worker relationships and a sense of control, fairness, values and reward are important for retaining staff and reducing turnover intent.
>
> (McFadden et al 2018, p213)

Unfortunately, social work teams under the greatest pressure may be less able to provide effective support. Each of us needs to monitor our levels of stress and well-being. This will be discussed further towards the end of the chapter.

Case Study   Cathy

Cathy is a newly qualified social worker. She has obtained a job in the family intervention team where she had her final practice learning opportunity. During placement Cathy had a protected caseload and a high level of support. Her weekly supervision focused primarily on her learning and her application of theory to practice. This involved in-depth discussion of specific cases and reflection on the ongoing work.

Now that she is a paid member of the team, Cathy feels that things have changed. The team are still supportive and there is some effort to manage her caseload, but the focus of supervision seems to have moved from development and support to management and compliance. Often the support and reflective aspects get squeezed out by caseload issues. Cathy says:

Supervision has become more about the organisation's needs than mine. It's nice to be treated like a competent team member but I don't feel like an expert yet and sometimes I would like to have my old practice teacher back.

1. In what ways is a practice teacher different to a line manager?
2. How could the support, development and reflective functions of supervision be promoted?
3. What could Cathy do to address her concerns?

Promote professional development

Assessment and decision making involve an interplay between knowledge, skills and values. While knowledge can be gained from a lecture or a book, the acquisition of skills and values is more complex. Much of the assessment process is a skill that can be learned and there is evidence that practitioner decision making improves during and after social work training (Devaney et al 2017). Similarly, expert practitioners seem to use information in a more sophisticated way than novices (Ghanem et al 2019). Supervision provides a form of mentoring or coaching where the practitioner can receive direction and feedback. This is particularly important for newly qualified staff who are learning the social work role as they go. It should be expected that your supervisor will be proactive in supporting and directing your practice and your analysis of information.

One very specific form of this support will be in promoting critical analysis and reflection. Chapter 5 has already discussed the value of a supervisor who will challenge your assumptions and interpretation of a situation. The practitioner should be able to use supervision as a sounding board, a reflective dialogue where they can unpick their experiences (Gregory 2023). Turney and Ruch (2023) argue that this safe and containing space is an essential part of information processing:

When supervision provides the opportunity for reflection, practitioners can bring together cognitive and affective knowledge to build a holistic understanding of the situations they encounter. In effect, social workers (and managers) are being individually and collectively supported to slow down, allowing them to feel and think.

(Turney and Ruch, p490)

The analytical questions in Chapter 5 including the 'Five whats?' could be used in supervision, but reflection importantly relates to the role of the practitioner. The supervisor may ask:

*   Why did you think that?
*   What were you hoping to achieve?
*   Do you feel you were understood?
*   How might the adult/child in question feel about that?
*   What other ways might you deal with that?

Houston (2015a) describes this questioning process as a critical-rational perspective and his Model for Supervision and Practice in Social Work (Houston 2015b) incorporates a range of questions to prompt reflection. Throughout this book we have encouraged practitioners to identify relevant knowledge and apply it to assessment practice. We have discussed how evidence can be used to support informed decision making. Accessing and applying knowledge are important aspects of professional practice. It is, however, possible that the knowledge or evidence that you need simply does not exist. As the range of social work interventions increases there are increasing gaps in the knowledge base. As practitioners we can highlight these areas, making them priorities for future research projects.

Case Study   The Manley Family

John is an experienced social worker who supports Mr and Mrs Manley in the care of their adult son Peter. Peter's behaviour at home can be challenging and his parents are fearful and distressed. There have never been any difficulties at the day centre that Peter attends five days each week. It seems that Mr and Mrs Manley struggle to be firm or consistent in their management of Peter's behaviour. The problem is escalating to the point where there is a risk of family breakdown. John has tried everything but nothing seems to work. He is at his wits' end.

- If you were John's line manager, what questions might help him reflect on this case?

Making supervision work for you

So far in this chapter we have naively presumed that every practitioner will have the perfect supervisor who will provide regular periods of structured and uninterrupted support. In the real world this is not always the case. Managers are overworked and they rarely receive training for the supervision role. As a result, they often supervise in the way that they were supervised. It may be necessary for a practitioner to proactively request that the critical reflection and development functions are prioritised. This might include:

1. Asking for a formal supervision agreement that includes developmental functions
2. Agreeing ways to respond to interruptions or cancelled supervision
3. Bringing an agenda that includes reflective discussions
4. Agreeing on a reflective model that you both like.

You cannot dictate how you are supervised, but it is possible that your line manager will welcome an approach that includes all elements of the supervision role.

The reality of compassion fatigue: when helping hurts

There is a harsh reality to social work and particularly assessment that all practitioners should recognise. Sometimes helping hurts. An empathetic approach to assessment can involve witnessing and engaging with another person's pain, trauma or distress. If not addressed, the accumulation of distress can lead to vicarious trauma or compassion fatigue (Méndez-Fernández 2022), which can have a negative impact on morale and social work practice. Practitioners who feel overwhelmed or emotionally exhausted may become unable or unwilling to engage in an empathetic manner. In an effort to protect themselves from further pain, they may distance themselves from emotional connection. This can take the form of depersonalisation or cynicism when the practitioner minimises the experience of the people they are supporting. Finally, compassion fatigue can cause the practitioner to feel hopeless about the people they are working with and the effectiveness of intervention (Long 2020). This could influence the process and the outcome of an assessment. Throughout this book we have stressed the importance of compassion and humanity when engaging with individuals and families. Many of the elements of good practice in assessment and decision making can be diminished by compassion fatigue, resulting in poor outcomes for individuals and families. It is in the interests of agencies, practitioners and ultimately people who use our services that staff remain motivated, compassionate and hopeful. Practitioner well-being is influenced by three factors, as shown in Figure 10.2.

Figure 10.2   Professional Well-being

Organisational aspects of professional well-being

Perhaps the most significant factors relating to professional well-being are the actions and expectations of employers. Staffing levels, caseloads, resources, training and support have a direct relationship to motivation and well-being. Employers have a duty of care to ensure that social work staff are equipped and supported to undertake a manageable workload. The culture within an organisation has a significant influence on a practitioner's experience of work pressure and stress (McFadden et al 2015). Some agencies take corporate responsibility for the social work task and outcomes, but in others practitioners feel they will be blamed for any shortcomings. Munro (2019) describes a shift in responsibility from the organisation to the individual practitioner. This blame culture has been discussed in earlier chapters and it has the potential to undermine the confidence of staff, leaving them feeling unsupported. Significantly, a defensive organisational culture limits the potential for curiosity and learning, two attributes that this book tries to promote. Organisations cannot learn and change if they always place the blame for negative outcomes on the individual worker. Equally, individuals cannot learn from their mistakes if they are not provided with a safe reflective space. Blame culture can lead to defensive practice, which has the potential to undermine positive risk taking within assessment and decision making. Practitioners are unlikely to consider risky solutions if they fear they will be held liable for negative outcomes. Sicora (2017) argues that a willingness to recognise mistakes and the ability to reflect on the cause and outcome are central to the development of understanding.

A further organisational aspect is the need for leadership in promoting good practice. Staff need to see management commitment to the principles and practicalities of any approach. The Department of Health and Social Care in the UK has provided recommendations for the implementation of strengths-based practice. The primary organisational requirement that they identify is strong leadership.

Having a clear vison by senior management of how the culture within the organisation will be shaped is essential in order to move towards a strengths and asset-based approach.

(Department of Health 2019, p51)

Changes in practice will rarely survive if they are not adopted at all levels of the organisation. Forrester et al (2018) found that training and support did not result in measurable changes in social work practice. They suggested organisational factors negated the positive impact of training quoting management expert Peter Drucker's phrase 'culture eats strategy for breakfast'.

Managerial aspects of professional well-being

Much of the managerial support function has been discussed earlier in this chapter. In social work the first line manager plays a key role in directing and supporting the service. Often the line manager is seen as making the decisions, overseeing the work and sharing the risk. Newcomb (2022) differentiated supportive supervision that was available and provided an opportunity for reflection with tokenistic supervision that focused purely on the administrative/management function. Staff interviewed by Newcomb saw supportive supervision as an act of care that evidenced their employer's commitment to their well-being. Newcomb described supportive supervision as

- accessible and timely
- educative and reflective

- emotionally supportive
- recognising alternate modes of supervision such as group support (Newcomb 2022, p1082).

Personal aspects of professional well-being

Personal attributes will not protect a practitioner in the absence of organisational and managerial support. However, personal factors do play a part in well-being. It is possible to use your social work skills and values to care for yourself in the same way that you use them to care for others. Apgar and Cadmus (2022) found that social work students were able to use strategies to help them deal with stressful events. These included positive reframing of the issue, meditation and using hobbies or exercise as a distraction. The value of coping strategies is echoed by Greer (2016), who argues that it is possible to build a 'psychology of resilience' that includes self-confidence, self-esteem and self-efficacy. He also discusses the impact of lifestyle issues like work–life balance.

Developing professional practice

The social work profession expects that practitioners' assessment skills will develop over the course of their careers, as illustrated in Figure 10.3. At the point of qualifying, social workers should have a broad understanding of needs and general skills in the assessment of needs, risks and capacity. Obviously, students have close supervision and support at this stage. Once in employment, practitioners will learn the knowledge, skills and values specific to their client group and setting. In-house training will introduce staff to the models and procedures used in the organisation. Staff will continue to be closely supervised, but will be expected to undertake some tasks independently. More experienced practitioners may receive additional training to undertake very specific assessments. These could relate to a statutory social work function regarding aspects of risk or capacity. Some specialist practitioners undertake assessments autonomously, although professional support should be available. The various levels of teaching for assessment and decision making are discussed further in Taylor (2020a).

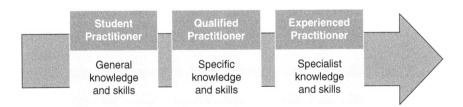

Figure 10.3   Levels of Assessment Skills

Specialist assessments include:

- Mental health risk assessments such as Approved Social Work;
- Mental capacity assessment;
- Parenting capacity assessment;
- Court assessments and reports;
- Adult safeguarding investigation;
- Joint investigation with police;
- Assessment for fostering or adoption;
- Assessment of student competence (Practice teaching).

Training may include the necessary knowledge as well as technical aspects of the assessment process. It should also recognise the complex and multifaceted nature of social work assessment discussed in earlier chapters. In some cases, candidates may undertake observed practice where their participation in a complex assessment process is evaluated by an experienced colleague. This feedback is an invaluable learning opportunity, but it is rarely available outside the initial training.

In some cases, support groups are provided to promote information sharing and learning relating to an assessment role. Often it is the practitioners who have the most up-to-date knowledge on the practicalities of the assessment task. These groups allow for reflection and the sharing of experience. They can also provide an opportunity to discuss policy changes or the implications of recent judicial rulings. If properly facilitated, a support group can also be a safe space where problems, near misses or negative outcomes can be considered to identify learning. This form of critical incident analysis (Lister 2013) allows for shared learning without the need to attribute blame. An evaluation of the effectiveness of our processes and practice is important if we want to meet the needs of individuals and families. This should be undertaken at individual and organisational levels. McPheat and Butler (2013) argue that organisations can foster a learning culture in which mistakes and near misses are used to adapt and innovate rather than attributing blame to individual employees.

The social work perspective

In the multidisciplinary context it is sometimes necessary to ensure that the social work perspective is heard. Although we are not the only profession that understands social needs, there are times when social workers must advocate for the rights and wishes of the person being assessed. This can be particularly difficult in settings dominated by a medical model like hospitals (Heenan and Birrell 2018), adult services (Kattari et al 2017) and mental health services (Fennig and Denov 2019).

Research Summary   Social Work in Acute Hospital Settings (McLaughlin 2016)

John McLaughlin used questionnaires and interviews to gather the views of patients, carers and staff in relation to the role of hospital social workers in Northern Ireland's integrated health and social services.

- Hospital social workers were described as being helpful, supportive and responsive.
- Healthcare staff commended hospital social workers' person-centred approach and assessment skills.
- Community staff felt hospital social workers were good at collaborating with other professionals and agencies.

Hospital social workers themselves worried that hospital procedures were hampering their ability to focus on the needs of patients and carers.

McLaughlin suggested that hospital social workers could strengthen their role by finding common purpose with patients and carers:

> …the time is now right for service users and professionals to collectively champion the vital contribution hospital social work can make to the quality of life, well-being and empowerment of patients and families during the hospitalisation process. Working in partnership, service users and healthcare social workers can help ensure that hospital social work not only survives but that it will be supported professionally so that it can continue to provide a holistic and person-centred service underpinned by the principles of social justice, human rights and anti-oppressive practice.

(McLaughlin 2016, p151)

The social work profession contributes a specific skill set to the assessment and decision-making process. It may be helpful to review how some social work roles can enhance a multidisciplinary or multi-agency assessment. The College of Social Work in the UK (2014) identified five aspects of social work practice. Each of these can be applied to assessment.

- Responding to complex need.
- Safeguarding and **risk management**.
- Addressing adversity and social exclusion.
- Promoting independence and autonomy.
- Prevention and early intervention.

The above aspects of social work suggest a needs-led rather than a process-led perspective. Such a holistic perspective encourages us to consider the extent to which needs have been met and identify limitations to service provision. There are a range of reasons why an assessment process may not result in all of the individual's needs being met. Hepworth et al (2010) include a 'resource development' phase within the social work process. This involves asking five resource questions:

1. What are the resource needs of a particular group?
2. How would client groups describe their resource needs?
3. Are there unmet needs or gaps in the services?
4. What are the barriers to the utilisation of existing resources?
5. Are the services that are provided effective? (Hepworth et al 2022, p333)

The potential for unmet need is often overlooked in an assessment process that endeavours to match people to existing services. This does the individual and the agency a disservice as there is no record of the gaps in provision.

Case Study   Thomas

Thomas is a 70-year-old retired businessman who lives with his wife, who is his primary carer. He has Motor Neurone Disease, which severely restricts his mobility. Thomas has two carers who assist him with dressing and toileting. A hoist is used to transfer him to and from his wheelchair.

Thomas has regular contact with family and friends, but the majority of the caring role falls to his wife. She provides constant care and has little time away from the house to buy groceries, etc. Thomas has been used to a busy lifestyle but now he spends most of his time watching television. He says that this can be monotonous, and he recognises that his wife is under pressure. The couple have asked for assistance.

The social worker undertook an assessment and agreed that there was a need for additional support. He brought Thomas to visit the local day centre, where people with disabilities participated in social activities and craft. A bus would be available to transport Thomas to the centre two days each week.

Thomas declined the service as he felt it did not meet his need. He had little interest in the activities and felt he had little in common with the other participants. The social worker recorded Thomas's decision, informed the centre and closed the file.

- What needs was Thomas expressing?
- What were his wife's needs?
- To what extent were these met?

In the above case, service planners were oblivious to the unmet need. There may be many people like Thomas who drop off the records and if the people who use the day centre are happy, any form of service development is unlikely. Concerningly, it is those people who are least able to demand services who will be most impacted by unmet need. Research suggests that there are significant gaps in services to groups including adults with disabilities (Zarkou and Brunner 2023), young carers (Addo et al 2021) and people in sexual minority groups (Steele et al 2017).

Theoretical underpinnings

This chapter draws on research and theory relating particularly to:

- professional development and supervision,
- leadership and management, and
- organisational systems and supports.

These themes are important to both practitioners and managers, as they can promote or hinder good practice and hence the value of service to our clients and families.

Knowledge and skills summary

- This chapter considers how social workers can learn and continue to develop assessment skills.
- The complexity of the assessment and decision-making process requires ongoing support and direction.
- Supervision has functions of accountability, support and professional development.
- The ability of the practitioner to undertake effective assessments is influenced by the culture of the employing organisation.
- The assessment task can be stressful and distressing and the support of professional well-being has organisational, managerial and personal components.
- Social work has a valuable contribution to make to multidisciplinary assessment and decision processes.

Further Reading

Scourfield, P. (2017). *Getting ready for direct practice in social work*. London: Sage.

This book is aimed at social work students. Chapter 1 provides a very accessible introduction to professional practice, including professional boundaries and the use of supervision.

Greer, J. (2016). *Resilience and personal effectiveness for social workers*. London: Sage.

This book discusses the pressures faced by social workers and suggests a range of self-care strategies.

Nickson, A.M., Carter, M.A. and Francis, A.P. (2019). *Supervision and professional development in social work practice*. London: Sage.

While this book was written primarily for supervisors, it provides a range of insights into professional development and the support that staff require.

Conclusion

The challenge

You are faced with a challenging task: to tell another person's story with understanding, empathy and accuracy. As a social worker, your judgements will need to incorporate knowledge, perspectives, probabilities, policies and law. You will need to develop skills of engaging others and exploring complex dynamic and sometimes conflicting information. You are required to uphold social work values as you manage ethical issues, dilemmas and conflicts. The professional task includes supporting clients and promoting their well-being through reasonable, reasoned risk taking. This creates tensions that are inherent in the professional task. Reasoned, reasonable professional judgement entails support for informed client risk taking, unless safeguarding duties and powers override or the client lacks decisional capacity or competence.

Let's look again at the case of Alice and Daniel that appeared in the introduction.

Case Study   Revisited: Alice and Daniel

Alice has been reported to social services by neighbours, who say that she and her partner, Daniel, are often drunk. Their three young children are unfed and unkempt. They are living in emergency accommodation that is dirty and unsafe. On occasions the family have been without heat or electricity. Daniel is described as a violent man who is known to police because of petty crime and anti-social behaviour. Alice has recently discovered that she is pregnant.

- How would you describe your role in this case?

In brief, our role is to understand the current family situation and to indicate potential areas for change or development. When undertaking assessment, we imagine alternative possibilities and invite the family members to share in that process. Before we ever meet the family, we can presume that the intervention is likely to be difficult. Alice and Daniel are unlikely to welcome our attention and we will be required to discuss tough issues. Merkel-Holguin et al. (2015) reviewed the literature and found that parents perceive child protection intervention as being:

- judgemental;
- fear-inducing;
- inhumane;
- difficult;

- humiliating;
- intimidating;
- shaming; and
- adversarial.

We cannot always control how people feel about our presence, but we can proactively seek ways to create emotional safety, trust and choice. The good news is that compassionate and authoritative social work seems to make a difference. Every day, people with a range of needs receive social work and social care services to promote their well-being. There is evidence that child protection services are impacting on levels of abuse (Pritchard and Williams 2009). In services for adults, practitioners' abilities to manage a complex range of tasks and perspectives has been recognised particularly in multidisciplinary settings (Moriarty and Manthorpe 2016). The range of social work interventions are diverse, but it seems that caring, trustworthy and approachable practitioners are able to achieve beneficial processes and outcomes (McLaughlin 2016).

We have provided an overview of the assessment and decision-making process that can be used with any client group. The family situation may be complex and some of the information may be subjective, but we believe that a structured approach will help us to better understand reality for this particular family. Assessment involves the purposeful use of knowledge skills and values to achieve this. We have discussed how it may be helpful to consider in advance how Alice and Daniel may be feeling about their situation and our involvement.

A primary objective of the early stages of assessment should be to develop some element of collaboration with the key individuals. We want the people who we are supporting to be involved in the decisions that are about them. This may involve an honest conversation about strengths and deficits and particularly the needs of children or vulnerable adults that are not being met. The professional task is to find ways to engage adults and children even when there are difficulties with language, perceptions or behaviour. Gaining experience can include tools and techniques to maximise involvement and empowerment. We are interested to know what Alice and Daniel want or need. It is equally important to ascertain the wishes and perspectives of their young children, and begin to appraise the needs that are or are not being met.

In some assessments our knowledge, skills and values can be supported by a framework that will help us recognise the issues and structure the information. Once we have got to know Alice and Daniel and their children better, we can discuss the key issues and identify tools that might be helpful. Some that may be relevant to this case are:

- experience of trauma (Levenson 2017);
- domestic violence (Stanley and Humphreys 2014);
- neglect (Srivastava and Hodson 2020);
- social inequality (Hyslop and Keddell 2018).

To provide an accurate overview of a complex social situation, it is often necessary to incorporate the views of a range of other professionals as well as family members. A health visitor (children's nurse) should be able to provide expertise on the children's development, and there may be professionals able to comment of the abuse of alcohol or the housing situation. Multidisciplinary working will require role clarity and effective communication, particularly when there is a need for group decision making.

The professional task is to develop and promote effective working between the range of professionals who are involved. It is necessary to recognise the potential for conflict and misunderstanding and proactively engage with others in a way that will minimise the potential for these barriers.

In Part Two of this book, we discussed how legislation and knowledge direct and inform the assessment and decision-making process. In social work roles, we often have a statutory duty to act to protect those who are at risk and provide specified services for identified needs, and our interventions need to be based on a solid knowledge base. Our intervention with Alice and Daniel and their children may be directed by legislation and policy. Social workers exercise an element of professional discretion, but in situations where there are substantial risks or concerns, this is managed within decision-making frameworks that provide opportunities for a wider breadth of knowledge to inform the decision.

Our interpretation of situations that we encounter is open to the possibility of bias, and we are required to be aware of our subjectivity and the influence that this may bring to assessment and decision making. In this book, we have promoted thoughtful analysis throughout the assessment process, and hopefully we have provided some tools that will support these skills. In cases like Alice and Daniel's we are required to make judgements about safeguarding (e.g. significant harm) or eligibility (e.g. do they warrant a family support worker). Risk of harm is one of the factors that will influence this decision, but we have stressed that risk should be understood within the broader context of family needs and strengths. Equally, when managing risk we need to recognise the costs and benefits of inaction as well as of intervention. We are right to be concerned about the safety of Alice, Daniel and their children, but measuring of risk – on its own – will not adequately describe the reality of their situation or produce the best outcomes. We have argued that reasoned, reasonable risk-taking decision making is core to the social work role in care planning to enable clients and families to achieve their life goals.

Compassion, courage, hope

A number of key social work values relate to the assessment and decision-making process. In particular, we believe that practitioners need to be able to exhibit compassion, courage and hope. Compassion is discussed in Chapter 2 and it includes the acceptance, approachability and empathy that individuals and families appreciate. It is an attitude that will support trust building and collaboration. Compassion should not be confused with blind acceptance, but rather it is the ability to be 'firm, fair and friendly' (Oliver and Charles 2015), echoing the character of 'good authority'. It takes courage to question the sources of information that support our assessments and decisions. Critical analysis, discussed in Chapter 5, involves challenging assumptions and assuring ourselves that we are doing the right thing. Fenton (2016, p15) suggests that moral courage might include, for example,

- taking responsibility for and arguing for a preferred decision; and
- advocating on behalf of people who use our services, even in the face of hostility and opposition.

Social workers should be agents of hope. It is our role to identify opportunities and possibilities even when the people we serve are unable to. This understanding of hope is more than an emotion. Hope can be a discipline (Collins 2015) and some suggest that it is a teachable skill (Kirby et al. 2019). Compassion, courage and hope support good practice in assessment and decision making. These qualities can also energise our practice, enabling us to deal with the challenges described at the start of this chapter. Sadly, the nature of social work can deplete our reserves of compassion, courage and hope. Emotional exhaustion or compassion fatigue can cause us to be uncaring, fearful and hopeless. Chapter 10 looked at how organisational supports and personal practices can support our well-being. It stressed the need for us to be compassionate to ourselves so that we can continue to care for others.

The reflective learning journey

The aim of this book is to support the trainee social worker in developing the knowledge and skills necessary for beginning practice in assessment and decision making in a context of risk or uncertainty. The scope and scale of the book has required robust decisions about what to include. The next stage of development as a newly qualified social worker is addressed in a companion volume (Taylor 2017).

Once in employment, do look for opportunities to continue to develop your knowledge and skills. There is much more to learn, and the world is not standing still! Look out for courses on aspects of assessment, decision making and risk relevant to your role, in particular on:

- child and adult protection knowledge, skills, policies and procedures;
- other protective frameworks for your area of work such as guardianship, enduring power of attorney, etc;
- human rights legislation and recent case law on negligence;
- risk factors, needs and helping processes for your own client group;
- decisional capacity and consent to care and treatment;
- your responsibility for health and safety at work, including personal safety for yourself and responsibilities to other staff;
- specialist assessment tools embodying sound research and theory; and
- clinical and social care governance, and related policies and procedures (including professional supervision) for managing decisions.

The state of knowledge and next steps

Social work has come a long way in the last 50 years. We have developed our knowledge, skills and values to support a diverse range of individuals, families and groups. We have found ways to empower, support and protect, and we have found ourselves increasingly held responsible for the outcomes of our decisions. Our understanding of need and social issues has changed as have the policies that define our role. There has been a rapid growth in the range of social work research and technology has made this accessible to students and practitioners.

Within this growth of the expertise and professionalism of social work, the study of decision making, assessment and risk has come a long way. The publication of *The SAGE handbook of decision making, assessment and risk in social work* (Taylor et al. 2023), with 49 chapters from across the globe, indicates the level of interest in academia and practice. It is probable that in future social work will continue to operate in a climate of complexity and uncertainty, and we are optimistic that the profession is up for the task. At the point of qualifying, students should have an understanding of the needs of individuals, the skills to engage with them and values to promote their well-being. Practitioners should have a balanced understanding of risk and they should be able to place this within the broader aspects of family needs. The coming years may see the development of more sophisticated assessment frameworks tools to facilitate gathering and collation of data, and communication between professionals. Already we are witnessing increased computerisation of processes, and the incorporation of statistical data on risks into care planning and decision making. Social work has shown that it can adapt to the ever-changing climate within which we work. Despite restructuring and reform within national systems for services and regulation, social work is still exploring ways to provide empowering, relationship-based practice. It is encouraging to see, in the literature and on social media, a continued emphasis on the best interests of the people we serve. We are hopeful that this will remain our central focus as we assess needs and make decisions in a context of changing technology, changing organisations and a changing society.

Take-home messages

1. **Try to be clear:** Understand your role and responsibilities with the people you support, your professional supervisor and other professionals.
2. **Try to be informed:** Familiarise yourself with the statutes, guidance, policies and procedures relevant to the risk, decision and assessment task.
3. **Try to be relational:** Find ways to engage with the people who are being assessed.
4. **Try to be open:** Maintain good communication with individuals, families, your professional supervisor and other professionals.
5. **Try to be balanced:** Consider the perspective of the various stakeholders, and the potential benefits, harms, mitigating factors and issues for each person.
6. **Try to be reflective:** Be aware of your own feelings, potential biases, pressures and influences.
7. **Try to be critical:** Evaluate sources of information and use specialist assessment tools where appropriate.
8. **Try to be knowledgeable:** Base your judgements on a good knowledge base and professional wisdom from experience.
9. **Try to be rational:** Ensure that your judgements are reasoned and reasonable.
10. **Try to be self-aware:** Recognise the supports that you and your colleagues need to face the challenges in making reasonable, reasoned risk-taking decisions in the best interests of clients and families.

Further Reading

Taylor, B.J. (2017). *Decision making, assessment and risk in social work* (Third edition). London: Sage (Post-qualifying social work series).

This book was written primarily for the newly qualified social worker in the first two years after qualifying. It goes into more depth on the topics in this book, with a greater focus on professional judgement and on contributing effectively to decision processes in complex risk situations.

Taylor, B.J., Fluke, J.D., Graham, J.C., Keddell, E., Killick, C., Shlonsky, A. and Whittaker, A. (Eds) (2023). *The SAGE handbook of decision making, assessment and risk in social work.* London: Sage.

This substantial reference work has been written by a team of over 100 authors from around the world, to provide a snapshot of research and theoretical understandings on decision making, assessment and risk in diverse social work contexts.

Taylor, B.J. and Whittaker, A. (Eds) (2019). *Professional judgement and decision making in social work: current issues.* London: Routledge.
Whittaker, A. and Taylor, B.J. (Eds) (2018). *Risk in social work practice: current issues.* London: Routledge.

These edited books comprise peer-reviewed contributions on current issues in professional judgement and decision-making processes, and in assessing, communicating and managing risk in social work respectively. The books give examples of a range of recent research on these topics.

Appendix 1

Professional capabilities framework for England

The 9 Domains

1. PROFESSIONALISM – Identify and behave as a professional social worker, committed to professional development.
2. VALUES AND ETHICS – Apply social work ethical principles and value to guide professional practices.
3. DIVERSITY AND EQUALITY – Recognise diversity and apply anti-discriminatory and anti-oppressive principles in practice.
4. RIGHTS, JUSTICE AND ECONOMIC WELLBEING – Advance human rights and promote social justice and economic well-being.
5. KNOWLEDGE – Develop and apply relevant knowledge from social work practice and research, social sciences, law, other professional and relevant fields, and from the experience of people who use services.
6. CRITICAL REFLECTION AND ANALYSIS – Apply critical reflection and analysis to inform and provide a rationale for professional decision-making.

7. SKILLS AND INTERVENTIONS – Use judgement, knowledge and authority to intervene with individuals, families and communities to promote independence, provide support, prevent harm and enable progress.

8. CONTEXTS AND ORGANISATIONS – Engage with, inform, and adapt to changing organisational contexts, and the social and policy environments that shape practice. Operate effectively within and contribute to the development of organisations and services, including multi-agency and inter-professional settings.

9. PROFESSIONAL LEADERSHIP – Promote the profession and good social work practice. Take responsibility for the professional learning and development of others. Develop personal influence and be part of the collective leadership and impact of the profession.

Published with kind permission of BASW – www.basw.co.uk

Appendix 2

Academic subject benchmark for social work in the UK

5 Knowledge, understanding and skills

Subject knowledge and understanding

5.1 During their qualifying degree studies in social work, students acquire, critically evaluate, apply and integrate knowledge and understanding in the following five core areas of study.

5.2 Social work theory, which includes:

1. critical explanations from social work theory and other subjects which contribute to the knowledge base of social work
2. an understanding of social work's rich and contested history from both a UK and comparative perspective
3. the relevance of sociological and applied psychological perspectives to understanding societal and structural influences on human behaviour at individual, group and community levels, and the relevance of sociological theorisation to a deeper understanding of adaptation and change
4. the relevance of psychological, physical and physiological perspectives to understanding human, personal and social development, well-being and risk
5. social science theories explaining and exploring group and organisational behaviour
6. the range of theories and research-informed evidence that informs understanding of the child, adult, family or community and of the range of assessment and interventions which can be used
7. the theory, models and methods of assessment, factors underpinning the selection and testing of relevant information, knowledge and critical appraisal of relevant social science and other research and evaluation methodologies, and the evidence base for social work
8. the nature of analysis and professional judgement and the processes of risk assessment and decision making, including the theory of risk-informed decisions and the balance of choice and control, rights and protection in decision making
9. approaches, methods and theories of intervention in working with a diverse population within a wide range of settings, including factors guiding the choice and critical evaluation of these, and user-led perspectives.

5.3 Values and ethics, which include:

1. the nature, historical evolution, political context and application of professional social work values, informed by national and international definitions and ethical statements, and their relation to personal values, identities, influences and ideologies

2. the ethical concepts of rights, responsibility, freedom, authority and power inherent in the practice of social workers as agents with statutory powers in different situations

3. aspects of philosophical ethics relevant to the understanding and resolution of value dilemmas and conflicts in both interpersonal and professional context

4. understanding of, and adherence to, the ethical foundations of empirical and conceptual research, as both consumers and producers of social science research

5. the relationship between human rights enshrined in law and the moral and ethical rights determined theoretically, philosophically and by contemporary society

6. the complex relationships between justice, care and control in social welfare and the practical and ethical implications of these, including their expression in roles as statutory agents in diverse practice settings and in upholding the law in respect of challenging discrimination and inequalities

7. the conceptual links between codes defining ethical practice and the regulation of professional conduct

8. the professional and ethical management of potential conflicts generated by codes of practice held by different professional groups

9. the ethical management of professional dilemmas and conflicts in balancing the perspectives of individuals who need care and support and professional decision-making at points of risk, care and protection

10. the constructive challenging of individuals and organisations where there may be conflicts with social work values, ethics and codes of practice

11. the professional responsibility to be open and honest if things go wrong (the duty of candour about own practice) and to act on concerns about poor or unlawful practice by any person or organisation

12. continuous professional development as a reflective, informed and skilled practitioner, including the constructive use of professional supervision

5.4   Service users and carers, which include:

1. the factors which contribute to the health and well-being of individuals, families and communities, including promoting dignity, choice and independence for people who need care and support

2. the underpinning perspectives that determine explanations of the characteristics and circumstances of people who need care and support, with critical evaluation drawing on research, practice experience and the experience and expertise of people who use services

3. the social and psychological processes associated with, for example, poverty, migration, unemployment, trauma, poor health, disability, lack of education and other sources of disadvantage and how they affect well-being, how they interact and may lead to marginalisation, isolation and exclusion, and demand for social work services

4. explanations of the links between the factors contributing to social differences and identities (for example, social class, gender, ethnic differences, age, sexuality and religious belief) and the structural consequences of inequality and differential need faced by service users

5. the nature and function of social work in a diverse and increasingly global society (with particular reference to prejudice, interpersonal relations, discrimination, empowerment and anti-discriminatory practices)

5.5   The nature of social work practice, in the UK and more widely, which includes:

1.   the place of theoretical perspectives and evidence from European and international research in assessment and decision-making processes
2.   the integration of theoretical perspectives and evidence from European and international research into the design and implementation of effective social work intervention with a wide range of service users, carers and communities
3.   the knowledge and skills which underpin effective practice, with a range of service users and in a variety of settings
4.   the processes that facilitate and support service user and citizen rights, choice, co-production, self-governance, well-being and independence
5.   the importance of interventions that promote social justice, human rights, social cohesion, collective responsibility and respect for diversity and that tackle inequalities
6.   its delivery in a range of community-based and organisational settings spanning the statutory, voluntary and private sectors, and the changing nature of these service contexts
7.   the factors and processes that facilitate effective interdisciplinary, interprofessional and interagency collaboration and partnership across a plurality of settings and disciplines
8.   the importance of social work's contribution to intervention across service user groups, settings and levels in terms of the profession's focus on social justice, human rights, social cohesion, collective responsibility and respect for diversities
9.   the processes of reflection and reflexivity as well as approaches for evaluating service and welfare outcomes for vulnerable people, and their significance for the development of practice and the practitioner.

5.6   The leadership, organisation and delivery of social work services, which includes:

1.   the location of contemporary social work within historical, comparative and global perspectives, including in the devolved nations of the UK and wider European and international contexts
2.   how the service delivery context is portrayed to service users, carers, families and communities
3.   the changing demography and cultures of communities, including European and international contexts, in which social workers practise
4.   the complex relationships between public, private, social and political philosophies, policies and priorities and the organisation and practice of social work, including the contested nature of these
5.   the issues and trends in modern public and social policy and their relationship to contemporary practice, service delivery and leadership in social work
6.   the significance of legislative and legal frameworks and service delivery standards, including on core social work values and ethics in the delivery of services which support, enable and empower
7.   the current range and appropriateness of statutory, voluntary and private agencies providing services and the organisational systems inherent within these
8.   development of new ways of working and delivery, for example the development of social enterprises, integrated multi-professional teams and independent social work provision
9.   the significance of professional and organisational relationships with other related services, including housing, health, education, police, employment, fire, income maintenance and criminal justice

10. the importance and complexities of the way agencies work together to provide care, the relationships between agency policies, legal requirements and professional boundaries in shaping the nature of services provided in integrated and interdisciplinary contexts

11. the contribution of different approaches to management and leadership within different settings, and the impact on professional practice and on quality of care management and leadership in public and human services

12. the development of person-centred services, personalised care, individual budgets and direct payments all focusing upon the human and legal rights of the service user for control, power and self-determination

13. the implications of modern information and communications technology for both the provision and receipt of services, use of technologically enabled support and the use of social media as a process and forum for vulnerable people, families and communities, and communities of professional practice.

Subject-specific skills and other skills

5.7 The range of skills required by a qualified social worker reflects the complex and demanding context in which they work. Many of these skills may be of value in many situations, for example, analytical thinking, building relationships, working as a member of an organisation, intervention, evaluation and reflection. What defines the specific nature of these skills as developed by social work students is:

1. the context in which they are applied and assessed (for example, communication skills in practice with people with sensory impairments or assessment skills in an interprofessional setting)

2. the relative weighting given to such skills within social work practice (for example, the central importance of problem-solving skills within complex human situations)

3. the specific purpose of skill development (for example, the acquisition of research skills in order to build a repertoire of research-based practice)

4. a requirement to integrate a range of skills (that is, not simply to demonstrate these in an isolated and incremental manner).

5.8 All social work graduates demonstrate the ability to reflect on and learn from the exercise of their skills, in order to build their professional identity. They understand the significance of the concepts of continuing professional development and lifelong learning, and accept responsibility for their own continuing development.

5.9 Social work students acquire and integrate skills in the following five core areas.

Problem-solving skills

5.10 These are subdivided into four areas.

5.11 Managing problem-solving activities: graduates in social work are able to:

1. think logically, systematically, creatively, critically and reflectively, in order to carry out a holistic assessment

2. apply ethical principles and practices critically in planning problem-solving activities

3. plan a sequence of actions to achieve specified objectives, making use of research, theory and other forms of evidence

4. manage processes of change, drawing on research, theory and other forms of evidence.

5.12 Gathering information: graduates in social work are able to:

1. demonstrate persistence in gathering information from a wide range of sources and using a variety of methods, for a range of purposes. These methods include electronic searches, reviews of relevant literature, policy and procedures, face-to-face interviews, and written and telephone contact with individuals and groups

2. take into account differences of viewpoint in gathering information and critically assess the reliability and relevance of the information gathered

3. assimilate and disseminate relevant information in reports and case records.

5.13 Analysis and synthesis: graduates in social work are able to analyse and synthesise knowledge gathered for problem-solving purposes, in order to:

1. assess human situations, taking into account a variety of factors (including the views of participants, theoretical concepts, research evidence, legislation and organisational policies and procedures)

2. analyse and synthesise information gathered, weighing competing evidence and modifying their viewpoint in the light of new information, then relate this information to a particular task, situation or problem

3. balance specific factors relevant to social work practice (such as risk, rights, cultural differences and language needs and preferences, responsibilities to protect vulnerable individuals and legal obligations)

4. assess the merits of contrasting theories, explanations, research, policies and procedures and use the information to develop and sustain reasoned arguments

5. employ a critical understanding of factors that support or inhibit problem-solving, including societal, organisational and community issues as well as individual relationships

6. critically analyse and take account of the impact of inequality and discrimination in working with people who use social work services.

5.14 Intervention and evaluation: graduates in social work are able to use their knowledge of a range of interventions and evaluation processes creatively and selectively to:

1. build and sustain purposeful relationships with people and organisations in communities and interprofessional contexts

2. make decisions based on evidence, set goals and construct specific plans to achieve outcomes, taking into account relevant information, including ethical guidelines

3. negotiate goals and plans with others, analysing and addressing in a creative and flexible manner individual, cultural and structural impediments to change

4. implement plans through a variety of systematic processes that include working in partnership

5. practice in a manner that promotes well-being, protects safety and resolves conflict

6. act as a navigator, advocate and support to assist people who need care and support to take decisions and access services

7. manage the complex dynamics of dependency and, in some settings, provide direct care and personal support to assist people in their everyday lives

8. meet deadlines and comply with external requirements of a task

9. plan, implement and critically monitor and review processes and outcomes

10. bring work to an effective conclusion, taking into account the implications for all involved

11. use and evaluate methods of intervention critically and reflectively.

Communication skills

5.15   Graduates in social work are able to communicate clearly, sensitively and effectively (using appropriate methods which may include working with interpreters) with individuals and groups of different ages and abilities in a range of formal and informal situations, in order to:

1. engage individuals and organisations, who may be unwilling, by verbal, paper-based and electronic means to achieve a range of objectives, including changing behaviour
2. use verbal and non-verbal cues to guide and inform conversations and interpretation of information
3. negotiate and, where necessary, redefine the purpose of interactions with individuals and organisations and the boundaries of their involvement
4. listen actively and empathetically to others, taking into account their specific needs and life experiences
5. engage appropriately with the life experiences of service users, to understand accurately their viewpoint, overcome personal prejudices and respond appropriately to a range of complex personal and interpersonal situations
6. make evidence-informed arguments drawing from theory, research and practice wisdom, including the viewpoints of service users and/or others
7. write accurately and clearly in styles adapted to the audience, purpose and context of the communication
8. use advocacy skills to promote others' rights, interests and needs, present conclusions verbally and on paper, in a structured form, appropriate to the audience for which these have been prepared
10. make effective preparation for, and lead, meetings in a productive way.

Skills in working with others

5.16   Graduates in social work are able to build relationships and work effectively with others, in order to:

1. involve users of social work services in ways that increase their resources, capacity and power to influence factors affecting their lives
2. engage service users and carers and wider community networks in active consultation
3. respect and manage differences such as organisational and professional boundaries and differences of identity and/or language
4. develop effective helping relationships and partnerships that facilitate change for individuals, groups and organisations while maintaining appropriate personal and professional boundaries
5. demonstrate interpersonal skills and emotional intelligence that creates and develops relationships based on openness, transparency and empathy
6. increase social justice by identifying and responding to prejudice, institutional discrimination and structural inequality
7. operate within a framework of multiple accountability (for example, to agencies, the public, service users, carers and others)
8. observe the limits of professional and organisational responsibility, using supervision appropriately and referring to others when required
9. provide reasoned, informed arguments to challenge others as necessary, in ways that are most likely to produce positive outcomes.

Skills in personal and professional development

5.17   Graduates in social work are able to:

1.   work at all times in accordance with codes of professional conduct and ethics
2.   advance their own learning and understanding with a degree of independence and use supervision as a tool to aid professional development
3.   develop their professional identity, recognise their own professional limitations and accountability, and know how and when to seek advice from a range of sources, including professional supervision
4.   use support networks and professional supervision to manage uncertainty, change and stress in work situations while maintaining resilience in self and others
5.   handle conflict between others and internally when personal views may conflict with a course of action necessitated by the social work role
6.   provide reasoned, informed arguments to challenge unacceptable practices in a responsible manner and raise concerns about wrongdoing in the workplace
7.   be open and honest with people if things go wrong
8.   understand the difference between theory, research, evidence and expertise and the role of professional judgement.

Use of technology and numerical skills

5.18   Graduates in social work are able to use information and communication technology effectively and appropriately for:

1.   professional communication, data storage and retrieval and information searching
2.   accessing and assimilating information to inform working with people who use services
3.   data analysis to enable effective use of research in practice
4.   enhancing skills in problem-solving
5.   applying numerical skills to financial and budgetary responsibilities
6.   understanding the social impact of technology, including the constraints of confidentiality and an awareness of the impact of the 'digital divide'.

© The Quality Assurance Agency for Higher Education, 2019 www.qaa.ac.uk/

Reproduced with kind permission of The Quality Assurance Agency for Higher Education.

Glossary

Assessing risk The professional task, working with the client, family and others as far as possible and appropriate, of gathering and analysing information relevant to the possibility of harm, in the light of relevant knowledge, in order to inform a risk-taking decision about care.

Assessment The professional task, working with the client, family and others as far as possible and appropriate, in gathering and analysing information – about the client problem and context in the light of relevant knowledge – in order to address problems and plan care.

Assessment tool The written or digital instrument that shapes what information is gathered for an assessment in a practice (clinical) context. The term 'assessment instrument' is often used for a comparable document for research rather than practice purposes.

Care plan This term includes plans to safeguard individuals and to support clients to take reasonable, reasoned risks as well as other forms of planning care such as where the focus is deciding about long-term care or provision of public resources such as home care. The term is used here as a generic term to include local and contextual variations such as 'protection plan', 'hospital discharge plan', 'prison discharge plan', 'safeguarding plan', 'home care services plan', 'individual risk management plan', 'case plan', etc.

Decision frame The psycho-social factors and events that give the decision and risk situation its meaning, limitations and possibilities.

Decision making A conscious process (individually or as a corporate exercise with one or more others) leading to the selection of a course of action from among two or more alternatives.

Decision tree A visual aid to illustrate the component parts or sequence of questions (or tests) which comprise a decision-making process. A simplified form of a decision tree, without a time element or numerical data on probabilities and seriousness of outcomes, may be used for visualising the options available and the decision path to particular outcomes.

Direct care risks Risks that relate to the direct care of clients, including those relating to:

1 standards of care (including provision of appropriately trained staff and skill mix);
2 ascertaining the facts (including ensuring care plans and interventions are appropriate and confidential);
3 consent to treatment (including ascertaining capacity to consent);

4   injury arising from failure in communication with clients and internally; and
5   working beyond one's competence (cf. Department of Health 1993).

Expected utility   See *Subjective expected utility.*

Hazard   Something that may cause harm (Health & Safety Executive 2015).

Health and safety risks   This includes all types of risks that relate to health and safety requirements, including:

1   provision of a safe place of work;
2   having safe systems of work (including in relation to personal safety);
3   control of substances hazardous to health; and
4   provision of information, instruction, training and supervision (cf. DH 1993).

Hindsight error   Assuming that because there is an undesirable outcome then the decision process must have been flawed, without taking due account of the context and the limited extent of information available at the time at which the decision was made.

Indirect care risks   This includes all types of risks that relate to indirect aspects of care such as:

1   security risks (including risks to personal safety of staff, clients and others);
2   fire risks;
3   risks arising from buildings, plants and equipment;
4   risks arising from waste; and
5   control of infection risks.

Integrated assessment system   A system of assessment in which there is more than one level of assessment depending upon the complexity of need and risk, and which coordinates specialised assessments into a cohesive administrative and holistic overview for analysis and decision making (cf. Taylor 2012a).

Judgement   The considered evaluation of evidence by an individual using their cognitive faculties so as to reach an opinion on a situation, event or proposed course of action based on values, knowledge and available information.

Likelihood   See *Probability.*

Managing risk   The professional task – working with the client, family and others as far as possible and appropriate – in reaching a judgement and participating in a decision-making process and its implementation, monitoring and review to support a client or act to protect a client in care planning that involves risk taking *(see also Risk management).*

Monitoring   Gathering information about the situation at regular time periods after the decision has been taken so as to initiate revision of the care plan if appropriate.

Organisational risks   This includes all types of risks that relate to the organisation being able to fulfil its purpose or mandate, including:

1   the exercise of statutory functions;
2   internal communications within and between teams and departments;
3   communications with external bodies;
4   legal liability and maintaining public credibility;
5   provision of goods and services to other organisations;
6   financial risks; and
7   information systems (cf. Department of Health 1993).

Probability   A numerical measure of the strength of a belief that a certain event will occur (Baron 2008 p104). Normally the term *probability* is used where there is data available about how frequently this type of event has occurred in the past (i.e. in relation to 'risk') and the term *likelihood* when the probability cannot be calculated (i.e. in relation to 'uncertainty'). This distinction between 'risk' and 'uncertainty' depends on the definition of what events in the past are defined as 'similar' and is perhaps not as useful in social work as in some other domains of knowledge. See also: *Likelihood.*

Problem solving   Finding, creating and evaluating options among which to select as part of the decision process.

Professional judgement   When a professional considers the evidence about a client or family situation in the light of professional knowledge to reach a conclusion or recommendation regarding a course of action.

Protective factor   By contrast with a Risk factor (q.v.) this is a factor that correlates with less probability of harm occurring. The terms 'mitigating factor' and 'desistance factor' (in criminal justice) are also used.

Review   When an *assessment* is repeated this is often called review. One difference from an *assessment* is that the effects of the planned intervention also need to be evaluated.

Risk   A time-bounded decision-making situation where the outcomes are not known and where benefits are sought but undesirable outcomes are possible. Sometimes contrasted with *uncertainty.*

Risk assessment   See *Assessing risk.*

Risk communication   The exchange of information between individuals receiving services, family members and professionals about possible harm and potential benefits of a course of action, usually in relation to a decision about a possible health and social care intervention. The term *risk-benefit communication* is also used.

Risk factors   Factors about a client, family or situation that have been shown through research to correlate significantly with the undesirable harm.

Risk management   The systems and processes of the organisation (including professional, decision-making, policy, procedural, strategic, communication, resource, legal and financial aspects) that support accountable professional judgement and reasonable risk taking for the benefit of clients and society, and that enable continued learning from mistakes and near misses as a means to improve safety and performance (See also *Managing risk*).

Risks   Undesirable, at least potentially quantifiable, possibilities that face an organisation providing social care services, including professional social work services. See *Direct care risks*; *Indirect care risks*; *Health and safety risks*; and *Organisational risks*.

Social construction of risk   Concepts and processes used to define risk in a certain context in a society at a particular time, even if the result does not correspond with measures of the probability of that particular harmful outcome (Stevenson et al 2018).

Subjective expected utility   A model of human judgement which posits that a rational person weighs up the options in terms of the benefit (utility) that is expected from each course of action. The attractiveness of the options is normally calculated by multiplying the value (utility) placed on that option (often calculated in monetary terms) by the probability of that outcome coming to pass.

Threshold judgement   A dichotomous (two-option) judgement about whether a situation is one side or the other of a predetermined level or 'line' in relation to some feature, condition or aspect of the situation being appraised. The threshold may relate, for example, to a compulsory safeguarding intervention on behalf of society or to eligibility for services.

Trigger factor   A situational element that may precipitate the occurrence of a possible or anticipated undesirable event that has been identified.

Uncertainty   Characterises a situation where the probability of an event (usually the outcome of a decision) cannot be calculated. Sometimes contrasted with *risk* when used in the sense that the probability of an unwanted outcome *can* be calculated. See also *Risk*.

Vulnerability   The susceptibility of an individual to suffer from a possible or anticipated undesirable event that has been identified.

The definitions in this Glossary have been developed over years of teaching and research on these topics, and are intended to be an aid to clear communication with clients and colleagues and within organisations. This list is a simplified version of the glossaries in Taylor (2017a) and Taylor et al (2023).

References

1 Crown Office Row (2019). *Protecting children from harm: CN & GN v Poole Borough Council*. London: 1COR.

Adams, R., Dominelli, L. and Payne, M. (Eds) (2009). *Critical practice in social work*. Basingstoke: Macmillan International Higher Education.

Addo, I.Y., Aguilar, S., Judd-Lam, S., Hofstaetter, L. and Poon, A.W.C. (2021). Young carers in Australia: understanding experiences of caring and support-seeking behaviour. *Australian Social Work*: 1–14.

Ægisdóttir, S., White, M.J., Spengler, P.M., Maugherman, A.S., Anderson, L.A., Cook, R.S., Nichols, C.N., Lampropoulos, G.K., Walker, B.S., Cohen, G. and Rush, J.D. (2006). The meta-analysis of clinical judgment project: fifty-six years of accumulated research on clinical versus statistical prediction. *The Counselling Psychologist*, 34(3): 341–382. DOI: 10.1177/0011000005285875.

Alfandari, R., Przeperski, J. and Taylor, B.J. (2023). Interprofessional decision making. In Taylor, B.J., Fluke, J.D., Graham, J.C., Keddell, E., Killick, C., Shlonsky, A. and Whittaker, A. (Eds), *The SAGE handbook of decision making, assessment and risk in social work* (Chapter 15, 176–184). London: Sage.

Alfandari, R. and Taylor, B.J. (2022). Community-based multi-professional child protection decision making: systematic narrative review. *Child Abuse and Neglect*, 123: 105432.

Alfandari, R. and Taylor, B.J. (2023). Processes of multi-professional child protection decision making in hospital settings: systematic narrative review. *Trauma, Violence, & Abuse*, 24(1): 295–312.

Alfandari, R., Taylor, B.J., Enosh, G., Killick, C., McCafferty, P., Mullineux, J., Przeperski, J., Rölver, M. and Whittaker, A. (2023). Group decision-making theories for child and family social work. *European Journal of Social Work*, 26(2): 204–217.

Alfandari, R., Taylor, B.J., Baginsky, M., Campbell, J., Helm, D., Killick, C., McCafferty, P., Mullineux, J., Shears, J., Sicora, A. and Whittaker, A. (2023). Making sense of risk: social work at the boundary between care and control. *Health, Risk & Society*, 25(1–2): 75–92.

Ambrose-Miller, W. and Ashcroft, R. (2016). Challenges faced by social workers as members of interprofessional collaborative health care teams. *Health & Social Work*, 41(2): 101–109.

Anand, J.C., Begley, E., O'Brien, M., Taylor, B.J. and Killick, C. (2013). Conceptualising elder abuse across local and global contexts: implications for policy and professional practice on the island of Ireland. *The Journal of Adult Protection*, 15(6): 280–289.

Apgar, D. and Cadmus, T. (2021). Using mixed methods to assess the coping and self-regulation skills of undergraduate social work students impacted by COVID-19. *Clinical Social Work Journal*: 1–12.

Aspinwall-Roberts, E. (2012). *Assessments in social work with adults*. Maidenhead: McGraw-Hill Education (UK).

Baginsky, M., Hickman, B., Harris, J., Manthorpe, J., Sanders, M., O'Higgins, A., Schoenwald, E. and Clayton, V. (2020). *Evaluation of MTM's signs of safety pilots. Evaluation report and evaluation report appendices*. The Department for Education.

Baginsky, M., Hickman, B., Moriarty, J. and Manthorpe, J. (2019). Working with signs of safety: parents' perception of change. *Child and Family Social Work*, 25(1): 154–164.

Bär, A.S. and Huber, O. (2008). Successful or unsuccessful search for risk defusing operators: effects on decision behaviour. *European Journal of Cognitive Psychology*, 20(4): 807–827.

Barkham, P. (2008). Hannah's choice. *The Guardian*, 12 November, *www.theguardian.com/society/2008/nov/12/health-child-protection#:~:text=I%27ve%20had%20too%20much,brother%20and%20her%20two%20sisters* (accessed 15 January 2024).

Baron, J. (2024). *Thinking and Deciding* (Fifth edition). Cambridge: Cambridge University Press.

Bartelink, C., van Yperen, T.A. and ten Berge, I.J. (2015). Deciding on child maltreatment: a literature review on methods that improve decision-making. *Child Abuse and Neglect*, 49: 142–153.

Bastian, P. and Schrödter, M. (2023). Decision aids, decision supports and managing risk. In Taylor, B.J., Fluke, J.D., Graham, J.C., Keddell, E., Killick, C., Shlonsky, A. and Whittaker, A. (Eds), *The SAGE handbook of decision making, assessment and risk in social work* (Chapter 30, 358–366). London: Sage.

Bates, J., Best, P., McQuilkin, J. and Taylor, B.J. (2017). Will web search engines replace bibliographic databases in the systematic identification of research? *Journal of Academic Librarianship*, 43(1): 8–17.

Baumann, D.J., Fluke, J.D., Dalgleish, L. and Kern, L.H. (2014). The decision-making ecology. In Shlonsky, A. and Benbenishty, R. (Eds), *From evidence to outcomes in child welfare: an international reader* (24–37). Oxford: Oxford University Press.

Beck, U. (1992). *The risk society: towards a new modernity*. London: Sage.

Beckett, C., Maynard, A. and Jordan, P. (2017). *Values and ethics in social work*. London: Sage.

Benbenishty, R., Davidson-Arad, B., López, M., Devaney, J., Spratt, T., Koopmans, C. and Hayes, D. (2015). Decision making in child protection: an international comparative study on maltreatment substantiation, risk assessment and interventions recommendations, and the role of professionals' child welfare attitudes. *Child Abuse & Neglect*, 49: 63–75.

Bentovim, A., Cox, A., Bingley Miller, L. and Pizzey, S. (2009). *Safeguarding children living with trauma and violence: evidence-based assessment, analysis and planning interventions*. London: Jessica Kingsley.

Bingham, T. (2011) *The rule of law*. London: Penguin.

Bostock, L., Patrizo, L., Godfrey, T. and Forrester, D. (2019). What is the impact of supervision on direct practice with families? *Children and Youth Services Review*, 105: 104428.

Brandon, M., Dodsworth, J. and Rumball, D. (2005). Serious case reviews: learning to use expertise. *Child Abuse Review*, 14(3): 160–176.

Brandon, S.E., Wells, S. and Seale, C. (2018). *Science-based interviewing: information elicitation*. Nebraska: DigitalCommons@University of Nebraska-Lincoln.

Brearley, P. (1982). *Risk in social work*. London: Routledge & Kegan Paul.

British Association of Social Workers (2018). *Professional capabilities framework*. Birmingham: British Association of Social Workers.

Bross, D.C. and Plum, H. (2023) Legal aspects of decision-making processes in social work. In Taylor, B.J., Fluke, J.D., Graham, J.C., Keddell, E., Killick, C., Shlonsky, A. and Whittaker, A. (Eds), *The SAGE handbook of decision making, assessment and risk in social work* (Chapter 31, 367–376). London: Sage.

Brown, L., Moore, S. and Turney, D. (2014). *Analysis and critical thinking in assessment* (Second edition). Dartington, Devon: Research in Practice.

Brown, R. (2019). *The approved mental health professionals' guide to mental health law* (Fifth edition). London: Sage.

Brown, R.A., Barbour, P. and Martin, D. (2015). *The Mental Capacity Act 2005: a guide for practice* (Third edition). London: Sage.

Brown, S., Brady, G., Franklin, A. and Crookes, R. (2017). *The use of tools and checklists to assess risk of child sexual exploitation: an exploratory study*. Coventry: Coventry University.

Brunswik, E. (1956). *Perception and the representative design of psychological experiments* (Second edition). Berkeley, CA: University of California Press.

Burke, C. (2006). *Building community through circles of friends: a practical guide to making inclusion a reality for people with learning disabilities*. Mental Health Foundation

Butler, I. and Williamson, H. (1994). *Children speak: children, trauma and social work*. London: Longman Publishing Group.

Campbell, A., Taylor, B.J. and McGlade, A. (2016). *Research design in social work: qualitative and quantitative methods*. London: Sage.

Campbell, J. and Campbell, R. (2023). Decisional capacity in mental health social work. In Taylor, B.J., Fluke, J.D., Graham, J.C., Keddell, E., Killick, C., Shlonsky, A. and Whittaker, A. (Eds), *The SAGE handbook of decision making, assessment and risk in social work* (Chapter 23, 261–268). London: Sage.

Carson, D. (2012). Reviewing reviews of professionals' risk-taking decisions. *Journal of Social Welfare and Family Law*, 34(4): 395–409.

Carson, D. (2016). *Precepts for professional risk decision-making which could and should be adopted by health and social care employers and managers*. Working Paper. DOI: 10.13140/RG.2.2.29491.22566.

Carson, D. and Bain, A. (2008). *Professional risk and working with people: decision-making in health, social care and criminal justice*. London: Jessica Kingsley.

Carson, D.C. and Mullineux, J.C. (2023). Accountability for risk decision making in social care. In Taylor, B.J., Fluke, J.D., Graham, J.C., Keddell, E., Killick, C., Shlonsky, A. & Whittaker, A. (Eds), *The SAGE handbook of decision making, assessment and risk in social work* (Chapter 42, 505–513). London: Sage.

Centre for Public Impact (2018). *The Allegheny county family screening tool: a case study on the use of AI in government*. Centre for Public Impact.

Chambers, M., Gallagher, A., Borschmann, R., Gillard, S., Turner, K. and Kantaris, X. (2014). The experiences of detained mental health service users: issues of dignity in care. *BMC Medical Ethics*, 15(1): 50.

Chouldechova, A., Benavides-Prado, D., Fialko, O. and Vaithianathan, R. (2018). A case study of algorithm-assisted decision making in child maltreatment hotline screening decisions. *Proceedings of Machine Learning Research: Proceedings of the 1st Conference on Fairness, Accountability and Transparency*. PMLR, 81: 134–148.

Clayton, V.M.E.L., Sanders, M., Schoenwald, E., Surkis, L. and Gibbons, D. (2020). Machine learning in children's services summary report. *What Works For Children's Social Care*. UK.

Coleman, H., Rogers, G. and King, J. (2002). Using portfolios to stimulate critical thinking in social work education. *Social Work Education*, 21: 583–595.

Collins, S. (2015). Hope and helping in social work. *Practice*, 27(3): 197–213.

Connolly, M. (2017). *Beyond the risk paradigm in child protection: current debates and new directions*. London: Palgrave.

Connolly, M., Harms, L. and Maidment, J. (Eds) (2009). *Social work: contexts and practice*. London: Oxford University Press.

Cook, A. and Miller, E. (2012). Talking points: personal outcomes approach. www.jitscotland.org.uk/wp-content/uploads/2014/01/Talking-Points-Practical-Guide-21-June-2012.pdf (accessed 25 Oct 2019).

Cook, L.L. (2017). Making sense of the initial home visit: the role of intuition in child and family social workers' assessments of risk. *Journal of Social Work Practice*, 31(4): 431–444.

Cook, L. (2023) Intuition in social work practice. In Taylor, B.J., Fluke, J.D., Graham, J.C., Keddell, E., Killick, C., Shlonsky, A. and Whittaker, A. (Eds), *The SAGE handbook of decision making, assessment and risk in social work*. (Chapter 7, 75–83). London: Sage.

Coulthard, B., Mallett, J. and Taylor, B.J. (2020). Better decisions for children with 'big data': can algorithms promote fairness, transparency and parental engagement? *Societies*, 10: 97.

Coulthard, B. and Taylor, B.J. (2022). Natural language processing to identify case factors in child protection court proceedings. *Methodological Innovations*, 15(3): 222–235.

Coulthard, B. and Taylor, B.J. (2023). Big data analytics for making decisions and managing risk. In Taylor, B.J., Fluke, J.D., Graham, J.C., Keddell, E., Killick, C., Shlonsky, A. and Whittaker, A. (Eds), *The SAGE handbook of decision making, assessment and risk in social work* (Chapter 33, 391–404) London: Sage.

Covell, N.H., McCorkle, B.H., Weissman, E.M., Summerfelt, T. and Essock, S.M. (2007) What's in a name? Terms preferred by service recipients. *Administration and Policy in Mental Health*, 34: 443–7.

Croisdale-Appleby, D. (2014). *Revisioning social work education: an independent review*. London: Department of Health.

Crossland, J. (2019). Implementing the Care Act: assessing need and providing care and support. In Braye, S. and Preston-Shoot, M. (Eds), *The Care Act 2014: wellbeing in practice*. London: Sage.

Cuccaro-Alamin, S., Foust, R., Vaithianathan, R. and Putnam-Hornstein, E. (2017). Risk assessment and decision making in child protective services: predictive risk modelling in context. *Children and Youth Services Review*, 79: 291–298.

Darragh, E. and Taylor, B.J. (2008). Research and reflective practice. In Higham, P. (Ed.), *Post qualifying social work practice* (148–160). London: Sage.

Davidson, G., Greer, K., Mulholland, A. and Webb, P. (2023). Engaging adults in the assessment process. In Taylor, B.J., Fluke, J.D., Graham, J.C., Keddell, E., Killick, C., Shlonsky, A. and Whittaker, A. (Eds), *The SAGE handbook of decision making, assessment and risk in social work* (Chapter 21, 243–251) London: Sage.

Davidson-Arad, B. and Benbenishty, R. (2016). Child welfare attitudes, risk assessments and intervention recommendations: the role of professional expertise. *British Journal of Social Work*, 46(1): 186–203.

Davys, A. and Beddoe, L. (2020). *Best practice in professional supervision: a guide for the helping professions*. London: Jessica Kingsley.

Dawes, R.M., Faust, D. and Meelh, P.E. (1989). Clinical versus actuarial judgment. *Science*, 243: 1668–1674.

de Bortoli, L. and Dolan, M. (2015). Decision making in social work with families and children: developing decision aids compatible with cognition. *British Journal of Social Work*, 45(7): 2142–2160.

de Jong, P. and Miller, S.D. (1995). How to interview for client strengths. *Social Work*, 40(6): 729–736.

Department of Health (2001). *Valuing people: a strategy for learning disability services in the 21st century*. London: Department of Health.

Department of Health (2007). *Independence, choice and risk: a guide to best practice in supported decision making*. London: Department of Health.

Department of Health (2012). *Caring for our future: reforming care and support* (Vol. 8378). London: The Stationery Office.

Department of Health (2017). *Strengths-based social work practice with adults: Roundtable report*. London: The Stationery Office.

Department of Health and Social Care (2019). *Strengths-based approach: practice framework and practice handbook*. London: Department of Health and Social Care.

Devaney, J., Hayes, D. and Spratt, T. (2017). The influences of training and experience in removal and reunification decisions involving children at risk of maltreatment: detecting a 'beginner dip'. *British Journal of Social Work*, 47(8): 2364–2383.

Dimond, B. (1997). *Legal aspects of care in the community*. London: Macmillan.

Dix, H., Hollinrake, S., and Meade, J. (Eds) (2019). *Relationship-based social work with adults*. St Albans: Critical Publishing.

Duffy, J., Davidson, G. and Kavanagh, D. (2016). Applying the recovery approach to the interface between mental health and child protection services. *Child Care in Practice*, 22(1): 35–49.

Duffy, J., Taylor, B.J. and McCall, S. (2006). Human rights and decision making in child protection through explicit argumentation. *Child Care in Practice*, 12(2): 81–95.

Duffy, M., Gillespie, K. and Clark, D.M. (2007). Post-traumatic stress disorder in the context of terrorism and other civil conflict in Northern Ireland: randomised controlled trial. *British Medical Journal*, 334: 1147–1150.

Dyke, C. (2019). *Writing analytic assessments in social work* (Second edition). St Albans: Critical Publishing.

Farmer, E. and Owen, M. (1995). *Child protection practice: private risks and public remedies*. London: Her Majesty's Stationery Office.

Fengler, J. and Schrödter, P. (2023). Engaging children in assessment and decisions. In Taylor, B.J., Fluke, J.D., Graham, J.C., Keddell, E., Killick, C., Shlonsky, A. and Whittaker, A. (Eds). *The SAGE handbook of decision making, assessment and risk in social work* (Chapter 19, 221–229). London: Sage.

Fengler, J. and Taylor, B.J. (2019). Effective assessment: a key knowledge and skill for a sustainable profession. *Social Work Education: The International Journal*, 38(3): 392–405.

Fennig, M. and Denov, M. (2019). Regime of truth: rethinking the dominance of the bio-medical model in mental health social work with refugee youth. *The British Journal of Social Work*, 49(2): 300–317.

Fenton, J. (2016). Organisational professionalism and moral courage: contradictory concepts in social work? *Critical and Radical Social Work*, 4(2): 199–215.

Ferguson, H. (2018). How social workers reflect in action and when and why they don't: the possibilities and limits to reflective practice in social work. *Social Work Education*, 37(4): 415–427.

Ferguson, T.H. (2017). *Child protection practice* (Second Edition). Basingstoke: Palgrave Macmillan.

Fife Child Protection Committee (2017). *Learning summary from a significant case review on Child C*. Fife: Fife Child Protection Committee.

Finlay, G. (2011). Let's talk about solutions! *Adult Learner: The Irish Journal of Adult and Community Education*, 99: 109.

Firmin, C. (2020). *Contextual safeguarding and child protection: rewriting the rules*. Abingdon, Oxfordshire and New York: Taylor & Francis.

Fisher, R.P. and Geiselman, R.E. (1992). *Memory-enhancing techniques for investigative interviewing: the cognitive interview*. Springfield, IL: Charles Thomas.

Flynn, M. (2007). *The murder of Steven Hoskin: a serious case review*. Cornwall: Cornwall Adult Protection Committee.

Fook, J. (2016). *Social work: a critical approach to practice*. London: Sage.

Forrester, D., Kershaw, S., Moss, H. and Hughes, L. (2008). Communication skills in child protection: how do social workers talk to parents? *Child & Family Social Work*, 13(1): 41–51.

Forrester, D., Westlake, D. and Glynn, G. (2012). Parental resistance and social worker skills: towards a theory of motivational social work. *Child & Family Social Work*, 17(2): 118–129.

Forrester, D., Westlake, D., Killian, M., Antonopoulou, V., McCann, M., Thurnham, A.,... and Hutchison, D. (2018). A randomized controlled trial of training in Motivational Interviewing for child protection. *Children and Youth Services Review*, 88: 180–190.

Forrester, D., Westlake, D., Killian, M., Antonopolou, V., McCann, M., Thurnham, A., Thomas, R., Waits, C., Whittaker, C. and Hutchison, D. (2019). What is the relationship between worker skills and outcomes for families in child and family social work? *The British Journal of Social Work*. bcy126: https://doi.org/10.1093/bjsw/bcy126

Frazer-Carroll, M. (2023). *Mad world: the politics of mental health*. London: Pluto Press.

Frith, L. and Martin, R. (2021). *Professional writing skills for social workers* (Second Edition). McGraw-Hill Education (UK).

Fuller, C., Taylor, P. and Wilson, K. (2019). *A toolkit of motivational skills: how to help others reach for change*. Chichester, West Sussex and Hoboken, NJ: John Wiley & Sons.

Furlong, M., Stokes, A., McGilloway, S., Hickey, G., Leckey, Y., Bywater, T., O'Neill, C., Cardwell, C., Taylor, B., Donnelly, M. and ENRICH Research Team (2018). A community-based parent-support programme to prevent child maltreatment: protocol for a randomised controlled trial. *HRB Open Research*, 1: 13.

Gale, L. (2022). Biopsychosocial-spiritual assessment: an overview. Cinahl Information Systems. www.ebsco.com/sites/default/files/acquiadam-assets/Social-Work-Reference-Center-Skill-Biopsychosocial-Spiritual-Assessment.pdf (accessed 9 January 2024).

Ghaffar, W., Manby, M. and Race, T. (2011). Exploring the experiences of parents and carers whose children have been subject to child protection plans. *British Journal of Social Work*, 42(5): 887–905.

Ghanem, C., Kollar, I., Pankofer, S., Eckl, M. and Fischer, F. (2019). Does probation officers' reasoning change in the light of scientific evidence? Analyzing the quality of evidence utilisation in social work. *Journal of Evidence-Based Social Work*, 16(4): 423–441.

Gillingham, P. (2019). Decision support systems, social justice and algorithmic accountability in social work: a new challenge. *Practice*, 31(4): 277–290.

Gillingham, P. (2020). The development of algorithmically based decision-making systems in children's protective services: is administrative data good enough? *British Journal of Social Work*, 50(2): 565–580.

Gillingham, P. and Whittaker, A. (2023). How can research and theory enhance understanding of professional decision-making in reviews of cases of child death and serious injury? *British Journal of Social Work*, 53(1): 5–22.

Goddard, C. (2021). The language of children's services. *Children and Young People Now Select*, 2021(5): 24–27.

Goldacre, A. and Hood, R. (2022). Factors affecting the social gradient in children's social care. *The British Journal of Social Work*, 52(6): 3599–3617.

HM Government (2018). *Working together to safeguard children: a guide to interagency working to safeguard and promote the welfare of children*. London: author.

Graham, J.C. and Fluke, J. (2023). Foundations of valid assessment. In Taylor, B.J., Fluke, J.D., Graham, J.C., Keddell, E., Killick, C., Shlonsky, A. and Whittaker, A. (Eds), *The SAGE handbook of decision making, assessment and risk in social work* (Chapter 26, 305–321). London: Sage.

Greer, J. (2016). *Resilience and personal effectiveness for social workers*. London: Sage.

Gregory, M. (2023). Decision making in organisational contexts. In Taylor, B.J., Fluke, J.D., Graham, J.C., Keddell, E., Killick, C., Shlonsky, A. and Whittaker, A. (Eds), *The SAGE handbook of decision making, assessment and risk in social work* (Chapter 16, 185–193). London: Sage.

Grove, W.M. and Meehl, P.E. (1996). Comparative efficiency of informal (subjective, impressionistic) and formal (mechanical, algorithmic) prediction procedures: the clinical–statistical controversy. *Psychology, Public Policy, and Law*, 2(2): 293–323. https://doi.org/10.1037/1076-8971.2.2.293

Gunnell, D. and Frankel, S. (1994). Prevention of suicide: aspirations and evidence. *British Medical Journal*, 308: 1227. DOI: https://doi.org/10.1136/bmj.308.6938.1227

Hagan, R., Manktelow, R., Mallett, J. and Taylor, B.J. (2014). Reducing loneliness amongst older people: systematic search and narrative review. *Aging and Mental Health*, 18(6): 683–693.

Hamilton, D., Taylor, B.J., Killick, C. and Bickerstaff, D. (2015). Suicidal ideation and behaviour among young people leaving care: case file survey. *Child Care in Practice*, 21(2): 160–176.

Hardiker, P., Exton, K. and Barker, M. (1991). The social policy contexts of prevention in child care. *British Journal of Social Work*, 21(4): 341–359.

Hardy, M. (2017). In defence of actuarialism: interrogating the logic of risk in social work practice. *Journal of Social Work Practice*, 31(4): 395–410.

Harris, P.M. (2006). What community supervision officers need to know about actuarial risk assessment and clinical judgment. *Federal Probation*, 70(2): 8–14.

Hayes, D. (2018). *Relationships matter: an analysis of complaints about social workers to the Northern Ireland Social Care Council and the Patient and Client Council*. Belfast: Northern Ireland Social Care Council.

Hayward, F. (2023). Ways of writing. In Moore, T. (Ed.), *Principles of practice by principal social workers*. St Albans: Critical Publishing.

Health and Safety Executive (2009). *Health and safety at work: what you need to know*. London: Health and Safety Executive. Contains public sector information licensed under the Open Government Licence v3.0. www.nationalarchives.gov.uk/doc/open-government-licence/version/3/ (accessed 9 January 2024).

Health and Safety Executive (2019). *Risk management*. London: Health and Safety Executive. www.hse.gov.uk/risk/index.htm (accessed 9 January 2024).

Heenan, D. and Birrell, D. (2018). Hospital-based social work: challenges at the interface between health and social care. *The British Journal of Social Work*, 19(7): 1741–1758.

Helm, D. (2023). Sense making in professional judgement. In Taylor, B.J., Fluke, J.D., Graham, J.C., Keddell, E., Killick, C., Shlonsky, A. and Whittaker, A. (Eds), *The SAGE handbook of decision making, assessment and risk in social work* (Chapter 10, 109–118). London: Sage.

Hennessey, R. (2011). *Relationship skills in social work*. London: Sage.

Hepworth, D.H., Der Vang, P., Blakey, J.M., Schwalbe, C. and Evans, C. (2022). *Empowerment series: direct social work practice* (Eleventh Edition). Boston, MA: Cengage Learning.

Hodge, D.R. (2013). Implicit spiritual assessment: an alternative approach for assessing client spirituality. *Social Work*, 58(3): 223–230.

Holland, S. (2001). Representing children in child protection assessments. *Childhood*, 8(3): 322–339.

Hollows, A. (2008). Professional judgement and the risk assessment process. In Calder, M. (Ed.), *Contemporary risk assessment in safeguarding children* (52–60). Lyme Regis, Dorset: Russell House.

Home Office (2005). *Strengthening multi-agency public protection arrangements*. London: HMSO.

Hood, R., Shute, S., Feilzer, M. and Wilcox, A. (2002). Sex offenders emerging from long-term imprisonment: a study of their long-term reconviction rates and of Parole Board members' judgements of their risk. *British Journal of Criminology*, 42: 371. DOI: 10.1093/bjc/42.2.371.

Horvat, S., Roszak, P. and Taylor, B.J. (2022). Is it harmful? A Thomistic perspective on risk science in social welfare. *Journal of Religion and Health*, 61(4): 3302–3316.

Horwarth, J. (2018). Assessing the needs of children living in chaotic and dysfunctional families. *Relational Social Work*, 2(2): 28–33.

Hothersall, S.J. (2014). *Social work with children, young people and their families in Scotland* (Third Edition). London: Sage.

Hothersall, S.J. and Maas-Lowit, M. (2010). *Need, risk and protection in social work practice*. London: Sage.

Hough, L.H. (1920). *On a letter from Simon Peter*. New York: The Christian Advocate.

Houston, S. (2015a). Reducing child protection error in social work: towards a holistic-rational perspective. *Journal of Social Work Practice*, 29(4): 379–393.

Houston, S. (2015b). *Reflective practice: a model for supervision and practice in social work*. Belfast: Northern Ireland Social Care Council.

Hyslop, I. and Keddell, E. (2018). Outing the elephants: exploring a new paradigm for child protection social work. *Social Sciences*, 7(7): 105.

Ingram, R. (2013). Emotions, social work practice and supervision: an uneasy alliance? *Journal of Social Work Practice*, 27(1): 5–19.

International Federation of Social Workers and International Association of School of Social Work (2014). *Global definition of the social work profession*. Switzerland: author.

Jack, G. and Gill, O. (2003). *The missing side of the triangle: assessing the importance of family and environmental factors in the lives of children*. Barkingside, Essex: Barnardo's.

Johnson, R., Smith, E. and Fisher, H. (2015). Testing the reliability and validity of the Graded Care Profile version 2 (GCP2). London: NSPCC.

Johnson, W., Clancy, T. and Bastian, P. (2015). Child abuse/neglect risk assessment under field practice conditions: tests of external and temporal validity and comparison with heart disease prediction. *Children and Youth Services Review*, 56(C): 76–85.

Jones, D. (2006). Assessments: a child mental health perspective. *Family Law in Practice*, 36(6): 471–477.

Kattari, S.K., Lavery, A. and Hasche, L. (2017). Applying a social model of disability across the life span. *Journal of Human Behavior in the Social Environment*, 27(8): 865–880.

Keaney, F., Strang, J., Martinez-Raga, J., Spektor, D., Manning, V., Kelleher, M., Wilson-Jones, C., Wanagaratne, S. and Sabater, A. (2004). Does anyone care about names? How attendees at substance misuse services like to be addressed by professionals. *European Addiction Research*, 10: 75–79.

Keddell, E. (2023). The devil in the detail: algorithmic risk prediction tools and their implications for ethics, justice and decision making. In Taylor, B.J., Fluke, J.D., Graham, J.C., Keddell, E., Killick, C., Shlonsky, A. and Whittaker, A. (Eds), *The SAGE handbook of decision making, assessment and risk in social work* (Chapter 34, 405–420). London: Sage.

Kelly, N. and Milner, J. (1996). Child protection decision-making. *Child Abuse Review*, 5: 91–102.

Kempe, H., Silverman, F., Steele, B., Drögemüller, W. and Silver, H. (1962). The battered child syndrome. *Journal of the American Medical Association*, 181(1): 17–24.

Kemshall, H. (2023). Risk, desistance and engagement: working with adult service users in Probation. In Taylor, B.J., Fluke, J.D., Graham, J.C., Keddell, E., Killick, C., Shlonsky, A. and Whittaker, A. (Eds), *The SAGE handbook of decision making, assessment and risk in social work* (Chapter 24, 269–279). London: Sage.

Kettle, M. (2023). The influence of optimism on analysis in professional judgement. In Taylor, B.J., Fluke, J.D., Graham, J.C., Keddell, E., Killick, C., Shlonsky, A. and Whittaker, A. (Eds), *The SAGE handbook of decision making, assessment and risk in social work* (Chapter 3, 33–41). London: Sage.

Killick, C. and Taylor, B.J. (2009). Professional decision making on elder abuse: systematic narrative review. *Journal of Elder Abuse and Neglect*, 21: 211–238.

Killick, C., Taylor, B.J., Begley, E., Anand, J.C. and O'Brien, M. (2015). Older people's conceptualisation of abuse: a systematic narrative review. *Journal of Elder Abuse and Neglect*, 27(2): 100–120.

Kinsella, P. (2000). *Person-centred risk assessment*. Liverpool: Paradigm.

Kirby, K., Lyons, A., Mallett, J., Goetzke, K., Dunne, M., Gibbons, W., Chnáimhsí, Á.N., Ferguson, J., Harkin, T., McGlinchey, E., McAnee, G., Belfer, M. and Stark, K. (2019). The Hopeful Minds programme: a mixed method evaluation of 10 school curriculum based, theoretically framed lessons to promote mental health and coping skills in 8–14 year olds. *Child Care in Practice*, 27(2008): 1–22.

Kirk, C.A., Killick, C., McAllister, A. and Taylor, B.J. (2019). Social workers perceptions of restorative approaches with families in cases of elder abuse: a qualitative study. *Journal of Adult Protection*, 21(3): 190–200.

Kirkman, E. and Melrose, K. (2014). *Clinical judgement and decision-making in children's social work: an analysis of the 'front door' system (Research Report 323)*. London: The Behavioural Insights Team, Department for Education.

Kopels, S. and Kagle, J.D. (1993). Do social workers have a duty to warn? *Social Service Review*, 67(1): 101–126.

Laming, H. (2003). *The Victoria Climbie Inquiry Report*. London: HMSO.

Levenson, J. (2017). Trauma-informed social work practice. *Social Work*, 62(2): 105–113.

Lewis, J. and Sanderson, H. (2011). *A practical guide to delivering personalisation: person-centred practice in health and social care*. London: Jessica Kingsley.

Lindsey, T. (2011). Coping, challenge and conflict in groups. In Taylor, B.J. (Ed.), *Working with aggression and resistance in social work* (102–113). London: Sage.

Lister, P.G. (2013). *Integrating social work theory and practice: a practical skills guide.* London: Routledge.

Lloyd, C., King, R. and Chenoweth, L. (2001). Social work, stress and burnout: a review. *Journal of Mental Health*, 11(3): 255–265.

Lloyd, C., King, R., Bassett, H., Sandland, S. and Saviage, G. (2001) Patient, client or consumer: a survey of preferred terms. *Australasian Psychiatry*, 9: 321–324.

Long, S. (2020). Supervisors' perception of vicarious trauma and growth in Australian refugee trauma counsellors. *Australian Social Work*, 73(1): 105–117.

López López, M., Wieldraaijer-Vincent, L. and ten Brummelaar, M. (2023). Re-imagining participation of young people in decision making in contexts of vulnerability. In Taylor, B.J., Fluke, J.D., Graham, J.C., Keddell, E., Killick, C., Shlonsky, A. and Whittaker, A. (Eds), *The SAGE handbook of decision making, assessment and risk in social work* (Chapter 20, 230–242). London: Sage.

Luan, S., Schooler, L.J. and Gigerenzer, G. (2011). A signal-detection analysis of fast-and-frugal trees. *Psychological Review*, 118(2): 316.

Lynch, A., Newlands, F. and Forrester, D. (2019). What does empathy sound like in social work communication? A mixed-methods study of empathy in child protection social work practice. *Child & Family Social Work*, 24(1): 139–147.

Maslow, A.H. (1954). *Motivation and personality.* New York: Harper and Row.

Maung, N.A. and Hammond, N. (2000). *Risk of reoffending needs assessments: the user's perspective: Home Office Research Study 216.* London: Home Office.

McCafferty, P. and Taylor, B.J. (2022). Barriers to knowledge acquisition and utilisation in child welfare decisions: a qualitative study. *Journal of Social Work,* 22(1): 87–108.

McColgan, M. and McMullin, C. (2017). *Doing relationship-based social work: a practical guide to building relationships and enabling change.* London: Jessica Kingsley.

McCormack, B., Taylor, B.J., McConville, J., Slater, P. and Murray, B.J. (2008). *The usability of the Northern Ireland single assessment tool (NISAT) for the health and social care of older people.* Belfast: Department of Health, Social Services and Public Safety.

Macdonald, G. (2001). *Effective interventions for child abuse and neglect: an evidence-based approach to planning and evaluating interventions.* Oxford: Wiley.

McFadden, P., Campbell, A. and Taylor, B.J. (2015). Resilience and burnout in child protection social work: individual and organizational themes from a systematic literature review. *British Journal of Social Work*, 45(5): 1546–1563.

McFadden, P., Mallett, J., Campbell, A. and Taylor, B. (2018). Explaining self-reported resilience in child-protection social work: the role of organisational factors, demographic information and job characteristics. *British Journal of Social Work*, 49(1): 198–216.

McFadden, P., Taylor, B.J., Campbell, A. and McQuilkin, J. (2012). Systematically identifying relevant research: case study on child protection social workers' resilience. *Research on Social Work Practice*, 22(6): 626–636.

McGinn, T., Taylor, B.J. and McColgan, M. (2019). A qualitative study of the perspectives of domestic violence survivors on behaviour change programmes with perpetrators. *Journal of Interpersonal Violence*, 36(17–18): NP9364–NP9390 [DOI: 10.1177/0886260519855663].

McGinn, A.H., Taylor, B.J., McColgan, M. and Lagdon, S. (2016). Survivor perspectives on IPV perpetrator interventions: systematic narrative review. *Trauma, Violence & Abuse*, 17(3): 239–255.

McGinn, A.H., Taylor, B.J., McColgan, M. and McQuilkin, J. (2016). Social work literature searching: current issues with databases and online search engines. *Research on Social Work Practice*, 26(3): 266–277.

McGlade, A. (2023). Getting evidence into organisations to support decision making and risk work. In Taylor, B.J., Fluke, J.D., Graham, J.C., Keddell, E., Killick, C., Shlonsky, A. and Whittaker, A. (Eds), *The SAGE handbook of decision making, assessment and risk in social work* (Chapter 43, 514–523). London: Sage.

McIvor, G. and Kemshall, H. (2002). *Serious, violence and sexual offenders: the use of risk assessment tools in Scotland*. Edinburgh: The Stationery Office.

Mackay, K. (2008). The Scottish adult support and protection legal framework. *Journal of Adult Protection*, 10(4): 25–36.

McLaughlin, J. (2016). Social work in acute hospital settings in Northern Ireland: the views of service users, carers and multi-disciplinary professionals. *Journal of Social Work*, 16(2): 135–154.

McLeod, A. (2010). A friend and an equal: do young people in care seek the impossible from their social workers? *British Journal of Social Work*, 40: 772–788.

McNellan, C.R., Gibbs, D.J., Knobel, A.S. and Putnam-Hornstein, E. (2022). The evidence base for risk assessment tools used in US child protection investigations: a systematic scoping review. *Child Abuse & Neglect*, 134: 105887.

McPheat, G. and Butler, L. (2014). Residential child-care agencies as learning organisations: innovation and learning from mistakes. *Social Work Education*, 33(2): 240–253.

Meehl, P.E. (1954). *Clinical versus statistical prediction: a theoretical analysis and a review of the evidence*. Minneapolis: University of Minnesota Press. https://doi.org/10.1037/11281-000

Méndez-Fernández, A.B., Aguiar-Fernández, F.J., Lombardero-Posada, X., Murcia-Álvarez, E. and González-Fernández, A. (2022). Vicariously resilient or traumatised social workers: exploring some risk and protective factors. *The British Journal of Social Work*, 52(2): 1089–1109.

Mental Health Commission (2006). *Multidisciplinary team working: from theory to practice*. Dublin: Mental Health Commission.

Merkel-Holguin, L., Hollinshead, D.M., Hahn, A.E., Casillas, K.L. and Fluke, J.D. (2015). The influence of differential response and other factors on parent perceptions of child protection involvement. *Child Abuse & Neglect*, 39: 18–31.

Miller, G.A. (1956). The magical number seven, plus or minus two: some limits on our memory for processing information. *Psychological Review*, 63(2): 81–97.

Miller, J. (2004). Critical incident debriefing and social work: expanding the frame. *Journal of Social Service Research*, 30(2): 7–25.

Miller, J. and Maloney, C. (2013). Practitioner compliance with risk/needs assessment tools: a theoretical and empirical assessment. *Criminal Justice and Behavior*, 40(7): 716–736.

Milner, J., Myers, S. and O'Byrne, P. (2015). *Assessment in social work*. Basingstoke, Hampshire: Macmillan. [Out of order]

Miller, W.R. and Rollnick, S. (2012). *Motivational interviewing: helping people change*. New York: Guilford Press.

Mitchell, R.J., Parker, V. and Giles, M. (2011). When do interprofessional teams succeed? Investigating the moderating roles of team and professional identity in interprofessional effectiveness. *Human Relations*, 64(10): 1321–1343.

Monahan, J. (1981). *Predicting violent behaviour: an assessment of clinical techniques*. Beverly Hills, CA: Sage.

Monahan, J. (1993). Limiting therapist exposure to Tarasoff liability: guidelines for risk containment. *American Psychologist*, 48(3): 242–250.

Monahan, J., Steadman, H.J., Silver, E., Appelbaum, P.S., Robbins, P.C., Mulvey, E.P., Roth, L.H., Grisso, T. and Banks, S. (2001). *Rethinking risk assessment: the MacArthur study of mental disorder and violence*. Oxford: Oxford University Press.

Montgomery, L., Anand, J.C., McKay, K., Taylor, B.J., Pearson, K. and Harper, C. (2016). Implications of divergences in adult protection legislation. *Journal of Adult Protection*, 18(3): 149–160.

Montgomery, L., MacDonald, M. and Walakira, E.J. (2023). Engaging client families in assessment and managing risks. In Taylor, B.J., Fluke, J.D., Graham, J.C., Keddell, E., Killick, C., Shlonsky, A. and Whittaker, A. (Eds), *The SAGE handbook of decision making, assessment and risk in social work* (Chapter 18, 211–220). London: Sage.

Mooney, S. and Bunting, L. (2019). *Family life stories workbook*. Belfast: Queen's University Belfast and South Eastern Health & Social Care Trust.

Moore, T. (2022). Relationships and reciprocity; where next for strengths-based social work in adult social care? *Journal of Social Work Practice*, 36(4): 451–463.

Moriarty, J. and Manthorpe, J. (2016). *The effectiveness of social work with adults: a systematic scoping review*. London: King's College London.

Mulheron, R. (2010). Trumping Bolam: a critical legal analysis of Bolitho's 'gloss'. *Cambridge Law Journal*, 69(3): 609–638. DOI: 10.1017/S0008197310000826

Mullineux, J.M., Taylor, B.J. and Giles, M. (2020). Professional judgement about reoffending: factorial survey. *Journal of Social Work*, 20(6): 797–816.

Munford, R. and Sanders, J. (2017). Harnessing resistance in interventions with young people. *Journal of Social Work Practice*, 31(1): 79–93.

Munro, E. (1996). Avoidable and unavoidable mistakes in child protection work. *British Journal of Social Work*, 26(6): 793–808.

Munro, E. (2008). *Effective Child Protection* (Second edition). London: Sage.

Munro, E. (2011). *The Munro review of child protection: final report: a child-centred system*. London: Her Majesty's Stationery Office.

Munro, E. (2019a). *Effective child protection*. London: Sage.

Munro, E. (2019b). Decision-making under uncertainty in child protection: creating a just and learning culture. *Child & Family Social Work*, 24(1): 123–130.

Munro, E., Cartwright, N., Hardie, J. and Montuschi, E. (2016). *Improving child safety: deliberation, judgement and empirical research*. Durham University: Centre for Humanities Engaging Science and Society.

Nathan, J. and Webber, M. (2010). Mental health social work and the bureau-medicalisation of mental health care: identity in a changing world. *Journal of Social Work Practice*, 24(1): 15–28.

Neill, M., Allen, J., Woodhead, N., Sanderson, H., Reid, S. and Erwin, L. (2009). A positive approach to risk requires person-centred thinking. *Tizard Learning Disability Review*, 14(4): 17–24.

Newcomb, M. (2022). Supportive social work supervision as an act of care: a conceptual model. *The British Journal of Social Work*, 52(2): 1070–1088.

Nickson, A.M., Carter, M.A. and Francis, A.P. (2019). *Supervision and professional development in social work practice*. Los Angeles: Sage Publications.

Ofsted (2019). *Focused visit to Devon local authority children's services*. London: Ofsted, www.devonscp.org.uk/ofsted-annual-conversation-and-focused-visit/ (accessed 15 January 2024).

Olaison, A. and Donnelly, S. (2023). Shared decision making with clients. In Taylor, B.J., Fluke, J.D., Graham, J.C., Keddell, E., Killick, C., Shlonsky, A. and Whittaker, A. (Eds), *The SAGE handbook of decision making, assessment and risk in social work* (Chapter 22, 252–260). London: Sage.

Oliver, C. and Charles, G. (2015). Enacting firm, fair and friendly practice: a model for strengths-based child protection relationships. *British Journal of Social Work*, 46(4): 1009–1026.

Osmo, R. and Landau, R. (2001). The need for explicit argumentation in ethical decision-making in social work. *Social Work Education*, 20(4): 483–492.

Parker, J. (2020). *Social work practice: assessment, planning, intervention and review* (Sixth Edition). London: Learning Matters.

Pawson, R., Boaz, A., Grayson, L., Long, A. and Barnes, C. (2003). *Types and quality of social care knowledge: stage two: towards the quality assessment of social care knowledge (working paper, 18)*. London: Economic and Social Research Council (UK) Centre for Evidence Based Policy and Practice.

Perry, J. and Sheldon, B. (1995). *Richard Phillips Inquiry report*. London: City of Westminster, and Kensington and Chelsea and Westminster District Health Authority.

Pipi, K. (2016). MĀRAMATANGA (Enlightenment): a creative approach to connecting facilitation and evaluation. *New Directions for Evaluation*, 2016(149): 43–52.

Platt, D. and Turney, D. (2014). Making threshold decisions in child protection: a conceptual analysis. *British Journal of Social Work*, 6: 1472–1490.

Platt, D. and Riches, K. (2016). Assessing parental capacity to change: the missing jigsaw piece in the assessment of a child's welfare? *Children and Youth Services Review*, 61: 141–148.

Platt, D. and Turney, D. (2018). The assessment process. In Horwath, J. and Platt, D. (Eds), *The child's world: the essential guide to assessing vulnerable children, young people and their families*. London and Philadelphia: Jessica Kingsley.

Ponton, L.E. (1997). *The romance of risk: why teenagers do the things they do*. New York: Basic Books.

Preston-Shoot, M. (2019). *Making good decisions* (Second Edition). Basingstoke, Hampshire: Palgrave Macmillan.

Preston-Shoot, M. (2023). Legally-literate decision making. In Taylor, B.J., Fluke, J.D., Graham, J.C., Keddell, E., Killick, C., Shlonsky, A. and Whittaker, A. (Eds), *The SAGE handbook of decision making, assessment and risk in social work* (Chapter 14, 163–175). London: Sage.

Pritchard, C., Davey, J. and Williams, R. (2013). Who kill children? Re-examining the evidence. *British Journal of Social Work*, 43: 1403–1438.

Pritchard, C. and Sharples, A. (2008). 'Violent' deaths of children in England and Wales and the major developed countries 1974–2002: possible evidence of improving child protection? *Child Abuse Review*, 17(5): 297–312.

Pritchard, C. and Williams, R. (2009). Comparing possible 'child-abuse-related-deaths' in England and Wales with the major developed countries 1974–2006: signs of progress? *British Journal of Social Work*, 40(6): 1700–1718.

Pritchard, C. and Williams, R. (2023). Assessment and risk: recognising the circularity of child-adverse-events and psychiatric disorders in children and adults. In Taylor, B.J., Fluke, J.D., Graham, J.C., Keddell, E., Killick, C., Shlonsky, A. and Whittaker, A. (Eds), *The SAGE handbook of decision making, assessment and risk in social work* (Chapter 17, 194–209). London: Sage.

Prochaska, J.O. and DiClemente, C.C. (1986). Toward a comprehensive model of change. In Miller, W.R. amd Heather, N. (Eds), *Treating addictive behaviors: processes of change* (3–27). Boston, MA: Springer.

Przeperski, J. and Taylor, B.J. (2022). Co-operation in child welfare decision-making: qualitative vignette study. *Child Care in Practice*, 28(2): 137–152.

Putnam-Hornstein, E., Needell, B., King, B. and Johnson-Motoyama, M. (2013). Racial and ethnic disparities: a population-based examination of risk factors for involvement with child protective services. *Child Abuse & Neglect*, 37(1), 33–46.

Quality Assurance Agency for Higher Education (UK) (2016). *Subject benchmark statement: social work*. London: author.

Raynor, P., Kynch, J., Roberts, C. and Merrington, S. (2000). *Risk and need assessment in probation services: an evaluation*. Oxford: Probation Studies Unit, University of Oxford.

Reder, P. and Duncan, S. (1999). Understanding communication in child protection networks. *Child Abuse Review*, 12: 82–100.

Reeves, A., Mckee, M., Gunnel, D., Chang, S.S., Basu, S., Barr, B. and Stuckler, D. (2015). Economic shocks, resilience and male suicides in the Great Recession: cross-national analysis of 20 EU countries. *European Journal of Public Health*, 25(3): 404–409.

Regehr, C., Bogo, M., Shlonsky, A. and LeBlanc, V. (2010). Confidence and professional judgement in assessing children's risk of abuse. *Research on Social Work Practice*, 20(6): 621–628.

Reith, M. (1998). *Community care tragedies: a practice guide to mental health inquiries*. Birmingham: Venture Press.

Rice, J., Mullineux, J. and Killick, C. (2022). Female care leavers' experience of the staff-child relationship while living in an intensive support children's home in Northern Ireland. *Child Care in Practice*, 28(1): 4–19.

Richardson, A. (2022). Personalisation as contribution-focused social work practice. *Journal of Social Work Practice*, 36(4), 385–399.

Robert Wood Johnson Foundation (2015). *Lessons from the field: promising interprofessional collaboration practices* (White Paper). rwjf.org

Rooney, R.H. and Mirick, R.G. (Eds) (2018). *Strategies for work with involuntary clients*. New York: Columbia University Press.

Ruch, G. (2005). Relationship-based practice and reflective practice: holistic approaches to contemporary child-care social work. *Child & Family Social Work*, 10(2): 111–123.

Rutter, D. (2013). *SCIE systematic research reviews: guidelines* (Third Edition). London: Social Care Institute for Excellence.

Rutter, L. and Brown, K. (2020). *Critical thinking and professional judgement for social work*. London: Sage.

Saltiel, D. (2017). Supervision: a contested space for learning and decision making. *Qualitative Social Work*, 16(4): 533–549.

Sanderson, H. (2000). *Person-centred planning: key features and approaches*. York: Joseph Rowntree Foundation.

Saunders, K., Brand, F., Lascelles, K. and Hawton, K. (2014). The sad truth about the SADPERSONS Scale: an evaluation of its clinical utility in self-harm patients. *Emergency Medicine Journal*, 31(10): 796–798.

Schön, D. (1983). *The reflective practitioner: how professionals think in action*. New York: Basic Books.

Schrödter, M., Bastian, P. and Taylor, B.J. (2020). Risikodiagnostik und Big Data Analytics in der Sozialen Arbeit [Risk diagnostics and big data analytics in social work]. In Kutscher, N., Ley, T., Seelmeyer, U., Siller, F., Tillmann, A. and Zorn, I. (Eds), *Handbuch soziale arbeit und digitalisierung [Handbook of social work and digitalisation]* (Chapter 19, 255–264). Weinheim, Germany: Beltz Juventa.

Schwalbe, J. (2004). Revisioning risk assessment for human service decision making. *Children and Youth Service Review*, 26(6): 561–576.

Scottish Government (2008). *Getting it right for every child*. Edinburgh: Scottish Government.

Scourfield, P. (2017). *Getting ready for direct practice in social work*. London: Learning Matters.

Secker, J. (1993). *From theory to practice in social work: the development of social work students' practice*. Hampshire: Avebury.

Seymour, C. and Seymour, R. (2007). *Courtroom skills for social workers*. Exeter: Learning Matters.

Shlonsky, A. and Wagner, D. (2005). The next step: integrating actuarial risk assessment and clinical judgement into an evidence-based practice framework in CPS case management. *Children and Youth Services Review*, 27(3), 409–427.

Shulman, L. (2009). *The skills of helping individuals, families, groups and communities* (Sixth edition). Belmont, CA: Brooks/Cole Cengage Learning.

Sicora, A. (2017). *Reflective practice*. Bristol: Policy Press.

Sicora, A., Taylor, B.J., Alfandari, R., Enosh, G., Helm, D., Killick, C., Lyons, O., Mullineux, J., Przeperski, J., Rölver, M. and Whittaker, K. (2021). Using intuition in social work decision making. *European Journal of Social Work*, 24(5): 772–787.

Slade, M., Oades, L. and Jarden, A. (Eds) (2017). *Wellbeing, recovery and mental health*. Cambridge: Cambridge University Press.

Smale, G., Tuson, G. and Statham, D. (2000). *Social work and social problems: working towards social inclusion and social change*. Houndmills, Basingstoke: Palgrave.

Søbjerg, L.M., Taylor, B.J., Przeperski, J., Horvat, S., Nouman, H. and Harvey, D. (2020). Using risk-factor statistics in decision making: prospects and challenges. *European Journal of Social Work*, 24(5), 788–801.

Sørensen, K.M. (2023). Implementing assessments using structured tools. In Taylor, B.J., Fluke, J.D., Graham, J.C., Keddell, E., Killick, C., Shlonsky, A. and Whittaker, A. (Eds), *The SAGE handbook of decision making, assessment and risk in social work* (Chapter 29, 347–357). London: Sage.

Spratt, T., Devaney, J. and Frederick, J. (2019). Adverse childhood experiences: beyond Signs of Safety; reimagining the organisation and practice of social work with children and families. *British Journal of Social Work*. bcz023: https://doi.org/10.1093/bjsw/bcz023

Spratt, T. (2023). Confirmation bias in social work. In Taylor, B.J., Fluke, J.D., Graham, J.C., Keddell, E., Killick, C., Shlonsky, A. and Whittaker, A. (Eds), *The SAGE handbook of decision making, assessment and risk in social work* (Chapter 1, 15–22). London: Sage.

Srivastava, O.P. and Hodson, D. (2020). Childhood neglect: a clinical perspective and introducing the Graded Care Profile 2. Paediatrics and Child Health, 30(11): 378–382.

Srivastava, O.P., Hodson, D. and Fountain, R. (2015). *Graded care profile version 2*. London: National Society for the Prevention of Cruelty to Children.

Stanley, N. and Humphreys, C. (2014). Multi-agency risk assessment and management for children and families experiencing domestic violence. *Children and Youth Services Review*, 47: 78–85.

Steele, L.S., Daley, A., Curling, D., Gibson, M.F., Green, D. C., Williams, C.C. and Ross, L.E. (2017). LGBT identity, untreated depression, and unmet need for mental health services by sexual minority women and trans-identified people. *Journal of Women's Health*, 26(2): 116–127.

Stevenson, M. and Taylor, B.J. (2016). Risk communication in dementia care: family perspectives. *Journal of Risk Research*, 18(1–2): 1–20.

Stevenson, M. and Taylor, B.J. (2017). Risk communication in dementia care: professional perspectives on consequences, likelihood, words and numbers. *British Journal of Social Work*, 47(7): 1940–1958.

Stevenson, M., McDowell, M.E. and Taylor, B.J. (2018). Concepts for communication about risk in dementia care: a review of the literature. *Dementia: The International Journal of Social Research and Practice*, 17(3): 359–390.

Stevenson, M., Savage, B. and Taylor, B.J. (2019). Perception and communication of risk in decision making by persons with a dementia. *Dementia: The International Journal of Social Research and Practice*, 18(3): 1108–1127.

Stevenson, M., Taylor, B.J. and Knox, J. (2016). Risk in dementia care: searching for the evidence. *Health, Risk and Society*, 18(1–2): 4–20.

Symonds, J., Williams, V., Miles, C., Steel, M., and Porter, S. (2018). The social care practitioner as assessor: 'people, relationships and professional judgement'. *The British Journal of Social Work*, 48(7): 1910–1928.

Taylor, B.J. (1999). Developing partnership between professions in implementing new children's legislation in Northern Ireland. *Journal of Inter-Professional Care*, 13(3): 249–259.

Taylor, B.J. (2006). Risk management paradigms in health and social services for professional decision making on the long-term care of older people. *British Journal of Social Work*, 36(8): 1411–1429.

Taylor, B.J. (Ed.) (2011). *Working with aggression and resistance in social work*. London: Sage.

Taylor, B.J. (2012a). Developing an integrated assessment tool for the health and social care of older people. *British Journal of Social Work*, 42(7): 1293–1314.

Taylor, B.J. (2012b). Models for professional judgement in social work. *European Journal of Social Work*, 15(4): 546–562.

Taylor, B.J. (2012c). Intervention research. In Gray, M., Midgley, J. and Webb, S. (Eds), *Social work handbook* (424–439). New York: Sage.

Taylor, B.J. (2017a). *Decision making, assessment and risk in social work* (Third edition). London: Sage.

Taylor, B.J. (2017b). Heuristics in professional judgement: a psycho-social rationality model. *British Journal of Social Work*, 47(4): 1043–1060.

Taylor, B.J. (2020a). Teaching and learning decision making in child welfare and protection social work. In Fluke, J., López, M., Benbenishty, R., Knorth, E. and Baumann, D. (Eds), *Decision making and judgement in child welfare and protection: theory, research and practice* (Chapter 13, 281–298). New York: Oxford University Press.

Taylor, B.J. (2020b). Using research in social work. In Parker, J. (Ed.), *Introducing social work* (160–171). London: Sage.

Taylor, B.J. (2021). Risk-managing decision making: a psycho-social rationality model. *British Journal of Social Work*, 51(7), 2819–2838.

Taylor, B.J. and Campbell, B. (2011). Quality, risk and governance: social workers' perspectives. *International Journal of Leadership in Public Services* [NOW the *International Journal of Public Leadership*], 7(4): 256–272.

Taylor, B.J. and Donnelly, M. (2006a). Professional perspectives on decision making about the long-term care of older people. *British Journal of Social Work*, 36(5): 807–826.

Taylor, B.J. and Donnelly, M. (2006b). Risks to home care workers: professional perspectives. *Health, Risk & Society*, 8(3): 239–256.

Taylor, B.J., Killick, C. and McGlade, A. (2015). *Understanding and using research in social work*. London: Sage.

Taylor, B.J. and McKeown, C. (2013). Assessing and managing risk with people with physical disabilities: development of a safety checklist. *Health, Risk and Society*, 15(2): 162–175.

Taylor, B.J. and Moorhead, A. (2020). The social sciences. In 'Part II: Tackling the challenges: considerations and methods for medicinal product risk communication research' of Bahri, P. (Ed.), *Communicating about risks and safe use of medicines: real life and applied research* (Chapter 8). Heidelberg: Springer.

Taylor, B.J. and Devine, T. (1993). *Assessing needs and planning care in social work*. Hampshire: Ashgate.

Taylor, B.J., Dempster, M. and Donnelly, M. (2003). Hidden gems: systematically searching electronic databases for research publications for social work and social care. *British Journal of Social Work*, 33(4): 423–439.

Taylor, B.J., Dempster, M. and Donnelly, M. (2007). Grading gems: appraising the quality of research for social work and social care. *British Journal of Social Work*, 37(2): 335–354.

Taylor, B.J., Fluke, J.D., Graham, J.C., Keddell, E., Killick, C., Shlonsky, A. and Whittaker, A. (Eds) (2023). *The SAGE handbook of decision making, assessment and risk in social work*. London: Sage.

Taylor, B.J., Killick, C., O'Brien, M., Begley, E. and Carter-Anand, J. (2014). Older people's conceptualisation of elder abuse and neglect. *Journal of Elder Abuse and Neglect*, 26(3): 223–243.

Taylor, B.J., Stevenson, M. and McDowell, M. (2018). Communicating risk in dementia care: survey of health and social care professionals. *Health and Social Care in the Community*, 26(2): e291–e303.

Taylor, B.J. and Whittaker, A. (Eds) (2019). *Professional judgement and decision making in social work: current issues*. London: Routledge.

Taylor, B.J., Wylie, E., Dempster, M. and Donnelly, M. (2007). Systematically retrieving research: a case study evaluating seven databases. *Research on Social Work Practice*, 17(6): 697–706.

Taylor, C. and White, S. (2006). Knowledge and reasoning in social work: educating for humane judgement. *British Journal of Social Work*, 36(6): 937–954.

Taylor, D.C. (2013). Social work: a critical approach to practice. *British Journal of Social Work*, 43(3): 618–619.

Teater, B., Devaney, J., Forrester, D., Scourfield, J. and Carpenter, J. (2017). *Quantitative research methods for social work: making social work count*. London: Palgrave Macmillan.

Tedam, P. (2020). *Anti-oppressive social work practice*. London: Sage.

Tedam, P. (2023) Cultural aspects of assessment and decision-making processes. In Taylor, B.J., Fluke, J.D., Graham, J.C., Keddell, E., Killick, C., Shlonsky, A. and Whittaker, A. (Eds), *The SAGE handbook of decision making, assessment and risk in social work* (Chapter 13, 153–162). London: Sage.

The College of Social Work (2014). Roles and Functions of Social Workers in England. Advice Note, London, The College of Social Work http://cdn.basw.co.uk/upload/basw_115640-9.pdf (accessed 12 February 2024).

Thom, B., Sales, R. and Pearce, J. (2007). *Growing Up with Risk*. Bristol: Policy Press.

Thomas, J. and Holland, S. (2009). Representing children's identities in core assessments. *British Journal of Social Work*, 40(8): 2617–2633.

Trevithick, P. (2008). Revisiting the knowledge base of social work: a framework for practice. *British Journal of Social Work*, 38(6): 1212–1237.

Trivedi, D., Goodman, C., Gage, H., Baron, N., Scheibl, F., Iliffe, S. ... and Drennan, V. (2013). The effectiveness of inter-professional working for older people living in the community: a systematic review. *Health & Social Care in the Community*, 21(2): 113–128.

Tunmore, J. (2017). Social constructionism and social work. In Deacon, L. and Macdonald, S. J., *Social work theory and practice*. London: Learning Matters.

Turnell, A. and Edwards, S. (1997). Aspiring to partnership: the *Signs of Safety* approach to child protection. *Child Abuse Review*, 6(3): 179–190.

Turner, C. (2003). *Are you listening?: what disabled children and young people in Wales think about the services they use: a consultation to inform the children and young people's national service framework*. Cardiff: Welsh Assembly Government.

Turney, D., Platt, D., Selwyn, J. and Farmer, E. (2011). *Social work assessment of children in need: what do we know? Messages from research: executive summary*. London: Department for Education.

Turney, D. and Ruch, G. (2023). The contribution of reflective practice to developing professional judgement and decision-making knowledge and skills. In Taylor, B.J., Fluke, J.D., Graham, J.C., Keddell, E., Killick, C., Shlonsky, A. and Whittaker, A. (Eds), *The SAGE handbook of decision making, assessment and risk in social work*. London: Sage (Chapter 40, 482–492).

Ward, H., Brown, R. and Hyde-Dryden, G. (2014). *Assessing parental capacity to change when children are on the edge of care: an overview of current research evidence*. Loughborough University.

Webb, C., Bywaters, P., Scourfield, J., McCartan, C., Bunting, L., Davidson, G. and Morris, K. (2020). Untangling child welfare inequalities and the 'inverse intervention law' in England. *Children and Youth Services Review*, 111: 104849.

Westheimer, I.J. (1977). *The practice of supervision in social work: a guide for staff supervision*. London: Ward Lock.

White, S., Hall, C. and Peckover, S. (2009). The descriptive tyranny of the common assessment framework: technologies of categorization and professional practice in child welfare. *British Journal of Social Work*, 39(7): 1197–1217.

Whittaker, A. (2011). Social defences and organisational culture in a local authority child protection setting: challenges for the Munro Review? *Journal of Social Work Practice*, 25(4): 481–495.

Whittaker, A. and Havard, T. (2015). Defensive practice as 'fear-based' practice: social work's open secret? *British Journal of Social Work*, 46(5): 1158–1174.

Whittaker, A. and Taylor, B.J. (Eds) (2018). *Risk in social work practice: current issues*. London: Routledge.

Winter, K. (2009). Relationships matter: the problems and prospects for social workers' relationships with young children in care. *Child & Family Social Work*, 14(4): 450–460.

Wood, J.M. (1996). Weighing evidence in sexual abuse evaluations: an introduction to Bayes Theorem. *Child Maltreatment*, 1(1): 25–36.

Wrench, K. (2018). *Creative ideas for assessing vulnerable children and families*. London: Jessica Kingsley.

Zarkou, N. and Brunner, R. (2023). How should we think about 'unmet need' in social care? A critical exploratory literature review. Glasgow: University of Glasgow, https://eprints.gla.ac.uk/297288/1/297288.pdf (accessed 9 June 2023).

Index

www.ingramcontent.com/pod-product-compliance
Ingram Content Group UK Ltd.
Pitfield, Milton Keynes, MK11 3LW, UK
UKHW010750060325
455854UK00002B/2